THE
National ⚾ Pastime

Endless Seasons
Baseball in Southern California

Edited by Jean Hastings Ardell and Andy McCue

Published by
The Society for American Baseball Research

EDITORS Jean Hastings Ardell and Andy McCue
MANAGING EDITOR Cecilia Tan
PRODUCTION AND DESIGN COORDINATOR Lisa Hochstein
COVER DESIGN Lisa Hochstein
FACT CHECKER Clifford Blau
PROOFREADERS Norman Macht, Cecilia Tan
FRONT COVER ART Ben Sakoguchi
BACK COVER ART David K. Anderson Sr.

PUBLISHED BY
The Society for American Baseball Research, Inc.
4455 East Camelback Road, Suite D-140
Phoenix, AZ 85018

PHONE (800) 969-7227
EMAIL info@sabr.org
WEB www.sabr.org

Contents

Note from the Editors

Endless Seasons: Baseball in Southern California

The title on the cover of this journal sums it up. With the sun shining 70 percent of the winter months, and annual rainfall of a mere 8 to 16 inches, usually from December through February, Southern California is as close to baseball Camelot as you are likely to get; the Mediterranean climate permits baseball to be played and enjoyed twelve months a year.

The weather has led to 220-game seasons in the Pacific Coast League and winter leagues that gave early twentieth century players a chance to pick up extra money playing ball rather than selling suits or singing on the vaudeville stage.

One result is that half again as many major league players have been born in California (1,977) than in any other state through the 2010 season. And that number doesn't include the numerous players born elsewhere but tutored in the sandlots, high schools, and colleges of Southern California after their parents moved them here. That's a substantial group, featuring Hall of Famers such as Jackie Robinson, Bert Blyleven, and George Brett.

Even more substantial is the way baseball permeates Southern California sports history, and we've tried to bring you just a sampling in this volume. There's organized baseball, from high schools and colleges up through the professional ranks. There's barely organized baseball, such as the California Winter League or the quirky Baseball Reliquary. There's baseball's impact on various ethnic groups—such as Latinos in East Los Angeles and Japanese Americans in an internment camp—and their impact on baseball.

There's Hollywood in these pages, and wooden ballparks, and pioneering women. It's another endless season of baseball writing to enjoy.

Working with the authors of the stories you are about to read was an abiding pleasure for the editors. SABR's Nick Frankovich, Cecilia Tan, and the staff were unfailingly helpful through all aspects of the editorial and production process, as was graphic designer Lisa Hochstein. The editors are grateful for the support of the men and women of SABR, particularly the Allan Roth chapter, which is headed by our president Stephen Roney. We'd also like to thank Tim Mead and the media department of the Los Angeles Angels of Anaheim; Josh Rawitch, Mark Langill, and the Los Angeles Dodgers media staff; the staff of the University of Southern California Athletic Department; Christina Rice and David Davis of the Los Angeles Public Library; Wayne Wilson and the staff at the LA84 Library; and Pat Kelly at the National Baseball Hall of Fame. SABR member David Eskenazi graciously provided a number of the photographs. Finally we deeply appreciate the generosity of Ben Sakoguchi for the use of his art on the cover.

— Jean Hastings Ardell and Andy McCue

ORANGES

FLY Ball
BRAND

Los Angeles, Calif.
Base Ball Team 1902

Los Chorizeros

The New York Yankees of East Los Angeles and the Reclaiming of Mexican American Baseball History

Richard A. Santillan and Francisco E. Balderrama

Baseball has been a major presence in the lives of Mexican Americans since the early twentieth century. Known as the Golden Age of Mexican American baseball, the years from the 1920s to the 1960s hold particular significance.[1] On any given Sunday, hundreds and even thousands of Mexican American fans watched games and cheered for their homegrown heroes and teams in such locations as Detroit, Chicago, St. Paul, Topeka, Omaha, Denver, San Antonio, Tucson, Seattle, Albuquerque, Boise, and East Los Angeles.

More than casual pick-up games for youth, these contests involved nearly the entire community. Players and their families loaded up their cars or chartered buses and headed off to their destination, arriving late Friday or early Saturday morning, according to recent work by historians.[2] They visited family and friends, and in the evening there were large receptions, with food, music, and dancing. The teams socialized at these events, but the next day baseball was serious business. Community pride was at stake. By Sunday night, the visitors were on their way home, having strengthened social and cultural ties with their brethren.

Nowhere was baseball more popular than in East Los Angeles, home to the largest concentration of Mexican Americans in the United States and second only to Mexico City in population of Mexican heritage during the early twentieth century. Over the decades, hundreds of industrial, religious, semipro, neighborhood, municipal, park, traveling, amateur, and pick-up teams have played on the fields of East L.A., a tradition that, as this article shows, would have a transformative effect upon the people of that time and place.

This article focuses on one of East L.A.'s great teams, the Carmelita Provision Company's *Los Chorizeros*. Often referred to as the New York Yankees of East Los Angeles by today's fans, journalists, and historians, *Los Chorizeros* won numerous city, county, community, and tournament championships between approximately 1948 and 1973, including, for example, the Los Angeles Municipal City championship in 1953, 1955, 1956, 1960, and 1964–65 with a roster of legendary players whose names live as part of community folklore.[3]

Moreover, long before Fernandomania, "Chorizeromania" galvanized Mexican Americans politically in the greater Los Angeles area. This article shows the direct connection between Mexican American baseball and the struggle for civil rights.[4] For much of the twentieth century, the Mexican American experience in the United States was deeply rooted in racial bigotry. This was a time of signs that read "No Mexicans Allowed," when it was common practice to segregate Mexican Americans in housing, swimming pools, employment, theaters, and restaurants, and deny them access to public parks and participation in organized sports. Even as late as the 1960s, Little League, Colt and Pony Leagues, and Babe Ruth baseball ignored many Mexican American communities, doing little to promote youth baseball. Mexican American communities responded to the racial intolerance in similar fashion as their African American neighbors, bt establishing their own teams, leagues, and tournaments. The history of Mexican American baseball and its socio-political implications in Southern California were largely ignored until the twenty-first century. The beginnings of that recognition are revealed in the accompanying sidebar on pages 12–13, the Latino Baseball History Project based at the John M. Pfau Library at California State University at San Bernardino.

LOS CHORIZEROS

The history of Mexican American baseball dates back to the massive immigration of Mexicans into East Los Angeles during the first two decades of the twentieth century. East L.A. is located east of the Los Angeles River and is linked to downtown Los Angeles by several concrete bridges built by the Works Progress Administration during the Great Depression. The community is both flat and hilly, and is divided into several distinct communities including City Terrace, Boyle Heights, Belvedere, Lincoln Heights, and Maravilla. With the emigration from Mexico, the area of "East Los," as its residents called it, became truly an American melting pot, with Jewish, Polish, Japanese, Chinese,

Armenian, Russian, Turkish, German, and Mexican residents. As other ethnic groups moved on after World War II, Mexican Americans became the predominant group. With this demographic, East L.A., or the Eastside, is now commonly regarded not so much as a particular geographical area but as a symbol of Mexican ethnic identity.[5]

This ethnic change was reflected in the flourishing of Mexican American businesses such as Mario's Service Station located on First Street and Hicks. Mario López, the owner of the gas station, had been an avid ballplayer in his native Chihuahua, Mexico, playing well enough on the outstanding Anahuac team to be recruited by the Cleveland Indians when he was only sixteen years old in 1925. But his family refused to allow him to turn professional. After immigrating to the United States in the late 1920s, he played on several teams in the Los Angeles area, including *Carta Blanca*. In 1942, López decided to sponsor a team under the name of Mario's Service Station. The team manager was Tommy Pérez, an outstanding right-handed pitcher from the desert area of Victorville-Barstow in California, who had learned to throw a mean knuckleball. Pérez had been a teammate of López on the *Carta Blanca* club, and the two men had become close, a friendship so strong that Pérez served as the manager of both of López's businesses, Mario's Service Station and later the Carmelita Provision Company. Besides being the team's ace pitcher, Tommy Pérez managed Mario's Service Station to at least two or three community championships, with López playing an outstanding shortstop. One major reason that López was able to recruit champion caliber players for his teams was that he liked to give them free gas when they had an outstanding game. After the games, López, Pérez, and the other players would return to the gas station to barbecue and drink beer. After the attack on Pearl Harbor and the outbreak of World War II, with many of the players serving in the military, baseball was suspended both in the community and at local high schools.[6]

By 1948 López had closed his gas station and was looking for new business opportunities. He remembered vividly that upon his arrival in East L.A. in the 1920s, few local markets carried popular Mexican food products, such as pigs' feet, *chicharrones* (pork rind),

Saul Toledo with son Saul Jr., Belvedere Park in East Los Angeles, circa 1964. This novelty photo, taken prior to the game, typifies how baseball was passed down from one generation of players to the next. In East L.A. families, it was common for two or more generations to play baseball.

LATINO BASEBALL HISTORY PROJECT

or *chorizo* (pork sausage). López, who had worked at a meatpacking plant from 1934 until 1942, began to produce *chorizo* and other popular Mexican pork items at the Carmelita Provision Company, named for Carmelita Avenue, where his factory was located. With the postwar demand increasing for familiar, good-quality food products by the rapidly growing Mexican community, the business prospered.[7]

Francisco "Pancho" Sornoso was an original co-owner of the *Chorizeros* for about six years along with Mario López. While he was not as active as López regarding baseball operations, Sornoso attended most of the games and traveled with the team to Mexico. His main responsibilities included customer service, purchasing pork, and selling Caremelita products.

According to his son Frank, López's focus on family, baseball, and business continued after he purchased the pork factory, and he soon formed a new team. Once again, López asked his good friend Tommy Pérez to be his manager. Just as they had done with the gas station team, both Pérez and López played on the team. López purchased the uniforms at the Bell Clothing Company. According to former players, the uniform had the team initials CPC stitched in cursive across the chest, smart-looking ball caps, and warm-up jackets. After winning its first community championship in 1948, one of the players, Saul Toledo, nicknamed the team *Los Chorizeros* (the Sausage Makers), and the moniker stuck.[8] The team logo was a pig with a baseball cap holding a glove and bat.

López used his new wealth to help those in the community who were less fortunate, giving away packages of *chorizo* to fans in the bleachers. After games he liked to invite his teammates to a local East L.A. restaurant-bar named the Joker's Den located near the famous *Cinco Puntos* (Five Points) for the five streets that intersect near Brooklyn and Lorena, or the Silver Dollar on Whittier Boulevard, or other watering holes, where he picked up the tab for tacos and beer. One of the players' wives, Louise Toledo, recalled that she and the other wives waited with their children in their cars while the men drank and ate at the pleasure of Mario López.[9]

Los Chorizeros were an amateur team, thus the players were not paid. They played for their great love and passion for baseball, according to Bea Armenta Dever, the daughter of Ray Armenta, one of the great local ballplayers. She noted that her father was fearless when challenging umpires' decisions and sometimes would go nose to nose with the men in blue. She added that, like most ballplayers of his era, her father sustained periodic injuries on the field, but they never stopped him from playing his heart out. Like many players, he was constantly whistling, chattering, and encouraging his team. When he made a mistake, he never put his head down or quit, regardless of the score.[10]

Former players grow nostalgic over those years when teams gave youngsters ten cents to shag fly balls, damaged bats and worn-out balls were almost completely wrapped with tape, players left their gloves on the field for the opposing team to use, rosin bags were on either side of the mound instead of the back of the mound, balls landed in nearby park swimming pools, young boys worked the manual scoreboard in center field, players wore wool uniforms, rookies learned to drink beer, spectators sat on the grass or makeshift stands to watch games and enjoy a picnic, players had to get the fields into shape, only two balls were used for the entire game, and the winning team took home the game balls.[11]

Los Chorizeros played at various local fields—Fresno, Belvedere, and Evergreen parks under the administration of the Los Angeles Department of Parks and Recreation, which established the rules and regulations of the games, including the responsibilities of the managers and umpires, and team equipment. Game day was usually Sunday. Ninety-year-old Saul Toledo, who played with the team from the early 1940s into the 1960s, is one of the oldest living *Chorizero* players. During his tenure, Toledo not only played baseball but also promoted the team through newspaper articles he wrote in the local press including "Midget" Martinez Sports Page and *La Publicidad*, hosted a local radio show on baseball, and served as a public address announcer after his retirement from playing baseball. Toledo's memories are sharp, and he speaks fondly of both the hard-fought games and the many friendships forged with players, their families, and loyal fans. He noted that the majority of teams they played against were Mexican American, but there were also teams made up of largely of African Americans, Asian Americans, and other ethnic groups. The teams that they played against, many times for the city championships, mirrored the ethnic diversity of the greater Los Angeles area—Jalisco Beer, Eagle Rock All Stars, Coast Meats, L.A. Braves, L.A. Coasters, Watts Giants, L.B. Grays, Hawthorne Merchants, North American Knights, Evergreen Cubs, Sons of Italy, Central Monarchs, L.A. Royals, Dow Painters, G.M.C. Trucks, *Carta Blanca*, and *Hermanidad Sastres*.[12]

After a few years, Tommy Pérez resigned as manager and another key individual in the history of *Los Chorizeros* was selected to manage the team, Manuel Pérez (no relation to Tommy Pérez), affectionately know as "Shorty." If *Los Chorizeros* were the New York Yankees of East L.A., Shorty was Joe McCarthy, Casey Stengel, and Joe Torre all wrapped into one. He, along

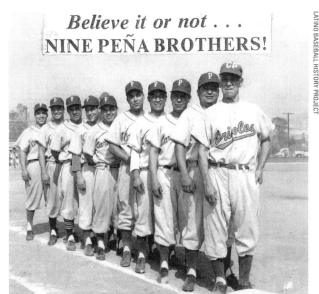

At Belvedere Park, the nine Peña brothers pose with their father William. This baseball family encompassed three generations, as grandfather, father, and all nine sons were baseball men. The grandfather, father, and five of the sons played the position of catcher. Their photograph appeared in *Ripley's Believe It or Not*.

Carmelita Chorizeros, 1948, Ross Snyder Park, home of the Watts Giants. Team manager Shorty Perez is wearing the National Auto Glass Company jersey. The two co-owners of the team, Mario López (*bottom left*) and Frank Sornoso (*bottom right*), are in civilian clothes. Outstanding players included Richard Alvarez, Larry Ochoa, Danny Salazar, and 17-year-old left-handed pitcher/outfielder Richard Peña (*top left*). This team won the East Los Angeles championship.

with Mario López, were the glue that kept the team together for nearly 35 years—an unprecedented number of years for any community team in the greater Los Angeles area and possibly in the United States. During his reign, Shorty's teams won numerous championships at the city and community levels. One of the great games of his managerial career took place at Wrigley Field in Los Angeles in 1961 when *Los Chorizeros* beat Venice, 3–2, in the Los Angeles City Finals, prevailing over pitcher Joe Moeller, who was about to sign a lucrative contract with the Los Angeles Dodgers and enjoyed a good professional career with the team.

As described by Saul Toledo, Shorty's typical Sunday began by attending Mass with his family, after which he returned home, loaded his car with bats, balls, gloves, chest protectors, and bases, and headed off to the baseball diamond. Shorty and his son would drag and water down the infield, chalk the foul lines, and make sure that all was ready for both teams and the thousands of fans. Once, when the team was short of catchers, Shorty went behind the plate and caught the entire game—at the age of 65.[13]

Game day was an exciting time for the entire community. The players would arrive early at the park to help prepare the playing field. Some of the wives and girlfriends would set up food stands, where they sold beef tacos, tamales, chorizo and egg burritos, beans and rice, and a variety of soft drinks and beer including *Dos Equis*, Lucky Lager, Brew 102, Pabst Blue Ribbon, and Eastside Beer. Music was often provided by an assortment of musicians including *mariachis*, strolling

trios, and individual *musicos*. In the stands, the fans cheered for their favorite teams and players, rooting and good-naturedly ribbing in both English and Spanish. There was loud laughter and gossip among friends and families. Dozens of children played in nearby sandboxes and on swings under the watchful eyes of their older brothers and sisters.

In a more serious vein, *Los Chorizeros* played during a turbulent time and place for Mexican Americans, for the 1930s to the 1960s saw a series of racially charged events and conflicts in Los Angeles. During the Great Depression, for instance, Southern California businesses and county charities targeted thousands of local residents for expulsion to Mexico. By conservative estimates one-third of the Mexican community was forced to flee Southern California to Mexico. Baseball player Al Padilla vividly recalled his mother's fear that the family would be sent to Mexico.[14] In the 1940s, racial intolerance directed specifically at young Mexican Americans again erupted. In 1942 The Sleepy Lagoon Case involved two dozen Mexican youths who were found guilty in a highly publicized murder trial. That led the following year to physical confrontations between U.S. servicemen and young Mexican Americans wearing the popular zoot suit. In the "Bloody Christmas Incident" of 1951, seven Mexican American prisoners were beaten by police officers at the Lincoln Heights jail. "Operation Wetback" of 1954 was yet another campaign to deport Mexicans. Then there was the eviction of the Mexican American community of Chávez Ravine in the 1950s to provide land for Dodger

Stadium. The 1960s marked the birth of the Los Angeles Chicano movement protesting the war in Vietnam, police brutality, deportations, and inferior public education.[15]

Chorizero baseball games provided both players and their supporters with a safe and convenient forum to discuss their labor struggles, political issues, and strategies to confront racial discrimination. Ethnic and political solidarity was manifested at games. Mexican American labor and political leaders attended games along with community leaders from local and national groups such as the Community Service Organization and the American G.I. Forum. "Smart politicians attended the games, because that was where the Mexican people were—at the church and ballpark," observed *Chorizero* ball player Johnny Peña.[16] For example, Los Angeles City Council member and later Congressman Edward R. Roybal and famous singer-guitarist and activist Eduardo "Lalo" Guerrero frequently attended games. Among the children was future film star Edward James Olmos.

The era in which Mexican American baseball flourished in Los Angeles, epitomized by the emergence of *Los Chorizeros* as a powerhouse, must be viewed within the context of the racial strife of the times and the community's ultimate response. Each intrinsically influenced the other. Mexican American players played ball on Sunday but during the rest of the week many became active in political and labor organizations to promote the preservation of the Mexican culture and language against cultural assimilation. A number of *Chorizeros* recalled that they and their families became involved in campaigns to secure a voice for their community, particularly in Edward Roybal's successful campaigns for Los Angeles City Council in 1949 and United States Congress in 1962.[17]

So baseball played an essential role in the life of the Mexican American community of East Los Angeles. Involvement in the game taught young people the rules of fair play, helped develop their physical and organizational skills, helped channel their competitiveness in a positive way, promoted civil and labor rights, reaffirmed cultural values and traditions, and forged a national identity for people of Mexican heritage by bringing them together across miles and circumstances to the baseball diamond. For some Mexican Americans, these games mirrored larger racial and class struggles that transcended the playing field, as community members often faced reprisals and harassment for being brown. On the field, what essentially mattered was that you played well, not the color of your skin. But what went on among the spectators

during and after the games was equally important, for such contests often had social, political, and cultural objectives. According to historian José M. Alamillo, Mexican Americans used baseball to demonstrate their equality through athletic competition and to broadcast community solidarity and strength.[18] Like family and religion, baseball was an institutional thread that united the community. These political conversations strengthened the communal sense of political empowerment and ethnic solidarity. The baseball field became another instrument for political organizing in the cause of civil and human rights. Mexican Americans in East Los Angeles had heroes to look to, teams to rally around, and shared experiences with which to build a stronger sense of cultural unity and common purpose for themselves and their children. One of the teams they looked up to was *Los Chorizeros*.

Many of the old ballplayers are now gone. Among them is Mario López who passed away at the young age of 57 in 1966. Unfortunately, López did not live to see his Mexican pork products become mainstream items in American chain stores and markets of the late twentieth century. Both Tommy Pérez and Shorty Pérez, the first and second managers of *Los Chorizeros*, also are gone. Tommy died in 1987 and Shorty in 1981. Shorty was buried in his uniform with a baseball autographed by his players and others. Shorty also had the distinction of being the first person inducted into the short-lived Carmelita Chorizeros Hall of Fame.[19]

Many of the *Chorizero* players went on to become educators, probation officers, political and business leaders, coaches, and professors.[20] And many of them continue to speak at schools, raise scholarships, and promote youth sports. *Los Chorizeros'* legacy continues whenever a Mexican American youth team takes the field. They were the foundation long ago that helped establish East Los Angeles into a true Field of Dreams for thousands of youths. To this day, the team logo sits prominently on the top of the Carmelita Provision Company factory building, where thousands of commuters on the Long Beach Freeway can still see the little pig with his bat and glove.[21] ■

Dedication
The authors wish to dedicate this article to the memory of Saul Toledo, who died on September 28, 2010, as we were completing this article.

Notes
1. The authors want to express their gratitude to a number of individuals who shared their memories of baseball and their families: Bea Armenta Dever, Isidro "Chilo" Herrera, Bob Lagunas, Mario and Frank López, Conrad Munatones, Al Padilla, Richard and Johnny Peña, Armando Pérez, Tom Pérez, Ernie Rodríguez, Saul Toledo, and Art Velarde. Executive Director of the Baseball Reliquary Terry Cannon and research assistant

Mark Ocegueda also provided special assistance. We especially want to acknowledge Jean Ardell for her excellent editing and baseball perspective. Finally, to the entire staff at the Pfau Library at California State University at San Bernardino for their tremendous support and assistance on this article.

2. The historical literature on Mexican American baseball in Los Angeles and elsewhere is quite limited. However, especially helpful were Samuel O. Regalado, "Baseball in the Barrios: The Scene in East Los Angeles Since World War II," *Baseball History* (Summer 1986), 47–59; Richard A. Santillan, "Mexican American Baseball Teams in the Midwest, 1916–1965: The Politics of Cultural Survival and Civil Rights," in *Perspectives in Mexican American Studies*, VII (Tucson: University of Arizona Press, 2000), 132–151; Francisco E. Balderrama and Richard A. Santillan, *Mexican American Baseball in Los Angeles* (Mount Pleasant: Arcadia Press, 2011).

3. Interview with Tom Pérez, 31 August 2010; Interview with Terry Cannon, 16 August 2010.

4. The article rests upon extensive oral history testimony including Isidro "Chilo" Herrera, Al Padilla, Richard Peña, Ernie Rodríguez, Saul Toledo, Art Velarde of the "Mexican American Baseball in Los Angeles: From the Barrios to the Big Leagues" project in the Special Collections at the John F. Kennedy Library, California State University Los Angeles.

5. The historiography of the Mexican in Los Angeles has grown rapidly recently but there remains no history of East LA. However, helpful for this period is Douglas Monroy, *Rebirth: Mexican Los Angeles From the Great Migration to the Great Depression* (Berkeley: University of California Press, 1999) for his incorporation of sports including baseball. Rodolfo Acuña, *A Community Under Siege: A Chronicle of Chicanos East of the Los Angeles River, 1945–1975* (Los Angeles: Chicano Studies Research Center, UCLA, 1984) for a discussion of key political-socio-economic changes.

6. Interviews with Padilla and Tom Pérez.

7. *Los Angeles Times*, 30 November 2008.

8. Interviews with Frank López, 7 September 2010, Saul Toledo, 12 March 2010; Tom Pérez interview.

9. Toledo interviews.

10. Correspondence of Bea Armenta Dever to the authors, 13 July 2010, 25 July 2010 as well as correspondence between Armenta Dever to Terry Cannon, 9 February 2008.

11. Interviews with Al Padilla, Richard Peña, Ernie Rodríguez Saul Toledo, and Art Velarde of the "Mexican American Baseball in Los Angeles: From the Barrios to the Big Leagues" project.

12. Ibid.

13. Toledo interview; KCET "Life and Times" Television Program, 19 April 2006; KTLA News, 30 April 2006; Regalado, "Baseball in the Barrios," 47.

14. Interview with Al Padilla, 3 August 2010.

15. Among the best and most recent studies of politics with significant information on the Los Angeles Mexican Eastside is Kenneth C. Burt, *The Search for a Civic Voice: California Latino Politics* (Claremont: Regina Press, 2007).

16. Interview with Johnny Peña, 8 September 2010.

17. Interviews with Padilla, Peña, Toledo.

18. See José Alamillo, "Peloteros in Paradise: Mexican American Baseball and Oppositional Politics in Southern California, 1930–1950," *Western Historical Quarterly*, XXXIV: 2, 191-212 as well as "Mexican American Baseball: Masculinity, Racial Struggle and Labor Politics in Southern California, 1930–1960," in John Bloom and Michael Willard, (eds.) *Sports Matters: Race, Recreation, and Culture*. (New York: New York University Press, 2002).

19. *Eastside Journal. Belvedere Citizen*, 2 December 1981.

20. Many Barrio baseball players including the Chorizeros dedicated their lives to careers in education as teachers and coaches such as Conrad Munatones, Al Padilla, Armando Pérez, and Ernie Rodríguez. See interviews of Al Padilla, Armando Pérez, Ernie Rodríguez, of the "Mexican American Baseball in Los Angeles: From the Barrios to the Big Leagues" project.

21. After the death of Shorty Pérez, Francisco "Frank" Corral managed the team until his untimely death in 2005. During his tenure *Los Chorizeros* won several more community, league, and tournament championships but not at the city level nor with the skillful players that dominated baseball from 1948 to the 1970s. *Los Chorizeros* still play today, appearing in August of 2010 as an all-star team in the city of El Monte. The club, however, can best be described as a pick-up team. Mario López's son, Frank, is often asked to throw out the first ceremonial pitch in respect to his father's legacy. Interview with Frank and Mario López, 8 and 9 September 2010.

The Latino Baseball History Project

Although the Mexican American community of East Los Angeles produced talented baseball players and managers and numerous teams, leagues, and tournaments that instilled a sense of community pride and achievement for more than 80 years, American society, especially the sports media and academia, paid little attention. This historical neglect has been exacerbated by the focus of historians on African American baseball. Since the birth of our nation, race relations have traditionally been socially framed as solely between white and black. Moreover, the Mexican American community has been often viewed in simplistic terms of where workers and their families live, without thorough investigation of its vibrant social institutions and established infrastructures. The reality is that the Mexican American community has had and continues to have a rich history of participation in the national pastime. As the following time line shows, the Latino Baseball History Project, a partnership between scholars and former players, has begun to reclaim that history through library exhibits, college courses, oral history interviews, documentaries, and scholarly and popular publications.

Fall 2004: For a library technology class assignment at Pasadena City College, Terry Cannon, the founder and executive director of the Baseball Reliquary, arranges an interview with Maggie Lu, a staff member at the John F. Kennedy Library at California State University Los Angeles (CSULA), where he notices empty display cases in the lobby. Cannon contacts David Sigler, in charge of Special Collections and coordinator of exhibits, with the idea to present an exhibition with the working title "Chicano Baseball: From the Barrios to the Big Leagues." Cannon follows up with César Caballero, acting university librarian at CSULA, who enthusiastically endorses a larger-scale exhibition on campus and enlists the support of Francisco E. Balderrama, a Professor of Chicano Studies and History at CSULA. Cannon establishes an advisory committee for the exhibition project, contacting historians and academicians who have done research on aspects of Mexican American baseball history in the Los Angeles area as well as other regions around the country. Out of their efforts come several significant developments and events as follows:

Fall 2005, Fall 2006: The Chicano Studies and History course, "Mexican American Baseball: An Oral History Approach," is taught by Professor Balderrama. The students collect photos and artifacts and interview dozens of former ballplayers and family members. The students' research uncovers evidence that baseball was an important means for Mexican Americans to celebrate ethnic identity, instill community pride, and promote socio-political awareness and activism.

March 2006: Drawing from the oral histories and artifacts from Balderrama's course, Terry Cannon presents "Mexican American Baseball in Los Angeles: From the Barrios to the Big Leagues" at CSULA. The exhibits attract hundreds of people, result in several media stories, and introduce the former ballplayers to a new generation of Mexican American baseball fans. It is one of the first Mexican American baseball exhibits at a major university in the U.S.[1]

November 2006: Former Mexican American ballplayers, including *Los Chorizeros*, serve as grand marshals of the 2nd Annual Boyle Heights Multicultural Parade.[2]

2007: The Project receives the Federation of State Humanities Councils' Schwartz Prize as the outstanding public funded humanities program in the United States.[3] Upon the recommendation of council member José Huizar, the Los Angeles City Council declares a special tribute in honor of the Mexican American ballplayers who contributed so much to the rich history of Los Angeles.[4]

May 2009: The John M. Pfau Library at California State University, San Bernardino is designated the official collection site for the Project, renamed the Latino Baseball

LATINO BASEBALL HISTORY PROJECT

The Carmelita Chorizeros logo has seen numerous changes over the years. Variations have included the baseball cap with or without the letter "C," the pig with both a glove and/or bat, and the use of black and white or color. The logo shown here is one of the earliest versions of the team mascot. The current color logo is displayed on the factory wall in East Los Angeles and appears on the sides of Carmelita's delivery trucks.

History Project. For the first time, a major university partners with the Mexican American community to establish a repository for Mexican American baseball history in Southern California. (The second stage of the project will broaden its scope to include Mexican American baseball throughout the United States and, eventually, other U.S. Latino groups.)

The Project continues to receive awards, grants, and public recognition from diverse organizations: the California Council for the Humanities; Los Angeles Trade-Technical College, Institute for Socio-Economic Justice, Brawley, California; Southwest Oral History Annual Conference; Natural History Museum of Los Angeles County; Pasadena Central Library; Pasadena City College; and the Pomona Public Library.

Notes

1. *Los Angeles Times*, 7 April 2006, 10 April 2006; *University Times*, 17 April 2006; *Daily News*, 23 April 2006; *The Press Enterprise*, 6 May 2006: KCAL Television News, 29 April 2006.
2. "You Tube, Boyle Heights Parade," 19 November 2006, www.youtube.com/watch?v=lvmZoUGViDA&feature (Accessed 25 August 2010).
3. Helen and Martin Schwartz Prize 2007, Federation of State Humanities Councils Program, www.statehumanities.org/programs/pastschwartz.htm. (Accessed 25 August 2010).
4. *Los Angeles Daily News*, 21 September 2007.

Post-Cooperstown Post Modernism

The Baseball Reliquary and the Future of Nostalgia

Don Malcolm

> BASEBALL is America's game: has the snap, go, fling, of the American atmosphere—belongs
> as much to our institutions, fits into them as significantly, as our constitutions, laws...
>
> —Walt Whitman

Just what is the Baseball Reliquary, anyway? There are as many answers to that question as there are multitudes contained by Walt Whitman, the Brooklyn-based author of *Leaves of Grass* and the first American artist to embrace the game and assimilate it into his poetic vocabulary.

What Whitman did for baseball during its formative years in the nineteenth century, the Baseball Reliquary—a homeless, "virtual Cooperstown" more akin to a floating crap game than a venerable shrine—is doing for it in the twenty-first. Despite its image as a kind of "trickster anti-institution" celebrating baseball's fringe elements, the Reliquary's stance is richly visionary, embodying an expansive concept of baseball's place in American culture that is as freewheeling for its time as Whitman's was in his.

From its inception, the Baseball Reliquary—with its many programs exploring stylistic and aesthetic elements embodied in the game, with its unique inversion of the Hall of Fame's enshrinement process (its "Shrine of the Eternals"), and with its commitment to shining a light on the underrepresented histories of the game—has defined itself as a hit-and-run organization that could carry its paraphernalia in a rucksack. (A museum without walls, the Reliquary's collection is displayed at periodic exhibitions around Southern California, when not occupying several storage units.) Reliquary devotee Ron Shelton, writer-director of *Cobb* and *Bull Durham*, and one who is deeply immersed in the game, was struck by this calculated impermanence: "It's as if they've created a Hall of Fame that is really just a state of mind."

And yet, this studied indifference to the rules of "institution-hood" has produced an alternative Hall of Fame concept that is bracing in its uncanny selection process. The voting membership of the Reliquary, year after year, has produced a virtually flawless set of inductees who represent a cross-section of baseball's cultural and athletic concerns. Their 39 inductees (the complete list can be found in the box on page 17) have a unique breadth of coverage that transcends Cooperstown.

———

"There are two things that the Baseball Reliquary is known for," says founder and executive director Terry Cannon of Pasadena. "We are known for being irreverent and we're known for having all those strange artifacts." Beginning in 1996 Cannon and right-hand man Albert Kilchesty clearly brought post-modern sensibilities to their mission. Kilchesty, an accomplished experimental filmmaker, is the organization's brilliant but wayward archivist and historian, whose flair for the surreal is pronounced. Taking Henry David Thoreau's "different drummer" dictum to its ultimate conclusion, Kilchesty and Cannon decided to invert the relationship of spectator and artifact from what is standard museum practice. "What if the imagination had some say in what the artifacts were?" Kilchesty suggests, with a faraway gleam in his eyes.

What if, indeed. As a result, the Reliquary's earliest artifacts follow this notion as rigorously as any modernist manifesto—the difference being, of course, that the items in question are as slapstick as they are surreal. Witness the Walter O'Malley tortilla, where the visage of the man who broke Brooklyn's heart by moving the Dodgers to Los Angeles mysteriously became manifest on an oblong hunk of hand-rolled, hand-patted flour. As is often the case, though, there is something more serious at work in the Reliquary's carefully crafted satire. Cannon and Kilchesty, while happy to traffic in cheap laughs, provide a more substantive payoff in their description of the tortilla's "provenance":

No other item of baseball memorabilia illustrates more succinctly the complex relationship between the Los Angeles Dodgers and their Mexican American fan base than this unusual artifact—a flour tortilla bearing a remarkable

PHOTO BY LARRY GOREN, COURTEST OF THE BASEBALL RELIQUARY

The fabled, mysterious Walter O'Malley Tortilla: post-modernism, prank-sterism, or divine manifestation?

likeness to former Dodger owner Walter O'Malley. Purchased from Ernesto Villafon in 1988 by Los Angeles artist and photographer Tom Meyer, who subsequently donated it to the Baseball Reliquary, the provenance of the tortilla is sketchy. According to Meyer, the tortilla was discovered by Mrs. Regina Flores, a resident of Chavez Ravine, who presented the object to her nephew, young Ernesto, shortly before her death in 1981. Villafon told Meyer that it was the sight of the Dodger patriarch's jowly visage on the tortilla that convinced Mrs. Flores and family to abandon their Chavez Ravine home peacefully in 1959 prior to the construction of Dodger Stadium. After resettling in Highland Park, Mrs. Flores became a zealous Dodger fan, much to the amazement of her family and friends, who, claims Villafon, had never heard her express any interest in baseball. Radio carbon dating indicates that the tortilla is approximately forty years old, lending credence to Villafon's story. En-cased originally in an ordinary picture frame, Reliquary preparators delicately removed the fragile artifact and enclosed it in a glass-covered scientific mount box for display.

The early years of the Baseball Reliquary produced a small but potent set of these post-modern artifacts, each imbued with the deadpan zest of a Jacques Tati sustaining a series of meta-commentaries on the inherent silliness of institutional puffery. Sight gags are the Reliquary's stock in trade, and many of their sub-sequent artifacts—the athletic supporter ("jock strap") of Eddie Gaedel, the only midget to play major league baseball; a partially-smoked cigar discarded by Babe Ruth; and the "potato ball" used in a ruse perpetrated by minor-league catcher Dave Bresnahan—amplify this approach.

In recent years, however, the Reliquary's exhibits have evolved from the ridiculous to the sublime. Witness, for example, the nimble merging of hard-boiled fact and freewheeling fantasy in the "Mother Teresa Baseball Forgeries":

In April of 2000, the FBI announced that 26 Southern Californians had been indicted in what the law enforcement agency called the largest, most lucrative, and most brazen fraud ring ever busted for trafficking in phony sports and celebrity autographs and memorabilia. In a case dubbed "Operation Bullpen," the FBI seized mer-chandise in California, Nevada, and other states that was designed to be sold for ten million dol-lars, including forged autographs of Marilyn Monroe, Joe DiMaggio, Mickey Mantle, the Marx Brothers, and Albert Einstein. The operation even produced a box of one dozen baseballs bearing the signature of Mother Teresa. "I think that pretty much says it all," said William Gore, spe-cial agent overseeing the FBI case. U.S. Attorney General Gregory Vaga seemed particularly ap-palled by the sacrilegious implications of the Mother Teresa forgeries, as he told reporters, "To so crassly exploit Mother Teresa, a woman the world has anointed as a saint and who spent a life of heroic virtue, is unconscionable."

"Operation Bullpen" involved undercover in-formants, a dummy company, wiretaps, and sixty search warrants. In just one month, the ring provided phony signatures on more than 10,000 baseballs. On the wiretaps, defendants were heard joking that Mickey Mantle and Mother Teresa had "one arm out of their graves" signing their names.

In a 72-page indictment, officials said that 50% to 90% of the one-billion-dollar-a-year memorabilia market is based on fraudulent goods. At the request of the Baseball Reliquary, federal law en-forcement authorities donated to the organization the box of one dozen baseballs bearing Mother

Baseball Reliquary Founder and Executive Director Terry Cannon with one of the Reliquary's most notable Shrine of the Eternals inductees, author/broadcaster/actor/pitcher Jim Bouton.

Teresa's forged signature to be used for exhibition purposes in order to alert consumers to the large amount of inauthentic memorabilia in the marketplace and to warn them to be cautious when purchasing autographed items.

Neither Cannon nor Kilchesty will confirm or deny the veracity of the above narrative: in fact, neither of them will cop to having written the narrative itself. When confronted, each merely points the finger at the other.

————

The resemblance of the Baseball Reliquary to another alternative Pasadena "anti-institution," the Doo-Dah Parade (which has been sending up the venerable city's annual flora-laden flotilla, the Tournament of Roses Parade, since the late 1970s), began to change in 1999 with the creation of its post-modern Cooperstown, the Shrine of the Eternals, whose induction ceremony is held at the Pasadena Central Library.

That July, an anti-traditional ritual was first devised, and the first three members of the Eternals—Dock Ellis, Curt Flood, and Bill Veeck, Jr.—were inducted. Over the years the ceremonies would become more elaborate, with additional awards given to ordinary fans and often-unheralded historians, but the perfect balance of whimsy and high seriousness was captured by Cannon in what has become an iconic opening signature for the festivities: the ringing of a cowbell in honor of

baseball's most raucous and extreme fan, Brooklyn's Hilda Chester, whose own incessant use of it was aptly described by Cannon as proof that she was "a master of the art of cacophony."

The Shrine of the Eternals ceremony would, from that point forward, mirror that idea. The flow of events would always drift between order and anarchy. The ceremony itself was a work of performance art, with a series of participants who added their own imagination to the inchoate tapestry that emerged out of thin air.

In his introduction during that first ceremony, Richard Amromin, chairman of the Reliquary's Board of Directors, spoke directly to the affinity between baseball and art:

> …art is not pre-defined…the freedom to make aesthetic, moral and social decisions, and face the consequence of those decisions, is the essence of art. And this is where today's honorees are true artists…they have transcended their chosen craft and exercised the freedom to make the same type of…decisions made by the greatest artists.

Thus began an induction process that, after twelve years, has built assiduously on this idea. Cooperstown would rarely be in congruence with the Reliquary voters, who recognized that their mission was to look for the forgotten, the legendary, the controversial, the visionary.

As the process evolved, those who paid attention began to see an emerging pattern in the type of individual honored by the Reliquary. "It wasn't about statistics," writer John Schulian notes. "It was about the impact that the person had on the game. And it was about the impact that the game had had on the person. It worked both ways."

The induction process gained in resonance as the years accumulated. "Somehow in the midst of this initially whimsical and irreverent Hall of Fame alternative, a mysterious thread began to appear in each threesome being honored," writer David Davis recalls. "An anonymous voter membership was suddenly creating themes and connections, adding a level of meaning that no one could possibly have expected to emerge out of such a process. It started to become mind-blowing."

The Reliquary voters were themselves becoming artists.

"I suppose one could see it as its own form of 'mass performance art,'" Terry Cannon suggests. "It seems as though we have defined a set of alternative categories for deserving individuals, and our voters have become locked into that process."

Terry Cannon, executive director of the Baseball Reliquary and deadpan comic, channels Brooklyn's Hilda Chester (the Queen of the Cowbell) as he calls to order the Reliquary's Shrine of the Eternals ceremony in Pasadena.

VOTING CATEGORIES
Baseball Reliquary Shrine of the Eternals, 1999–2011
39 inductees

Visionary (7)
Roberto Clemente,* Curt Flood, Bill James, Marvin Miller, Jackie Robinson,* Lester Rodney, Bill Veeck

Controversial (7)
Dick Allen, Jim Bouton, Dock Ellis, Ted Giannoulas, Shoeless Joe Jackson, Bill Lee, Pete Rose

Pioneering (13)
Jim Abbott, Roger Angell, Emmett Ashford, Ila Borders, Jim Brosnan, Rod Dedeaux, Jim Eisenreich, Josh Gibson,* Satchel Paige,* Pam Postema, Fernando Valenzuela, Maury Wills, Kenichi Zenimura

Forgotten/Overlooked (6)
Moe Berg, Bill Buckner, Pete Gray, William "Dummy" Hoy, Roger Maris, Minnie Minoso

Incandescent/Legendary (6)
Yogi Berra,* Steve Dalkowski, Mark Fidrych, Buck O'Neil, Jimmy Piersall, Casey Stengel*

* Inductee is also enshrined in the Baseball Hall of Fame

"It shifts around every year," adds Kilchesty. "But somehow, some way, the results keep blending into new shadings."

There is not much overlap with the Hall of Fame, as the accompanying chart shows. Only six of the 39 Eternals have plaques in Cooperstown. The other 30 represent the Reliquary's unique agglomeration of child-like wonder and aesthetic-historical sophistication.

"Pioneers" have emerged as the most conspicuous category of honorees—often individuals who broke a significant cultural barrier in their pursuit of the game. Players either officially barred from Cooperstown (Joe Jackson, Pete Rose), shunned for cultural reasons (Dick Allen), or overlooked for reasons of historical expediency (Marvin Miller) have been embraced by the Reliquary voters.

The Reliquary's roots in Southern California do show up in the voting results now and then, local heroes (Jackie Robinson, Jim Abbott, Rod Dedeaux, Fernando Valenzuela), natives (Bill Lee, Dock Ellis), and transplants (Lester Rodney, Kenichi Zenimura) are well represented. But the stories embedded in these baseball people's lives, and their cultural interaction with the sport, are what make them Eternals. The formula that comes to mind has little do with whether the individual played baseball, rather, it is how that person found self-expression through interaction with the game. Simply put, each of the honorees in the Shrine of the Eternals has some combination of adversity, extremity, and "otherness" that has made his or her life narrative unique and praiseworthy.

"Singularity is the key ingredient, I think," Kilchesty posits. "A member of the Eternals is one-of-a-kind, no matter how you might categorize them."

The Reliquary's most fruitful symbiosis in its evolution from "puckish irreverence" to "cultural synthesis" is clearly in its association with Southern California painter Ben Sakoguchi, whose ongoing "Unauthorized History of Baseball" fully embodies the qualities discussed above: adversity (a second-generation Japanese American, Sakoguchi was one of thousands detained in internment camps during World War II), extremity (Sakoguchi regularly incorporates jarring cultural juxtapositions in his work), and "otherness" (the work strongly exhibits anti-institutional and antinomian themes) are combined in an epic series of small (10" x 11") paintings that also pay homage to the storied "orange crate art" that was once ubiquitous in California.

Fifteen years ago, when Sakoguchi began the series (which now comprises nearly 250 paintings), it appeared that the symbiosis between his work and the Reliquary project was nothing more than a happy coincidence. Over the subsequent span of time, however, it's clear that there has been a convergence of sensibilities.

"It was interesting how almost all of our inductees would wind up with a painting of their own," says Cannon. "We never asked Ben to do that—we've never commissioned him. Ben doesn't work that way. I like to think that it's because we haven't asked him that he's found his own way to embrace our efforts. Perhaps he sees us as a variant of the type of inspiration that artists have. It's a delicate connection to a special realm of reality."

Sakoguchi breathes new life—an often pointedly scabrous life—into a quaint, undervalued art form. It is the essence of post-modernist artistic strategy, adding bark and bite, embodying the "snap, go, fling" that so captivated Walt Whitman (who was, after all, an avant-garde poet in his own day). The peculiar, indefinable energy that Whitman sensed in America, and that he saw exemplified in baseball, has not been severed from either the game or the nation in the time span separating his day from ours.

"It just seems that it has," muses Cannon. "We tend to forget that baseball emerged as a major force in America at the same time that the robber barons were carving up the nation's wealth. There's always been that tension between myth and reality in American culture, and baseball is right there in the middle of it all. It's a miracle that the game hasn't been completely sullied by corporatization, and we just want to do our part to make sure that it doesn't happen."

Kilchesty agrees. "No more uncritical nostalgia!" he shouts. When Walt Whitman is mentioned, he nods. "Whitman was no apologist—he was an enthusiast. He saw that art and play were vital therapies for the task of living. And baseball was where that was at for America. It still is."

Perhaps we can best explain the emergence of this most improbable anti-institution to the continuing need for cultural evolution, and its protection against the all-too-prevalent forces of ossification. If Whitman were here today, it's quite possible that he'd see the Reliquary, and not Cooperstown, as the embodiment of what should be celebrated about baseball and its connection with America. By inverting its uses, the Reliquary transforms nostalgia from a simple longing for the past into an engagement with the future as it rushes to greet us. Every third Sunday in July, the Reliquary's induction day, it is Whitman's notion of baseball as "the hurrah game" that animates the Reliquary's singular synthesis of art and ceremony, anarchy and ritual, past and future. ■

Manzanar

Family, Friends, and Desert Diamonds Behind Barbed Wire

Kerry Yo Nakagawa

"There was always the wind."
—Dennis Tojo Bambauer, orphaned internee living
in the Manzanar Children's Village

Growing up in the small farm town of Fowler, California, we used to travel east towards the Sierra Nevada mountains to go fishing or picnic at the river or lakes. I remember hearing stories about camp life on the "other side" of those mountains—at Manzanar—from my cousins. My relatives and community lived in the animal stalls of the Santa Anita Race Track because of President Roosevelt's Executive Order 9066. Six months later, they transferred to the permanent Manzanar Detention Camp between the towns of Lone Pine and Independence, in California's Owens Valley over the mountains from where we [later] fished.

My cousin, Aiko Harada, was one of 10,046 inmates/internees and had her first child at Manzanar. "We had to stuff our mattresses with hay and shared our tiny space with my husband's parents. The only privacy we had was the blanket hung between us," Aiko said.

My relatives were a small part of the 120,000 West Coast persons of Japanese American ancestry who were removed from their homes in 1942, neighborhood by neighborhood. The temporary Assembly centers were built throughout California at racetracks, fairgrounds, and similar facilities. Detainees spent much of the spring and summer of 1942 in these facilities. Conditions were generally poor, as might be expected given the haste in which they were built. Residents complained of overcrowding, shoddy construction, communal showers, and toilets with no partitions. The worst indignity was being housed in the odorous horse stables or animal stalls at the race tracks of Santa Anita, Tanforan (near San Francisco), and Fresno. Military police patrolled the perimeters and regulated visitors. Internal police held roll calls and enforced curfews. Inside the animal stalls of the assembly centers, families reflected on their lost homes, educational opportunities, businesses, cars, furniture, and heirloom artifacts, which had been sold for ten cents on the dollar. They had been able to bring only what they could carry in two suitcases. One of the first problems facing the internees was to establish a sense of routine in the face of totally disrupted patterns of life. Cultural, recreational, and work activities took on tremendous importance. There were schools for the children and many adults were government employees earning standard G.I. wages. Doctors and other professionals earned the top $19 monthly wage. Teachers, secretaries, and other support staff earned a $16 monthly wage, and laborers were paid $12 per month.

Through the hardships of the searing summers and harsh winters, Japanese Americans and baseball began to flourish. Although the government took away constitutional rights, freedom, radios, cameras, religion, and for the immigrant Issei, their native language, Uncle Sam did not deny Japanese Americans the right to play the All-American Pastime of baseball. George Omachi, a former Nisei (first generation born in the US) baseball player, manager and Houston Astros scout said, "Without baseball, camp life would have

EFT Storytellers on Manzanar Baseball Field. *Left to right*: Kerry Yo Nakagawa (Nisei Baseball Research Project), Pete Mitsui (Founder of San Fernando Aces), Jeff Arnett (former director of education at the National Baseball Hall of Fame).

Manzanar Champions. The prewar San Fernando Aces team were the camp champions. Top row, fourth from left: Founder of the Aces Pete Mitsui.

been miserable.... It was humiliating, demeaning, being incarcerated by our own country." Assembly center baseball teams began to organize and develop almost immediately. Baseball played a major role in an effort to create a degree of continuity and recreation. Playing, watching, and supporting baseball inside America's concentration camps brought a sense of normalcy to then very abnormal lives, creating a social and positive atmosphere for the internees. Arts and sports practiced by the internees were not entertainment but approaches for finding, articulating, and preserving meaning in a senseless situation. Former internee Pete Mitsui, founder of the San Fernando Aces and coach of the Manzanar camp champions, said, "The ballclub was an important part of the community identity. Examining that history today is a way to explain not only what happened but why the internment camps episode occurred, as well as how the 1942 events connect to today's issues."

All ten permanent camps in the US built diamonds and established teams and leagues. At Manzanar, the teams took turns driving a dump truck to the hills for decomposed granite. They would lay granite down in the bleacher and dugout sections of the ball field, as well as the infield to cut down on the dust that stirred up during the games. San Francisco Aces catcher Barry Tamura worked for the camp fire department and ensured the field was watered down by conducting frequent fire drills on the diamond. At Manzanar's "A"

Field, thousands of fans gathered to watch their home-town heroes from the San Fernando Aces, San Pedro Skippers, Scorpions, Padres, Manza Knights, Oliver's, Has-beens and other organized teams of the camp's twelve leagues. The Aces and Skippers were prewar, semipro powerhouse teams coming into the camp established, while other teams formed in the camps. By the summer of 1942, the camp newspaper, *The Manzanar Press*, was covering nearly 100 men's and 14 women's softball teams like the Dusty Chicks, Modernaires, Stardusters, and Montebello Gophers. The four primary "A" teams who were considered semipro were the Guadalupe YMBA in Gila River, Arizona, the Florin AC at Jerome, Arkansas, the San Fernando Aces at Manzanar, and the Wakabas at Tule Lake, California. "If it wasn't for the war, I think we could have had a Japanese American major leaguer even before Jackie Robinson," said Tets Furukawa, a pitcher for the Gila River Eagles.

Rosie Kakauchi played on that field with the Dusty Chicks and was an all-star catcher. "We were so good we even challenged the men to play us and we beat them," she said. Rosie's husband Jack would enlist and play third base for Camp Grant, an Illinois Army team. In 1943, the Camp Grant team would beat the Chicago Cubs in an exhibition, 4–3.

Baseball serves as a touchstone to compare and contrast different cultures, since Japanese Americans in the internment camps had white teachers who

Famed prewar photographer Toyo Miyatake took this photo from centerfield looking into the grandstands of Manzanar. He smuggled his lenses into camp, building boxes around them to make homemade cameras, and took over 40,000 images.

reinforced mainstream values. No matter how remote, how desolate the camps were, baseball was a vehicle to give focus to lives and link the prisoners to their culture and their community. Baseball serves as a lens to examine camp history and provide an opportunity for people to discuss the delicate and troublesome stories of internment. Baseball provides the common grounds with which these people can identify with all diverse cultures. American citizens of the Issei and Nisei generations were imprisoned by their own government primarily because they looked like the enemy, while German and Italian Americans were not. As a result, internment camps are central to Japanese American culture. Japanese American baseball is a story of inclusion within the context of exclusion. Against their backdrop of exclusionary laws, baseball was passionately played within the community by local teams. In the beginning, internment camp conditions were dismal and morale was low. The adults sought out baseball as a way to bring a sense of normalcy to the futility of daily life. Baseball not only created a positive atmosphere, but encouraged physical conditioning, and maintained self-esteem despite the harsh conditions of desert life and unconstitutional incarceration.

The irony of baseball behind barbed wire was that Japanese Americans were considered enemy aliens and confined to camps. Donning a baseball uniform, however, gave them free passage to road trips from Gila River, Arizona to Heart Mountain, Wyoming or Amache, Colorado. "The ball players would usually travel in small groups of five or six so that we would not create attention," said Howard Zenimura. "None of the citizens of the different towns and cities we passed through paid us much attention." The players would travel by Greyhound bus hundreds of miles for a one- or two-week road trip. The other irony is that most of the diamonds were built outside of the barbed wire. Sab Yamada, an outfielder with the Fresno Assembly Center team, said, "Where would you run to? There were hundreds of miles of desert and most of the government officials were upset that they were in the desert too...[T]here was no treachery or espionage going on in the camps."

————

On February 13, 2007, the Nisei Baseball Research Project joined the National Park Service, Ball State University, and the National Baseball Hall of Fame for an "electronic field trip" (where classrooms all over the country are taken to an interesting place via a television satellite hookup). A group of students from Kansas schools won the contest to host the show. Through the prism of Manzanar, students learned about Japanese American internment. Secretary of the Interior Dirk Kempthorne, with Nisei veterans Joe Ichiuji (liberated Dachau with the highly decorated all-Nisei 442nd Regiment Combat Team) and Grant Hirabayashi (Army Ranger Hall of Fame) helped facilitate questions.

We met that frigid morning to clear out sagebrush and tumbleweeds on the baseball fields of Manzanar. Pete Mitsui, manager and former player of the Manzanar champions, led us to where the bases used to be. At first base, we discovered a rusty peg that had anchored the base back in 1942.

"Seeing our kids so excited and getting the opportunity to host a live show was the highlight of my educational career," said Dan Brown, a teacher from Kansas. For Tom Leatherman (former superintendent of Manzanar), it was all about the kids telling the story of internment. "Watching the students become the voice and engage and share their discoveries with millions of other kids across the country was powerful."

I personally will treasure looking at the towering slopes of the Sierra Nevada mountains, being part of this historic event with my peers and Nisei "Pioneers" and playing catch with Tom Leatherman after clearing, leveling, grooming, and lining the "new" Manzanar baseball field. Manzanar is a Spanish term meaning "apple orchard" and reminds us that the interned Japanese Americans were as American as mom, apple pie, and baseball. They kept the All-American Pastime alive, even from behind barbed wire. In their world, life brought a desert and they built these diamonds in the rough, persevered, and eventually made it home.

After 1945, most Japanese Americans had very little. Most came back to nothing, but they could still meet every Sunday at the ball field, forging community and fellowship. Through its positive identity and image, baseball helped salve the deep wounds of war. Similarly, the story about baseball behind barbed wire contains the potential to transform not only Japanese-American communities, but American communities throughout the nation because of its heroic triumph over discrimination and xenophobia. ■

References

Nakagawa, Kerry Yo, *Through A Diamond, 100 Years of Japanese American Baseball*, (San Francisco; Rudi Publishing, 2001), Chapter Six.

Author Interviews

Kakauuchi, Rosie (2010), Mitsui, Pete (1997, 2010), Lynch, Alisa (2010), Leatherman, Tom (2010), Brown, Dan (2010), Zenimura, Kenso (1996, 1997, 2010), Yamada, Sab (1997), Omachi, George "Hats" (1996), Harada, Aiko (2010) Furukawa, Tets (2010).

For More Information

Manzanar National Historic Site. www.nps.gov/manz (760) 878-2194 Manzanar is located on the west side of U.S. highway 395, 9 miles north of Lone Pine, California and 6 miles south of Independence, CA.

Ball State University.www.bsu.eft-2000 W. University Ave. Muncie, IN 47306. (800) 382-8540 and (765) 289-1241.

National Baseball Hall of Fame and Museum. www.baseballhall.org, 25 Main Street Cooperstown, NY 13326-1300. (888) 425-5633.

Nisei Baseball Research Project. www.niseibaseball.com.

Toyo Miyatake Studios—285 West Fairview Avenue, San Gabriel, CA 91776. (626) 289-5674.

Stanford Program on International and Cross-Cultural Education. www.spice.stanford.edu (650) 723-1116.

American Pastime. Film. Warner Bros. (2007). www.warnervideo.com/ American Pastime.

The Asian-American jazz-fusion band Hiroshima has a song entitled "Manzanar" on its album *The Bridge* (2003). It is an instrumental song inspired by Manzanar and the Japanese American internment.

The Sandlot Mentors of Los Angeles

Rick Obrand

Southern California has long been fertile ground for major-league talent. Walter Johnson, Jackie Robinson, Bob Lemon, Duke Snider, Don Drysdale, George Brett, Tony Gwynn, and Ozzie Smith all began their careers on the sandlots and high school diamonds of the greater Los Angeles area. So many gifted athletes—but it takes more than raw talent to achieve big-league success. A strong work ethic, the opportunity to play regularly, good health, luck, and the proper development of skills are vital to reaching the Show. Many major-league stars credit their success to a coach who in their youth helped refine their natural skills. This article presents those little known but important men, who helped to launch so many players from the sandlots of Los Angeles to baseball stardom.

PLAYGROUND SUPERVISORS

Arthur Dietz (1874–?) led a life one might think was fictional. A graduate of Yale University, he mined for gold in Alaska, worked as a strongman in the Barnum & Bailey Circus, and was a professional long-distance swimmer. A train accident in Clarksburg, West Virginia, however, left Dietz with two broken legs and two broken arms, derailing his adventurism. Settling in the Los Angeles area in the early years of the twentieth century, he began a new career as a City of Los Angeles Parks and Recreation Supervisor. Working at the Slauson Playground, located at 62nd and Hoover in southeast Los Angeles, Dietz is credited with developing the baseball talents of Emil "Irish" Meusel (National League RBI leader in 1923), Bob Meusel (of the New York Yankees' famed Murderers' Row) and Pete Schneider (a big-league twenty-game winner who hit five home runs in a single PCL game in 1923). Along the way Dietz fathered fourteen children (twelve boys), though none achieved baseball success. During World War I he enlisted in the Army, where he served as the athletic director of US troops stationed in Paris. Following the end of the war, Dietz resumed his Los Angeles recreation career, working at Arroyo Seco Playground in north Los Angeles and Anderson Play-ground in San Pedro. At Arroyo Seco and Anderson, Dietz emphasized track and field athletics, and his athletes were always among the leaders in the Los Angeles Junior Pentathlon.

Bill Duvernet (1906–1991) played semipro baseball in Los Angeles, but spurned offers to turn professional to pursue a career as a Los Angeles City Playground Supervisor at Manchester Playground (1931–41). Located at Manchester and Hoover in southwest Los Angeles, the playground had four magnificent diamonds and, beginning in 1931, became a baseball hotbed under Duvernet's direction. More than 80 of his players enjoyed professional baseball careers; many of them credit Duvernet with their growth as ballplayers. Mickey Owen felt that "Duvernet was very encouraging and a big factor in my career development."[1] Bobby Doerr recalled, "He was always talking baseball."[2] Bud Stewart said, "Duvernet was a fine gentleman, so enthusiastic and encouraging to all his players."[3]

Among others with praise for Duvernet were Nippy Jones, Lou Stringer, Eddie Malone, Steve Mesner, Gerry Priddy, and Herschel Lyons. Owen, Doerr, Mesner, and Lyons all played on the same sandlot team at Manchester in 1932. Like Dietz a generation before him, Duvernet left his recreation career to serve during wartime. Stationed in New Guinea during World War II, he was in charge of organizing sports activities there. Following his military discharge, Duvernet continued his recreation career at Griffith Playground in north Los Angeles. At Griffith he became a big proponent of basketball and lobbied the recreation department to build more basketball courts, as Duvernet foresaw basketball gaining popularity.

Benny Lefebvre (1912–94) attended Manual Arts High School in Los Angeles, where he was better known for football than baseball. Following graduation, he played semipro football for the Los Angeles Maroons, Los Angeles Spoilers, and Long Beach Longshoremen, before beginning a career as a playground supervisor at

Rancho Cienega Playground in West Los Angeles. He also coached the Crenshaw Post American Legion team. The 1951 Crenshaw Legion team, featuring Billy Consolo and Sparky Anderson, won the National American Legion championship.

A legendary hitting instructor, Lefebvre tutored Consolo, Anderson, Norm Sherry, Larry Sherry, Don Buford, Marcel Lachemann, and Rene Lachemann. It's no coincidence that Anderson, Norm Sherry, and both Lachemanns became big league managers, as they were all schooled in Lefebvre fundamentals. Sparky Anderson did not live in the Dorsey High School district, but transferred there to play with the guys from Rancho. Anderson said, "Lefebvre made me realize that hard work was the only way."[4] Rene Lachemann said, "Benny Lefebvre was the most influential in developing my skills."[5]

Lefebvre also ran the Lefebvre Baseball and Summer Camp of Catalina Island 1954–63. Late in his career he coached baseball at St. Bernard's High School in Westchester and football at Pius X High School in Downey. He also coached his own sons, including Jim Lefebvre, the 1965 National League Rookie of the Year. Sons Gil and Tip also enjoyed professional baseball careers.

Chet Brewer (1907–90) grew up in Des Moines, Iowa. He debuted in the Negro Leagues in 1925, pitching off and on through 1952 in the Negro Leagues and elsewhere, with much success. In 1938 Brewer became the first African American to play in the Mexican League. Like many other Negro League stars of that era, he often spent the winter months playing in the California Winter League. Following fourteen seasons in the Winter League and enjoying the Los Angeles area, Brewer decided to make it his permanent home. A longtime scout for the Pittsburgh Pirates, he also established youth baseball programs in the Los Angeles and Compton areas. Among the major leaguers he helped develop were Roy White, Dock Ellis, Don Wilson, and Bobby Tolan. Dock Ellis felt Brewer "had a tremendous influence on my career."[6] Chet Brewer Field in south Los Angeles is named in his honor.

Earl Brown Jr. (1943–) grew up in Los Angeles and played baseball at legendary Fremont High School. Following a short stint at Los Angeles City College, he signed a pro contract with Tom Lasorda of the Los Angeles Dodgers. After two minor league seasons, however, Brown realized he would never reach the big leagues, retired from the game, and returned to Los Angeles. He went to work full-time for the Southern Pacific Railroad and

part-time as a playground supervisor at Manchester Playground in southwest Los Angeles. At Manchester he coached the 1968 Manchester Hawks, a youth team of nine to 12-year-olds that featured Eddie Murray, Ozzie Smith, Chet Lemon, and Rich Murray. He later led teams that featured Darryl Strawberry, Eric Davis, and Chris Brown. As Davis commented, "Earl prepared us for the next level."[7] Chris Brown said, "He was the coach who really taught us how to play."[8]

Brown's teams often played three or four games a day during the summer months, under the belief that the more you play, the more you learn. While Brown was involved in his youth coaching endeavors, he also scouted for the Oakland Athletics and Cincinnati Reds.

HIGH SCHOOL AND COLLEGE COACHES

Les Haserot (1904–57) starred at shortstop for Hollywood High in 1923 on a team that featured future PCL star Solly Mishkin and Helms Hall of Fame creator Bill Schroeder. Following high school, Haserot became a three-sport (football, baseball, basketball) star at Occidental College in Los Angeles. Upon graduation, he entered professional baseball, playing for the PCL's Portland Beavers and Mission Bells in 1927–28. A fine defensive shortstop but unable to hit the curveball, he quit the pros in 1929 to become the baseball coach at Fremont High School in Los Angeles. Fremont, by the way, is only about a mile from Manchester Playground.

Haserot became known for running his program like a professional training camp, stressing the fundamentals, conditioning, and playing the percentages. Bobby Doerr commented, "Haserot gave us the knowledge to prepare for pro ball."[9] According to Glenn Mickens, "Haserot was a great motivator and you could feel his love of the game."[10] So great was Haserot's reputation that fifteen-year-old Gene Mauch commuted several miles from his mid-city Los Angeles home to play for him. Haserot's teams reeled off a string of Los Angeles City Baseball Championships in 1932, 1933, 1939, 1942, 1943, 1946, 1947, and 1948. Bob White, the successful coach at archrival Washington High School said, "Playing a Haserot team was like playing a big league team."[11]

Les Haserot coached at Fremont through 1956, when the effects of leukemia began to weaken him. He died the following year from a self-inflicted gunshot. Among the players he groomed were Hal Spindel, Bobby Doerr, Dick Conger, Merrill Combs, George Metkovich, Nippy Jones, George McDonald, Larry Barton, Gene Mauch, Glenn Mickens, Al Grunwald, Vic Marasco, and Clint Conatser. Haserot's name still lives in Los Angeles baseball circles. On June 5 he was inducted into the Los Angeles City Sports Hall of Fame.

John Scolinos (1918–2009) did not develop large numbers of big leaguers, but he was known as one of Southern California's finest baseball teachers. A graduate of Manual Arts High School in Los Angeles, he played high school baseball, but was better known as an All Los Angeles City High School football center. He briefly gave pro baseball a whirl, performing in the California League and others, but World War II interrupted his career. During the war Scolinos served as a radio operator on a B-29. Following the war he joined the staff of Pepperdine College in Los Angeles, serving as football and baseball coach 1946–60. In 1962 he moved to Cal Poly Pomona as baseball coach and his teams won NCAA Division II Championships in 1976, 1980, and 1983. A student of the game, Scolinos is often described by two words: inspiration and integrity. He is a member of the American Baseball Coaches Hall of Fame. Cal Poly's Scolinos Field is named in his honor.

John Herbold (1929–) like Les Haserot before him, graduated from Hollywood High School. At Stanford University he was Phi Beta Kappa and a fourth string catcher on the baseball team. While at Stanford he communicated with Haserot, who inspired him to embark on a coaching career. Following coaching concepts of Haserot, Herbold was a strong believer in fundamentals and conditioning. He coached on the high school and college level for 50 years, beginning at Long Beach Poly High School in 1956. At Long Beach Poly and Lakewood High School he produced numerous championship teams. His 1970 Lakewood team was rated number one in the United States. During his high school coaching years Herbold produced many future big leaguers, including Tommy Sisk, Brian McCall, Ollie Brown, Oscar Brown, Randy Moffitt, Willie Norwood, Floyd Chiffer, John Flannery, Mike Fitzgerald, Larry Casian, and Craig Grebeck.

In 1984 Herbold moved to the college level, guiding Cal State Los Angeles for twenty years. There he developed Jay Gibbons for the big leagues. USC's legendary coach Rod Dedeaux (whose career is covered in another article in this journal) said, "Herbold was one of the most fundamentally sound baseball coaches of all time."[12] While coaching, Herbold was a part-time scout for five organizations. He also found time to work as a featured columnist for *Collegiate Baseball* for twenty years. Herbold was elected to the American Baseball Coaches Hall of Fame in 1998.

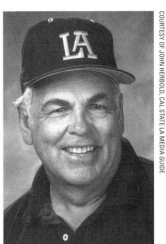

John Herbold, award-winning coach at Cal. State Los Angeles, circa 1995. Herbold coached high school and college baseball in Southern California for fifty years.

John Stevenson (1933–2010) graduated from Redondo Union High School and UCLA, where he was greatly influenced by a class taught by legendary UCLA basketball coach John Wooden. A disciplinarian, he became the baseball coach at El Segundo High School in 1960 and remained in that position until his death. His teams won a California state record 1,059 games and garnered CIF Southern Section titles in 1965, 1966, 1971, 1973, 1979, and 1989. He developed future Hall of Famer George Brett, as well as Ken Brett, Bobby Floyd, Scott McGregor, Zak Shinall, and Billy Traber.

"El Segundo is a baseball town because of John Stevenson,"[13] said Bobby Brett, another Brett brother who played for Stevenson. Like so many of the above-mentioned coaches, Stevenson was a stickler for fundamentals, alert to all mental aspects of the game. Bobby Brett added, "He gave you all the tools to be successful."[14]

BASEBALL PROMOTERS
Joe Pirrone (1896–1973) was born and raised in Los Angeles where he developed a lifelong love for baseball. He played for Polytechnic High School of Los Angeles, as well as many of the sandlot teams of the area. After a brief career in pro ball, he began showing talent as an entrepreneur, owning a vegetable store, a nightclub, and a restaurant. Baseball remained in his blood, however, and with his brother, John, helped build the new California Winter League into a showcase for Negro Leaguers and local African American talent. The Pirrone brothers sponsored their Pirrone All Stars in the league from 1920–45, which featured such stars as Babe Herman, the Meusel brothers, Smead Jolley, Fred Haney, Willie Ludolph, and Ernie Orsatti competing against stars of the Negro Leagues. In 1929 the Pirrone brothers invested $16,000 to construct Pirrone Park

(later known as White Sox Park) at 38th and Compton Avenue on the southeast side of Los Angeles. Here major leaguers, Negro Leaguers, local African American players like Jim Direaux and Joe Filmore, and the Pirrone All Stars played winter baseball in a harmonious, integrated setting. Pirrone will long be remembered as "the Father of the California Winter League."

Dan Crowley (1907–1994) was born in Los Angeles and played baseball at Manual Arts High School. He entered pro ball and rose as high as the PCL in 1933. When Crowley began his pro career in 1925 he got the idea to form an offseason pro team to compete with the local college teams. The "Crowley All Stars" became a tradition and played exhibition games with USC for sixty years, ending in 1984. Over the years the "Crowley All Stars" featured such big-league stalwarts as Bob Lemon, Ralph Kiner, Mel Almada, Harry Danning, Jack Salveson, Rip Russell, and Steve Mesner. Crowley also worked many years as a scout for the New York Yankees and as a longtime college baseball umpire. The next time you view the 1941 baseball film classic, *Pride of the Yankees*, notice the plate umpire, Dan Crowley.

Willrich "Bill" Schroeder (1904–87) was not a playground supervisor, baseball coach, or baseball scout, but he was a pivotal influence in the development and popularity of high school baseball in the Los Angeles area. Schroeder was born in Beaumont, Texas, but grew up in Hollywood, where he played third base for the 1923 Los Angeles City Baseball Champs, Hollywood High School. Schroeder loved to reminisce about his idolization of Frank Shellenback and playing with Solly Mishkin and Les Haserot. While working as a banker, Schroeder enlisted the funding of Paul Helms (Helms Bakery) and established the Helms Athletic Foundation in 1936. The Foundation established a sports museum with an amazing collection of exhibits and the largest sports library in the world. Schroeder, however, wanted to have an active foundation that not only enabled fans to recall the past, but also kept pace with the present. The Foundation selected Athletes of the Year and Athletes of the Month in many sports. Awards programs were developed to honor local high school all-star teams. Bob Lemon, Duke Snider, Tony Gwynn, Rollie Fingers, Don Drysdale, and many other major league stars were honored by the Foundation. Helms became the center for high school sports in Southern California and flourishes today as LA 84. Braven Dyer Jr., Schroeder's longtime assistant director said, "Schroeder was the most influential individual in

Bill Schroeder standing with the Helms Foundation World Trophy, presented annually to the world's top amateur athlete. Schroeder was a great advocate of high school baseball in Southern California.

Los Angeles sports during the forties, fifties, and sixties."[15] Schroeder also found time to compile the first PCL Record Book and was the president of three minor leagues: the California League, the Sunset League, and the Far West League.

John Young (1949–) grew up in the south Los Angeles neighborhood that was a baseball hotbed. He did not attend the local public high school, but instead the parochial, Mt. Carmel High School. In fact, Young is the only big-leaguer to come out of Mt. Carmel, while the public schools in the area—Locke, Fremont, Compton, and Centennial—were producing numerous big leaguers. Young went off to play ball at Chapman College (later known as Chapman University) and enjoyed a brief career with the Detroit Tigers.

Following his playing days, Young began a long career as a scout. As the years rolled by, he noticed that fewer and fewer baseball players were coming out of the old neighborhood. The park diamonds that once were the most fertile major league baseball incubators in America were now gang-infested, preventing young prospects from playing baseball. In 1989 Young founded RBI (Reviving Baseball in Inner Cities) to help return the game to inner city youth. His goal was to encourage participation in baseball, provide youth with a positive team-oriented activity, and to keep kids off the streets. The program has grown tremendously and now operates in 240 sites around the world, adding a softball element and academic element. Is the program successful? Just ask James Loney or Coco Crisp. They're both graduates of RBI.

SCOUTS

Kenny Myers (1920–72) grew up in Los Angeles and played baseball at the "bad boy" school, Riis High School. After signing a professional contract, Myers spent many years as a minor league player and manager, once hitting four home runs (two grand slams) in a single game. He became a scout for the Los Angeles Dodgers (signing Willie Davis and Jim Merritt) and later for the California Angels. Myers was more than just a scout. He was a teacher, an analyst, and a batting innovator. Former big league manager and player Norm Sherry wrote, "Myers was the most knowledgeable baseball man in all phases of the game."[16] "He was the finest hitting instructor of all time," observed famed coach, John Herbold.[17]

Myers had innovative ways to teach all phases of hitting. John Roseboro and Willie Davis felt he made them major league hitters. Davis, in particular, was a Kenny Myers success story. In high school Davis was a 9.5 sprinter who batted from the right side. Myers patiently taught Davis to hit from the left side to utilize his blazing speed. Eventually Willie Davis became a baseball all-star. When baseball people speak of legendary scouts, Kenny Myers's name is always in the conversation.

Harold "Lefty" Phillips (1919–72) was a highly regarded All Los Angeles City pitcher at Franklin High School. He signed with the St. Louis Browns, but arm trouble quickly derailed his playing career. Phillips came home to Los Angeles and briefly worked for the railroad. He eventually became a scout for the Cincinnati Reds (1948–50) and then in 1951 moved to the Brooklyn Dodgers. He eventually became the Dodgers' head Southern California scout. Mining the wealth of baseball talent in Los Angeles, Phillips signed Bobby Lillis, Sparky Anderson, Larry Sherry, Don Drysdale, and Ron Fairly for the Dodgers. With his great knowledge of pitching, Phillips was elevated to Dodgers pitching coach for a staff that included Sandy Koufax, Don Drysdale, and Claude Osteen. Phillips then became the manager of the California Angels 1969–71. Sparky Anderson said, "Phillips was one of the biggest brains baseball ever produced. He was the biggest influence in my career."[18] ■

Notes

1. Letter from Mickey Owen to author, 1997.
2. Letter from Bobby Doerr to author, 30 June, 1997.
3. Letter from Ed "Bud" Stewart to author, 17 March, 1998.
4. Letter from George "Sparky" Anderson to author, 1997.
5. Letter from Rene Lachemann to author, 17 February, 1998.
6. Oral presentation by Dock Ellis to author's class, 1995.
7. Waters, Sean. "He Has a Real Eye For Talent." *Los Angeles Times*, 27 June 1993.
8. Ibid.
9. Letter from Bobby Doerr to author, 30 June 1997.
10. Letter from Glenn Mickens to author, 2 March 1998.
11. Bob White interview with author, June 1962.
12. Rod Dedeaux interview with author, 3 January 1998.
13. Bolch, Ben. Record-setting El Segundo Baseball Coach," *Los Angeles Times*, 13 January 2010: A21.
14. Ibid.
15. Braven "Bud" Dyer interview with author, 1986.
16. Letter from Norm Sherry to author, 1998.
17. John Herbold interview with author, 2004.
18. Letter from George "Sparky" Anderson to author, 1997.

Sources

De La Vega, John. "Manchester Alma Mater of Many Stars," *Los Angeles Times*, 19 February 1948: A9.

Drennen, Andrew. "Salute to John Stevenson," *Cal Hi Sports State Record Book*, 2009: 249.

Eckhoff, Irving. "Dietz Hailed as Coach of Champions," *Los Angeles Times*, 26 June 1932: E6.

McNeil, William F.. *The California Winter League*, Jefferson, North Carolina, McFarland & Company, Inc. 2002.

Ostler, Scott. "An All Star and His Collection of Stars," *Los Angeles Times*, 2 February 1984: E1.

Jimmie Reese

The Career and the Man

Tom Willman

I was driving us down Westwood Boulevard in L.A. headed toward lunch at Junior's, when we had this conversation. This was maybe 1990. I think I asked Jimmie if he'd ever seen any of the Chicago Black Sox.

"Swede Risberg," he said.

"Really? What was he like?"

"Hard-nosed," he said matter-of-factly. "A hard-nosed ballplayer, but a nice guy."[1]

I still replay that snippet of conversation in my head. It contrasts so sharply with the memorable description that Shoeless Joe Jackson hung on Risberg: "The Swede was a hard guy."[2]

Just a little twist on a word, Jackson's implication of menace, versus Jimmie Reese's context of baseball as it was properly played in the 1910s. At the time, though, what brought me up short was the revelation that I was sitting next to a man who in his mind's eye could still see the way a young Swede Risberg had ranged after grounders in the year 1915. Risberg played for the Venice-Vernon Tigers of the old Pacific Coast League that year. In fact, Jimmie remembered Lefty Williams and Fred McMullin, too, and likely saw Sleepy Bill Burns and Joe Gedeon on the diamond as well. Four years before each played a fateful hand in the Black Sox scandal, they were all playing ball in the Coast League. And Jimmie Reese was there.[3]

The year Jimmie Reese was born, the American League played its first games as a major league. On his second birthday, Pittsburgh beat Boston, 7–3, in the very first World Series game. When he was six, they wrote "Take Me Out to the Ball Game."

The first time Jimmie himself came to any attention on a baseball diamond was at Washington Park, the PCL home of the Los Angeles Angels. He was a quick, blond youngster with a dazzling smile and boundless energy. He had fallen in love with baseball at about the usual age, and had begun sneaking into the ballpark, hanging around the practices, making himself useful.[4] By 1917, the manager of the Angels was the luminary Frank Chance, as in Tinker to Evers, and Jimmie had earned the title of "mascot." Every Sunday, Chance gave him a dollar and a baseball. And

how's that for bookends? Frank Chance's rookie year in the majors was 1898. When Jimmie died, in his 23rd year as a big-league coach, he lay in state in his Angels' uniform. That was 1994. The unparalleled baseball life of Jimmie Reese—as player, and as witness—nearly spanned the twentieth century.

By the usual statistics, the big-league career of Jimmie Reese was modest. Drill down to fielding, and he is in the upper echelon of big-league second basemen by common standards. Methodical observers may double-take at his pinch-hitting numbers—15-for-33 over three seasons. But the point is not to invite analysis. It's that most of the amazing baseball life of Jimmie Reese was lived beyond statistics.

His youth was the storybook stuff of Horatio Alger. The son of Russian Jewish immigrants, he was born Hyman Solomon (no middle name) in New York City on October 1, 1901.[5] Jimmie said his widowed mother moved him and his sister to L.A. when he was little. He became a family breadwinner, a hustling newsboy, hawking papers on the streets. In an orphan trade, he lived by his wits and his charm, inventing the man he would become. He took the name Jimmie Reese. When World War I loomed and the Navy built a

Reese as a newsboy in navy cap in 1918 selling papers at the San Pedro Submarine Base, where he was already playing with major leaguers. The pinholes in the corners and the glue splotches testify to how many times Reese showed the picture to visitors and moved it around his workshop.

submarine base at San Pedro, Jimmie wound up distributing papers and living on base, wearing a sailor's uniform and mascoting for its champion Navy ball team. He left San Pedro High, where he was on the team, fudged his age, set off into the long Southern California summer and became a semipro baseball gypsy. In the '20s he rose to stardom with the Coast League's Oakland Oaks. In the '30s, after his brief turn in the majors, he would star again for the 1934 Angels, always nominated as the best minor league team ever. When his playing days ended, he spent more than 30 years coaching, sometimes scouting, for a procession of Coast League teams, including a long run in San Diego. And then, from 1972 until his death in 1994, Jimmie Reese lived in the glow of fable as the California Angels' conditioning coach, No. 50, the master of the fungo and onetime roommate of Babe Ruth. His own achievements as a player—and so much of the rich history he had lived—receded gently into the past.

But here's a magical thing. We can know the story of the young Jimmie Reese, and the long-ago game as he played it, because he left a carefully assembled record—scrapbooks filled with news clippings, photographs, telegrams, with his hopes and dreams as he rose toward his baseball destiny. Players' scrapbooks aren't new. But reemerging into the light 17 years after his death, almost 100 years after he began to assemble them, Jimmie's have the aura of a lost treasure map.[6]

Jimmie's work ethic was staggering. As a kid, he made headlines practicing with both teams before a game.[7] He asked permission to report to spring training early. He hustled through the long Coast League season. He stayed around the park to practice after the season ended. Then he played winter ball.[8] Fast-forward to 1930, when Jimmie went to Yankee Stadium early to throw extra BP for a slumping Lou Gehrig. Fast-forward again to 1972 and a propitious meeting on the first day of Angels' spring training in Holtville, California. Newcomer Nolan Ryan, just 25, "was standing around...when an older man, who seemed to be one of the California coaches, hollered to me, 'Get out in the infield. Get some practice.'" For the next 20 minutes, until he was ready to throw up, Ryan was trapped in a pitiless fungo marathon. He was rescued by pitching coach Tom Morgan calling him to warm up. It was the beginning of a beautiful friendship.[9] Fast-forward again to 1994, the last spring of Jimmie's life, when he did much the same thing to pitcher Julio Valera.[10] It was a lifelong pattern.

When Jimmie Reese was young, his fielding left baseball people agog wherever he went. He was a nat-

A throw to Reese forces out San Francisco Seals runner Carl Dittmar.

ural fielder with acrobatic skills. By the middle '20s, he was regarded as spectacular, always diving and tumbling.[11] Fans loved his showmanship, and in the box scores, where panache never registers, he still looked like what he was—the best second baseman in the league.[12] He set a PCL single-season fielding record for chances handled with 1,294.[13] Baseball veterans compared him to the best they had known, up to and including Eddie Collins.[14] Coast hyperbole? When he got to the Bronx, Yankees GM Ed Barrow called him one of the best fielders he had ever seen.[15] Jimmie would eventually set the Coast League career record for fielding, with 9,890 chances, and be named the second baseman on the all-time PCL team.[16]

You wonder how many young hopeful infielders, parading through the Angels' camp every spring in the 1970s and '80s, had any idea who he was.

To them he was the conditioning coach. With his trademark flat-sided fungo bat, he could hit a player's outstretched glove. Once on a bet he hit a flagpole. He could slap balls through the strike zone from the mound. Or he could hit grounder after grounder, right, left, right, precisely at the limits of a players' reach. Until lungs and legs burned. Until agility and endurance began to show. It is ironic that in the end, the exquisite fielder was known only for his work with the bat.

And yet, what ultimately became singular was not how he had played the game, but how he had lived it.

Yes, Jimmie Reese roomed with Babe Ruth as a Yankee and spelled Frankie Frisch with the Cardinals. But he was mentored by Doc Crandall, who pitched with Christy Mathewson for John McGraw's Giants. He grew up on the field in L.A. with Sam Crawford, who led the National League in homers in 1901. He played behind Wilbur Cooper, who'd pitched for Pittsburgh with Honus Wagner on his infield, and with Harry Krause, who in 1909 led the American League in ERA. Krause pitched for Connie Mack that year. His

TOM WILLMAN

A monogrammed mug from his Angels days juxtaposed with a Babe Ruth-Jimmie Reese photo from his time with the Yankees.

REESE SCRAPBOOKS

Reese in San Francisco Seals uniform surrounded by cutouts of him in uniform from high school to the PCL.

second baseman was Eddie Collins. Home Run Baker was at third. The Navy players who took Jimmie under their wing during World War I included Harry Heilmann, Howard Ehmke, and Bob Meusel. Jimmie was a teammate of the young Paul Waner in the '20s, and the young Ted Williams in the '30s; he played against the young Joe DiMaggio. One day in 1927, one of Jimmie's Oakland games was preceded by an old-timers' contest. Aging catcher Fred Lange played in

old-fashioned style, bare-handed. His batterymate was George Van Haltren, who had pitched for the Chicago Nationals of 1887 under manager Cap Anson.[17]

All this sketches the cumulative baseball awareness of a man who, in his last year in a big-league uniform, was a teammate of Jim Edmonds, who would still be in the majors in 2010.

So it was that in a game which reduces so absorbingly by statistical cross-section, Jimmie Reese was the sum of a cannier, more elemental understanding of the game and its players.

One day in the 1980s, Jimmie was talking about Nolan Ryan throwing 100 miles an hour, and the thought began triggering associations. Ryan led him to Dizzy Dean, and then Bobo Newsom. The speed and agility of PCL outfield star Jigger Statz brought him to Gary Pettis. The catcher on the wonderful 1934 PCL champion Angels, Gilly Campbell, led to Bob Boone. Campbell was the better hitter, but Boone "makes it up right there," said Jimmie, tapping his head. "And you see, that's the intangible that you don't notice. There's no stats on those things."

The monologue that day ran to 42 players, from Grover Cleveland Alexander to Bo Jackson. Like Swede Risberg, they would all be on lifelong instant replay for Jimmie Reese.[18]

I first met Jimmie early in 1986. He was living in L.A., near Westwood Village. One visit and interview led to another. My wife and little boy (soon enough, two little boys) always came along. At first, our visits were arranged around the interviews. Soon they were being arranged around lunch at Junior's. Jimmie sat next to the kids.

The living room of Jimmie's apartment was a shrine to baseball history with row upon row of autographed player photographs reaching across 70 years. The collection was crowned by inscribed photos from his old friends Babe Ruth and Lou Gehrig. But it was out back in his picture-framing workshop where his own values were best displayed. Family-photo Christmas cards from friends in and out of baseball shared space with pictures of "his" kids, generations of them, ours soon included. Jimmie Reese famously gave away baseball artifacts, even treasured relics, without a twinge of nostalgia, while the things he kept closest around him were family keepsakes, obscure photos, pasted on cardboard and filled with thumbtack holes.

This should be understood about Jimmie Reese. He could have walked through life without ever touching a baseball and still been unforgettable to those who met him. He truly liked people, and in a way that is not given to many of us.

But baseball was his life. He loved the locker-room give-and-take. He challenged generations of young players with his precision fungoes, teased them, worked them, helped bring out the best in them, gave to each the sympathetic ear of a friend. The local Baseball Writers Association chapter gave him its "Good Guy Award" year after year after year. And it was the same with those of us outside of baseball. I don't know where the lineage of "his" kids started. Maybe in the '30s with the children of teammate Jigger Statz. In the '50s Jimmie became godfather to little Bonnie Baker, the daughter of close friends and neighbors. As a child, she earned pennies using a magnet to find fallen nails around his workshop.[19] As for me, I think my favorite recollection of Jimmie would date to about 1990. It's of him walking down the sidewalk toward Junior's, towing each of our little boys by a hand, speculating happily about what kind of cookies they were going to find in the bakery case.

People do not name their children after just plain nice guys, they name them after the exceptional. One thinks of Nolan Reese Ryan, Connor Reese Narron, to mention just two names familiar in baseball circles. The friends—the extended family—of Jimmie Reese share this, the realization that we will probably not meet his like again, on the baseball field or off. When you were around Jimmie, you felt as if you'd walked into a Frank Capra movie. It was a wonderful life.

In August 1994, the ballplayers went on strike. They would not come back that season. On July 13, amid the rancorous runup to that strike, on a summer day when there was no baseball, Jimmie Reese died. He was 92. Two days later, on July 15, the Disney movie *Angels in the Outfield* came out. It was about a boy who grew up on his own a lot, who loved baseball, who snuck into Angels' games, and who saw something so wondrous on the field that it became a life-changing epiphany.[20]

And how's that for bookends? ∎

Notes

1. Undated interview notes; about 1990.
2. *Eight Men Out*, by Eliot Asinof, Ace Publishing, NY, 1963. 208.
3. "Jimmie Reese: In His Own Words," by James D. Smith III, 89, *Baseball Research Journal* No. 24, SABR, 1994.
4. "Jimmy Reese First Young Player Oaks Are Developing Since 'Busher Rule' Began," by John J. Connolly. Undated clipping (1925), Scrapbook 1, 5.
5. State of New York, Certificate and Record of Birth, copy of document in collection of Bonnie Baker Blish.
6. Three scrapbooks and assorted ephemera and keepsakes. Collection of the author.
7. Undated clipping, Scrapbook 2 (1926), 45.
8. Undated clipping (1924), Scrapbook I, 37.
9. *Throwing Heat: The Autobiography of Nolan Ryan*, by Nolan Ryan and Harvey Frommer. Doubleday, NY, 1988. 74-75.
10. "An Angel Remembered: Jimmie Reese was Known for His Love of Baseball—and People", by Bob Nightengale and Chris Foster. Obituary sidebar, *Los Angeles Times*, 14 July 1994.
11. Scrapbooks, various clippings. Example: "The Second Guess," by A.J.B., undated column 1926, Scrapbook 2, 49: "It is amusing to sit close to the Hollywood bench in Emeryville this week and listen to the highly-paid splinter-gatherers ridiculing and sneering at Jimmy Reese… . He will go through more acrobatic contortions in one game than most players will use in a season. BUT JIMMY GETS THERE. He apparently has no fear of injury to himself. He tumbles, falls, spraddles, somersaults and whatnot. BUT HE COMES UP WITH THE BALL AND HE GENERALLY GETS HIS MAN."
12. Undated clipping (1926), "All-Star Team of Youngsters," Scrapbook 2, 50.
13. Undated clipping, (December 1927), Scrapbook 2, 72.
14. "Reese-Lary Pair Fastest of All Time: Hollander," by Clyde Giraldo, undated clipping, 1926, Scrapbook 2, 58.
15. Undated clipping with Scrapbooks, apparently June 6, 1930. By James M. Kahn, Special to The [N.Y.] *Evening Graphic*, dateline Chicago.
16. "Remembering Jimmie Reese, 1901-1994," by Tom Singer, *Halo Magazine* (Angels' scorebook), Vol. 5, 1994, 15. Beverage, Richard E. *The Angels: Los Angeles in the Pacific Coast League: 1919–1957*. Placentia, CA: The Deacon Press, 1981, 13.
17. *History of Baseball in California and Pacific Coast Leagues, 1847–1938: Musings of an Old Time Baseball Player*. By Fred W. Lange, Oakland, CA. 19, 30–31, 174.
18. Interview notes, Sept. 11, 1986.
19. "Jimmie Reese: An Extraordinary Life," DVD reminiscence by Don and Bonnie Baker Blish, privately produced.
20. July 15, 1994 release date for *Angels in the Outfield*. the Internet Movie Database. www.imdb.com.

Baseball at Sepulveda Dam

One Afternoon, Three Hall of Famers

Bob Timmermann

Since Southern California is one of the major sources of baseball talent today, few if any of the top prospects ever go unnoticed by the media now. But on one day in May 1973, on one large field out in the San Fernando Valley, four baseball games were played simultaneously. In those games, three future Hall of Famers were on the field, with seven other future major leaguers also taking part. Only one suburban newspaper took significant note of the goings-on, but even they could not have guessed at the significance of that day's play.

May 29, 1973, the day of the quarterfinals of the Los Angeles City Section baseball tournament. The four games in this round all started at 2 PM at the Sepulveda Sports Center in suburban Encino. The center had four diamonds that shared an expansive outfield. Each diamond had an all-dirt infield and there were no pitching mounds. There were also no fixed seats for spectators, who could just roam the complex.

The headline event of the day was a matchup between Taft High of Woodland Hills and Monroe High of Sepulveda (now North Hills). Taft's star was its shortstop, Robin Yount, although two newspapers covering the event, the *Van Nuys News and Valley Green Sheet* and the *Los Angeles Times*, barely mentioned Yount in its stories. The *Times* stories of the games were just brief summaries, while the *Van Nuys News* did not publish every day, so its game stories came out two days after the games were played.

Both teams had scratched across single runs before Monroe won it, 2–1, in the bottom of the seventh inning on a bloop double that just eluded Yount's dive, and a game-ending single that the Taft left fielder lost in the sun. On another corner of the diamond, Locke High from South Central Los Angeles showed up with pitcher/catcher Eddie Murray and a little-known shortstop referred to in the papers as "Osburn" Smith. Locke faced John F. Kennedy High of Granada Hills, a school that was just two years old. Murray started on the mound in this one, but Kennedy had the better of him, winning 4–3. The winning run scored on an error by Smith on the rock-strewn infield.

The third diamond matched defending champion Venice against Granada Hills High. Although there were no Hall of Famers in this one, future MLB pitcher Dave Schmidt (just a sophomore) was playing right field for Granada Hills. Venice won the game, 4–3.

In the fourth quarterfinal, Lincoln High from the city's Eastside took on Sylmar High. Lincoln started Bobby Castillo, considered the best pitcher in L.A. Castillo was 12–0 for a team that was 18–1 overall entering the game. Castillo fanned 12 in the game, but Sylmar scored four runs in the sixth and seventh for a 4–2 win.

In addition to Hall of Famers Yount (who would be picked third in the amateur draft about a week later), Murray, and Smith, you could also see several other future major leaguers:

Lincoln High: Castillo
Granada Hills High: Schmidt
Taft High: Kelly Paris
Kennedy High: Jim Anderson, Darryl Cias
Locke High: Rich Murray (Eddie's brother), Darrell Jackson.

The championship (played at Dodger Stadium) would ultimately be won by Sylmar, a team which sent no players to the major leagues, although one player, Kevin Kopp, would spend a year in the minors.

High school baseball would start to change after this year. The seasons became longer as more preseason tournaments were held. (Champion Sylmar finished 1973 by playing 24 games. The 2010 champion, El Camino Real, played 33 games.) Players would become better known. Darryl Stroh, who coached Granada Hills in 1973, said he never saw Yount play in high school, even though his school and Taft are fairly close together. They were in separate leagues, and there were few interleague matches outside of the playoffs. The *Los Angeles Times* did not mention Yount's name in its main sports section until Yount's high school career was over and he was earning Player of the Year awards as well as being the third overall pick in the draft. Murray's name was consigned to the agate section, and his draft status was not immediately released to the public. (He was a third round pick of the Orioles.)

"Osburn" Smith, aka Osborne, would not be drafted out of high school, where he was better known for basketball than baseball. Instead, the future Wizard of Oz went to Cal Poly San Luis Obispo and would end up as a fourth round pick by the Padres in 1977 and make it to the majors the following year.

When Murray was inducted into the Hall of Fame in 2003, he joined Smith (inducted the year before) as the only pair of high school teammates enshrined in Cooperstown.

The high school baseball playoffs for Los Angeles are now played on far-better manicured fields. Numerous media representatives show up to track the best prospects. The bigger games get live blog updates. Scouts still find gems, but their gleam isn't hidden as thoroughly as it was. You might find a gem of a player at one of these games now, but it most assuredly won't be a diamond in the rough as it looked to be back in 1973. ■

Sources
Van Nuys News and Valley Green Sheet, 31 May 1973.
Los Angeles Times, 30 May 1973 and 7 June 1973.
Interview with Darryl Stroh.

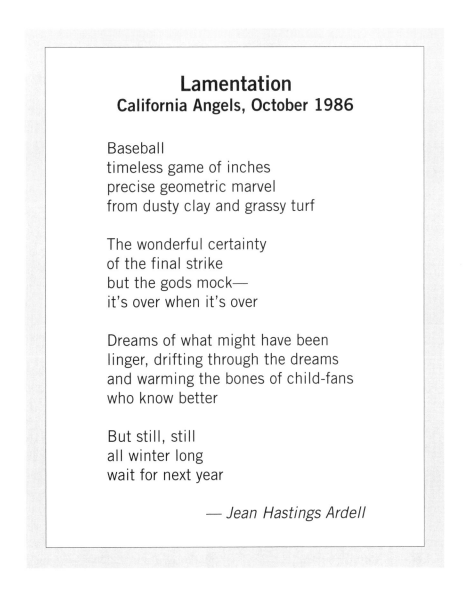

Lamentation
California Angels, October 1986

Baseball
timeless game of inches
precise geometric marvel
from dusty clay and grassy turf

The wonderful certainty
of the final strike
but the gods mock—
it's over when it's over

Dreams of what might have been
linger, drifting through the dreams
and warming the bones of child-fans
who know better

But still, still
all winter long
wait for next year

— *Jean Hastings Ardell*

Greater Los Angeles Area Colleges

Major League Mass-Production

David K. Anderson Sr. and David K. Anderson Jr.

In 1910, pitcher William "Dutch" Hinrichs from Occidental College joined the Washington Senators for three games. With his "cup of coffee," Hinrichs became the first major leaguer to have played baseball at a current Los Angeles area college.

However, Hinrichs wasn't the first local collegian to reach the major leagues. Fred Snodgrass, best remembered for his dropped fly ball in the 1912 World Series, attended the defunct St. Vincent's College in Los Angeles. Snodgrass broke in with the New York Giants in 1908—two years ahead of Hinrichs. St. Vincent's eventually grew and evolved into what is now Loyola Marymount University.

Hinrichs and Snodgrass are unknown to most fans, but many Los Angeles area collegians who followed them are not. Local schools have produced such greats as Jackie Robinson, Tom Seaver, Randy Johnson, and Mark McGwire, as well as a host of other all-star caliber players.

Within the Los Angeles area, there are 32 colleges and universities that play baseball in the National Collegiate Athletic Association's Division I, II, or III or in the National Association of Intercollegiate Athletics. Of those, 25 have produced at least one major leaguer, and that group of schools has combined to send over 400 players to the big leagues. And that doesn't take into account the area's two-year colleges, which have produced players such as the Braves' Tommy Hanson from Riverside Community College.

It isn't surprising that Los Angeles area colleges and universities have been prolific producers of major league talent. The region is ideal for baseball because its balmy winter weather allows year-round play. Of course, the area's colleges can also draw from a population base of well over 18 million people.

As a result, many of the Los Angeles area colleges and universities have established themselves as collegiate baseball powerhouses. Here's a quick look at some of the major programs.

SOUTHERN CALIFORNIA (USC) TROJANS

The Trojans have appeared in 21 NCAA College World Series and have won twelve NCAA titles—twice the number of any other school nationwide. Eleven of those NCAA titles were won by head coach Rod Dedeaux, who had an amazing span of 37 consecutive years at USC without a losing season. Dedeaux, himself a former major leaguer from Southern California, was named "Coach of the Century" in 1999 by *Collegiate Baseball* magazine.

Southern Cal has produced 103 major leaguers, which is more than any other college in the country. (The University of Texas is second with 100.)

Interestingly, major league pitchers from Southern Cal have collected nine Cy Young awards—Johnson (5), Seaver (3), and Barry Zito (1).

Coach Rod Dedeaux and the USC Trojans after beating Pepperdine to earn a berth at the College World Series in Omaha.

UCLA BRUINS

The Bruins have appeared three times in the College World Series, most recently as the championship game runner-up in 2010.

The Bruins have sent 67 players to the majors—only nine colleges nationwide have produced more. Other Bruins major league hopefuls are on the way, with ten UCLA players having been selected in the 2010 major league draft.

CAL STATE FULLERTON TITANS

Cal State Fullerton has won four College World Series titles, ranking them behind only Southern Cal (12), Texas (6), LSU (6), and Arizona State (5). The Titans have appeared in 16 College World Series—six of those have been since 2001.

It wasn't until 1980 that a former Titan, catcher Dan Whitmer, reached the big time with the California Angels. Since that time, however, 48 Cal State Fullerton alums have reached the major leagues, an average of over three major leaguers every two years.

PEPPERDINE WAVES

In 1992, the Waves became the third Southern California school to win a College World Series. The championship came after one previous CWS and 19 NCAA tournament attempts, dating back to 1955.

CAL STATE LONG BEACH 49ERS

Officially nicknamed the 49ers, Cal State Long Beach's baseball team is affectionately known to students and alums as the Dirtbags. CSULB has participated in four College World Series, the last being in 1998. Through 2008, the school had appeared in 17 NCAA tournaments over a 20-year period.

Amazingly, 12 former Dirtbags—over 36 percent of the school's 33 major leaguers—were big leaguers in 2010.

LOYOLA MARYMOUNT LIONS

The current Loyola Marymount University is the end-result of an evolution involving several predecessor schools. One of those, St. Vincent's College, produced outfielder Fred Snodgrass who debuted with the New York Giants in 1908. In 1938, first baseman Les Powers also debuted with the New York Giants after attending Loyola College, another predecessor.

In 1986, Loyola Marymount participated in its only College World Series.

UC SANTA BARBARA GAUCHOS

UC Santa Barbara has produced 19 major leaguers since third baseman Joe Martin's debut with the New York Giants in 1936. At that time, the institution was known as Santa Barbara State College.

CAL STATE NORTHRIDGE MATADORS

Before upgrading to Division I, Cal State Northridge appeared in four NCAA Division II title games, winning two (1970 and 1984). When the school won its first title, it was still known as San Fernando Valley State College.

Jackie Robinson (*second from left*) starred in baseball at Pasadena's Muir High, then at Pasadena Junior College before transferring to UCLA.

In 1940, Jackie Robinson became the Bruins' only four-sport letterman—in baseball, football, basketball, and track and field.

LOS ANGELES PUBLIC LIBRARY

LOS ANGELES PUBLIC LIBRARY

CAL STATE LOS ANGELES GOLDEN EAGLES

Before moving its program to Division II, Cal State Los Angeles—then known as the Diablos—played in the 1977 College World Series.

UC IRVINE ANTEATERS

Before upgrading to Division I, UC Irvine won two NCAA Division II titles, in 1973 and 1974. More recently, the school also competed in the 2007 College World Series.

UC RIVERSIDE HIGHLANDERS

A perennial NCAA Division II power, the Highlanders moved to Division I in 2002.

CHAPMAN PANTHERS

The NCAA's first Division II championship game was played in 1968, when Chapman University defeated Delta State, 11–0.

LA VERNE LEOPARDS

In 1995, La Verne defeated Methodist (NC) to win its only NCAA Division III title.

CALIFORNIA STATE POLYTECHNIC (POMONA) BRONCOS

Cal Poly Pomona has won three NCAA Division II titles (1976, 1980, and 1983) and has made four other NCAA tournament appearances.

WHITTIER POETS

Whittier produced its first major leaguer in 1937, when

In a reunion of St. Vincent's College, Fred Snodgrass (*right*) takes a seat with fellow alums Art "Tillie" Shafer (*middle*) and Los Angeles Police Chief William H. Parker (*left*). Snodgrass and Shafer were also teammates on the New York Giants.

infielder Tony Malinosky broke in with the Brooklyn Dodgers. While attending Whittier, Malinosky was a friend and classmate of Richard Milhous Nixon. At this writing, Malinosky was the oldest living ex-major league player, at 101, when he died earlier this year.

BIOLA EAGLES

The school name "Biola" was originally the acronym for "Bible Institute of Los Angeles." Biola has produced two major leaguers—brothers Todd and Tim Worrell. ∎

MAJOR LEAGUE PLAYERS FROM LOS ANGELES AREA COLLEGES

College/University	Div	City Location	Began Play	First MLB Alum	1st Yr MLB	Most Notable MLB Player	# In MLB
Azusa Pacific	NAIA	Azusa	1960	Paul Moskau	1977	Jeff Robinson	5
Biola	NAIA	La Mirada	1960	Todd Worrell	1985	Todd Worrell	2
Cal Lutheran	III	Thousand Oaks	1962	Kevin Gross	1983	Kevin Gross	2
Cal Poly Pomona	II	Pomona	1960	Mark Wiley	1975	Wayne Gross	9
Cal State Dominguez	II	Carson	1972	LaRue Washington	1978	Craig Grebeck	5
Cal State Fullerton	I	Fullerton	1965	Dan Whitmer	1980	Tim Wallach	48
Cal State Los Angeles	II	Los Angeles	1950	Brock Davis	1963	Jay Gibbons	14
Cal State Northridge	I	Northridge	1959	Paul Edmondson	1969	Lyman Bostock	13
Chapman	III	Orange	1926	Randy Jones	1973	Randy Jones	7
Claremont-McKenna	III	Claremont	1959	Wes Parker	1964	Wes Parker	1
La Verne	III	La Verne	1921	Ewell Blackwell	1942	Dan Quisenberry	9
Long Beach State	I	Long Beach	1954	Dick Nen	1963	Jason Giambi	37
Loyola Marymount	I	Los Angeles	1922	Fred Snodgrass ##	1908	Fred Snodgrass	30
Occidental	III	Los Angeles	1887	Dutch Hinrichs	1910	Bud Teachout	5
Pepperdine	I	Malibu	1939	Gail Hopkins	1968	Mike Scott	30
Pomona	III	Claremont	1889	Harry Kingman	1914	Harry Kingman	1
Southern California	I	Los Angeles	1889	Fay Thomas	1927	Randy Johnson	103
The Master's	NAIA	Santa Clarita	1965	Mark Redman	1999	Jerry Owens	2
UC Irvine	I	Irvine	1970	Gary Wheelock	1976	Brady Anderson	6
UC Riverside	I	Riverside	1958	John Lowenstein	1970	Troy Percival	14
UC Santa Barbara	I	Santa Barbara	1925	Joe Martin	1936	Michael Young	20
UCLA	I	Los Angeles	1920	Marv Gudat	1929	Jackie Robinson	67
Vanguard	NAIA	Costa Mesa	1977	Tim Fortugno	1992	Tim Fortugno	2
Westmont	NAIA	Santa Barbara	1949	Jerry DaVanon	1969	Jerry Davanon	2
Whittier	III	Whittier	1901	Tony Malinosky	1937	Jim Colborn	6

Shown are four-Year Colleges & Universities Only; Two-Year Community Colleges are not included

= Fred Snodgrass attended St. Vincent's College, which later evolved into Loyola Marymount.

All-Time Collegiate Team: Greater Los Angeles Area		
Brady Anderson	UC Irvine	RF
Jackie Robinson	UCLA	2B
Fred Lynn	Southern Cal	CF
Mark McGwire	Southern Cal	1B
Jason Giambi	Long Beach State	DH
Troy Glaus	UCLA	3B
Dave Kingman	Southern Cal	LF
Michael Young	UC Santa Barbara	SS
Don Slaught	UCLA	C
Chase Utley	UCLA	PH
Lyman Bostock	Cal State Northridge	PH
Don Buford	Southern Cal	PR
Bret Boone	Southern Cal	UT
Tim Wallach	Cal State Fullerton	UT
Todd Zeile	UCLA	UT
Randy Johnson	Southern Cal	SP
Tom Seaver	Southern Cal	SP
Mike Scott	Pepperdine	SP
Barry Zito	Southern Cal	SP
Ewell Blackwell	La Verne	SP
Randy Jones	Chapman	SP
Dan Haren	Pepperdine	SP
Dan Quisenberry	La Verne	RP
Todd Worrell	Biola	RP
Troy Percival	UC Riverside	CL

Southern California	
Jeff Cirillo	3B
Brett Boone	2B
Fred Lynn	CF
Mark McGwire	1B
Dave Kingman	DH
Geoff Jenkins	LF
Ron Fairly	RF
Roy Smalley Jr.	SS
Dave Engle	C
Randy Johnson	SP
Tom Seaver	SP
Tom House	RP

UCLA	
Dave Roberts	CF
Shane Mack	RF
Jackie Robinson	2B
Troy Glaus	3B
Eric Karros	1B
Jeff Conine	DH
Eric Byrnes	LF
Don Slaught	C
Mike Gallego	SS
Tim Leary	SP
Bill Bonham	SP
Dave Schmidt	RP

Cal State Fullerton	
Reed Johnson	LF
Mark Kotsay	RF
Aaron Rowand	CF
Phil Nevin	1B
Tim Wallach	3B
Jeremy Giambi	DH
Brent Mayne	C
Andy Mota	2B
Mike Rouse	SS
Mike Harkey	SP
Ricky Romero	SP
Chad Cordero	RP

Cal State Long Beach	
Harold Reynolds	2B
Troy Tulowitzki	SS
Evan Longoria	3B
Jason Giambi	DH
Terrmel Sledge	LF
John Bowker	1B
Jeff Liefer	RF
Jeremy Reed	CF
Brad Davis	C
Steve Trachsel	SP
Jered Weaver	SP
Randy Moffitt	RP

37

"Never Make the Same Mistake Once"

Remembering USC Baseball Coach Rod Dedeaux

Bob Leach

Actor Jack Lemmon toes the rubber, looks in for the sign, and takes a deep puff from a sizeable Cuban cigar. He throws a fastball down the heart of the plate, and I whistle a line drive inches from his famous visage for a single.

This was no dream or fantasy—just one of the Hollywood Celebrity Games that Coach Dedeaux arranged between the icons of the film and television industries and alumni of the University of Southern California (USC) baseball program. When I played outfield for Dedeaux in 1974–1976, mixing with the rich and famous was commonplace. Other stars who typically showed up for a celebrity event or ballgame were John Wayne, a USC football player in the 1920s when he was known as Marion Morrison, Tom Selleck, who played basketball at USC in the 1960s, and Mickey Mantle, the New York Yankees Hall of Famer who hit two of his longest tape-measure home runs in a 1951 exhibition game against the Trojans at Bovard Field on the USC campus.

I met Mantle when he suited up in his Yankee pinstripes to play in the 1975 celebrity game, seven years after his playing career had ended. Casey Stengel, a mentor and later a close friend of Dedeaux's, was a frequent spectator at our Saturday conference games until his death in 1975. But competing against and talking with icons such as Jack Lemmon and John Wayne was only a part of what made playing for Rod Dedeaux a magical experience.

Walking onto historic Bovard Field as a freshman in 1972, I was thrilled to be a part of collegiate baseball history. In his 45-year career at USC (1942–1986) Dedeaux compiled 1,332 wins, 571 losses, 11 ties—a Division I record that stood until 1994, 28 conference championships, and 11 College World Series championships, including five straight 1970–1974. He coached more than 50 future major leaguers, including Fred Lynn, Tom Seaver, Mark McGwire, Dave Kingman, Roy Smalley, and Randy Johnson. After World War II, he was a primary factor in re-establishing connections between USand Japanese baseball, and, in the 1980s, in establishing baseball as an Olympic sport. All the while he was building a highly successful trucking line, Dart Transportation, Inc. This article examines a few of the reasons why in 1999 *Collegiate Baseball* magazine named Rod Dedeaux the Coach of the Century and why his former players feel a bond with him that endures to this day.

Part of Coach Dedeaux's genius was using every available resource to benefit his teams. His drills stressed the essential fundamentals of the game. He often told us that "taking infield" had become a lost art, stressing that fans would come out early to the College World Series games just to watch the Trojans take infield practice. About 45 minutes before the start of a game, Rod would take a fungo bat—he was superb at hitting fungoes—and hit to each infielder. After fielding a grounder and throwing to first, the player would cover his base to receive a throw from the catcher. He would then return the throw or toss the ball to a player at another base. Dedeaux would frequently yell, "Get rid of it; get rid of it!" reminding

USC ATHLETIC DEPARTMENT

The Mamas & the Papas were wrong. It does rain in Southern California. When our game was rained out after three innings, Rod took Jim Barr (a former right-hander with the Giants and Angels), Dave Kingman, and me out to lunch, where, as usual, Coach was the consummate raconteur.

It was always a party when Coach got together with his friend, Dodgers manager Tommy Lasorda.

us that it was essential to make the transition from glove to bare hand and throw the ball as quickly as possible. "Move your puppies, Tiger!" he shouted frequently, reminding us to move our feet with quick short steps before making a throw. When USC "took infield" it was with a very flashy style and beautiful to watch. For whatever reason, the professionals quit the tradition years ago, and it is rare for college teams to "take infield" with the quickness, flair, and efficiency of the Trojans teams of the Dedeaux era. Coach Dedeaux put plenty of pressure on us to excel. He believed that if you could handle the stress he put on you during practice, you'd find it easier to handle when you were playing in front of 20,000 people in Omaha, Nebraska, at the College World Series. It was "taking infield" with the intensity that Coach Dedeaux demanded that prepared you for the pressure of big-game situations.

Being physically prepared was only part of Dedeaux's teaching. He once said, "I always felt that the game was a lot more than just a bat, a ball, and a glove. The mental side is so important. And I always believed in doing everything right, whether it be on the field or off the field."[1]

Coach believed in learning from others' mistakes, so that you could avoid making them yourself. One of his favorite expressions, "Never make the same mistake once," wasn't asking his players to be perfect but to be closely observant and wise. He called all of us "Tiger" and expected us to be "in the game" at all times. When Coach Dedeaux corrected a player after he returned from the field to the dugout, the player would often defend himself by saying, "I thought—"

Dedeaux would always interrupt with, "Tiger, don't think. You'll hurt the ballclub." Throughout my life I've realized that so much of the time we are better off staying in the moment and reacting rather than analyzing and thinking too much.

Dedeaux understood that bad bounces can happen, but considered a poorly thrown ball a mental mistake. While most coaches would consider an errant throw to be a physical error, Coach Dedeaux believed that, if you moved your puppies properly, you would always throw accurately. He kept a fine book for mental errors. Base-running mistakes, errant throws, throwing to the wrong base, and missed signs were considered mental mistakes. The most expensive was the first mental error of the day ($1.00); subsequent fines were 25 cents. Coach figured that if no one made the first mental error, we would play a perfect game. Like most college students, we were short on funds, so it behooved us to learn to do things the right way.

Dedeaux's teams were not just mentally prepared. We were mentally tough. He was highly skilled in the art of bench jockeying—the ability to heckle your opponents from the dugout with a diverse array of putdowns without using profanity. (In today's vernacular it's called trash talking; this type of banter is no longer allowed in college baseball.) Certainly our opponents were no shrinking violets when it came to bench jockeying, but no team was as good at it as the Trojans.

While many thought this type of behavior was poor sportsmanship, Coach saw it as gamesmanship that we could use to gain an edge. (Still, Dedeaux had his limits. Late in the game, if we were far ahead, he would exclaim in his deep voice, "Let 'em die, Tigers," a signal to not rub any more salt in the wound of our opponents.) If an opposing player had a big nose, we might holler, "What would your rather have, a million dollars or a nose full of nickels?" Or, if he carried some extra weight, he was likely to hear, "Don't go near the ocean, you're liable to get harpooned!" Not only did this serve to distract opposing teams, more importantly, it kept the players on the bench actively involved in the game. Perhaps the Trojans'

USC ATHLETIC DEPARTMENT

Left to right: Steve Kemp, Roy Smalley, Rod Dedeaux, Fred Lynn, and Dave Kingman. During the mid-1970s an Alumni Game was played in which the Trojans' opponents were former USC players who were current major leaguers. Additional bleachers were set up down the foul lines to accommodate overflow crowds. Today's lucrative contracts have prevented this type of an exhibition.

finest moment in bench jockeying came during a crucial game in the playoffs for the CWS in 1973. As Dedeaux recalled:[2]

Dave Winfield was pitching a great ballgame for the University of Minnesota. Going into the bottom of the ninth, the score was 7–0 against USC, and we'd only had one hit, an infield single. I've not talked much about this before, but Minnesota was doing a lot of hot-dogging, which made us mad. And a lot of people felt we were in trouble, what with the lead and Winfield pitching…. But we were a disciplined team, and you had to credit the patience of our batters, who had made him throw a lot of pitches…. He was up to some 150-odd pitches, and yes, our guys were counting, helping him to realize what he was doing. They were putting a thought in his mind. They'd say, '152, 153…' And he'd look at his arm. But he was tiring, there's no doubt about it. So they took him out, and he moved to the outfield. Well, we rallied—and they talked to Winfield about coming back in to pitch, but he didn't do it. And we beat them…. They say this may have been the greatest come-from-behind victory in the history of college baseball.

One of the reasons Coach Dedeaux was so beloved by his players was that it was so much fun to play for

him. Whether it was in the locker room, on the field, or at a banquet, he was a fabulous storyteller and comedian. He had a resonant voice that took command of any setting. I am pretty sure he developed his biting sense of humor from his close friend, Casey Stengel. Both were long-time residents of Glendale, a suburb north/northwest of downtown L.A.

Coach Dedeaux encouraged fun and a light-hearted approach that he felt kept us loose and relaxed under pressure. One of his favorite routines was the singing of "McNamara's Band" after each win. A former player from the 1950s, Bill Doyle, told me how this tradition began. Rod was a big fan of the singer Dennis Day, a regular on the old *Jack Benny Program* on CBS-TV, and loved Day's version of "McNamara's Band." He decided to make that our signature song. When Coach entered our locker room after a win, he would scream, "That Trojan horse is out in front and they'll never catch us! When you sing it, sing it loud! 'Oh, me name is McNamara, I'm the leader of the band. Although we're few in number, we're the finest in the land….'" We were loud and celebratory, though no one would ever have confused us with the Mormon Tabernacle Choir.

I have been teaching teenagers at Duarte High School, near Pasadena, for the past 33 years. For the last ten years I have incorporated a "Friday" song, similar to Coach Dedeaux's "McNamara's Band." I play Loverboy's "Working for the Weekend" for my students to celebrate that we made it to Friday. They absolutely love it! Believe it or not, each senior class requests that the song be played during the prom, and they make sure that I stick around to dance with them. It shocks me that they get such a charge out of it, but I must thank Coach Dedeaux for the idea.

Baseball has a tradition in which rookies are made to do something unusual. Back in his youth at Hollywood High School, Dedeaux had acquired a red wig from the drama department. Years later, as coach of the Trojans, he decreed that a player on his first road trip had to wear the hideous-looking wig at the airport in a way that would cause his teammates to break into laughter. Tom Seaver did, Billy ["Spaceman"] Lee did, and then there was Randy Johnson. As Dedeaux recalled, "It was on a Sunday afternoon, at LAX, I think, with a crowd around. Johnson comes sliding down the chute with a baggage tag, just stretched out, and that long body going around and around, with the wig on. Well, it did shake things up."

I once asked Marvin Cobb, who earned two championship rings as a defensive back for Coach John McKay's football team and two championship rings as shortstop/second baseman for Dedeaux, about what made Dedeaux so good. "He was far and away the greatest coach I have ever had," Cobb replied, adding that it was not only all the championships. "It was the psychological aspects of baseball that have translated into all the facets of my life." Marvin's favorite maxim of Dedeaux's is, "Just the way we like it!" "Number One," as the players affectionately called our coach, used this expression any time the weather was bad, the odds were against us, or we were dealing with a very difficult situation. Ever the master psychologist, Coach Dedeaux never let us grow negative about anything. Cobb pointed out that there have been countless challenges throughout his adult life when this outlook helped him to succeed.

Coach Dedeaux was masterful at making you a tough competitor and person. But if he made you the butt of a joke, he would soon point out the positives about your game. While I was initiated with the "red wig in the airport" treatment and endured some teasing by Coach Dedeaux, he made up for that many times over with some of the most genuine compliments I have ever received. At the beginning of 1977,

he introduced me as head coach for our junior varsity team. He told our new players that when I came to USC he didn't see how I'd ever be able to play for our varsity. Through hard work and determination, I became the cleanup hitter. As Coach Dedeaux said, "That's really saying something."

———

Most of us players thought we were training under Coach Dedeaux to become major leaguers. In reality, we were all serving an internship for life, for in addition to making great baseball teams, he was, more importantly, passing on his wisdom and experience so that we could thrive in any setting. In 2008 the USC Baseball Alumni Association was organized to support the university's baseball program. That's the official reason it exists. Unofficially, most of its members, who are now in their fifties, sixties, and seventies and played for Coach Dedeaux, want to keep his memory alive. All of us treasure being with those who loved him as much as we did. The time we spent playing for Coach Dedeaux lasted only a few short years, but what made him so fabulous for those fortunate to have been under his supervision is that his emphasis on mental toughness, optimism, and fun translated not only to winning baseball games but to succeeding in life. ■

Notes

1. Rod Dedeaux, personal interview, Dan and Jean Hastings Ardell, March 6, 2002.
2. Ibid.

Mis-Management 101
The American League Expansion for 1961

Andy McCue and Eric Thompson

Responding to six decades of demographic change, the National and American leagues moved to expand as the 1960s dawned. While the National League took a measured approach to analyzing markets, identifying ownership groups and giving them time to organize, the American League followed a stumbling, reactive path. One new franchise was given merely eight days to find personnel and plan for an expansion draft. And then, to conform to a Byzantine set of rules, the league president had to secretly revise the draft with a series of mandated trades before announcing the results.

The path to expansion for both leagues was a combination of new markets and old politics.

By 1953, the 50-year-old lineup of American and National League cities had been left in the demographic dust. Population had moved from the northeast quadrant to the vibrant cities of the West and South. The less financially successful clubs in two-team cities were finding it increasingly difficult to compete.

This situation was ameliorated with the moves of the Boston Braves to Milwaukee (1953), the St. Louis Browns to Baltimore (1954), and the Philadelphia Athletics to Kansas City (1955). But these shifts barely strayed from the Northeast. There was talk of further franchise shifts, or maybe expansion, but nothing actually happened. That pattern was shattered in late 1957 with the announcement that the National League's New York Giants and Brooklyn Dodgers would move to San Francisco and Los Angeles.

The reaction in New York was swift. Within a few weeks, the Mayor's Baseball Committee, headed by well-connected lawyer William Shea, was created to bring National League baseball back to the city.

The reaction in major league baseball was slower. It wasn't until December of 1958 that the owners formed the Major League Baseball Expansion Committee, and it was here that the American League's stumbles began.

For its representatives, the National League owners chose two powerful owners, Walter O'Malley of the Dodgers and Philip Wrigley of the Cubs. Wrigley was a well-connected, wealthy owner, who'd played a quiet role in the westward expansion of the National League. O'Malley was particularly important because the implicit assumption behind any expansion was that if the National League wanted back into New York, the American League would have to be allowed into Los Angeles.

The American League owners chose Arnold Johnson, the man who had just moved his Athletics to the smallest market in major league baseball, and George Medinger, a minority shareholder and a vice president of the Cleveland Indians. No Del Webb, whose Yankees were now the sole major league team in New York. No Tom Yawkey.

Six months later, the expansion stew was complicated by the unveiling of Branch Rickey's plan for a third major league to be called the Continental League. Rickey promised to respect major league baseball's player contracts, but he was clearly eyeing their best existing and potential markets. The Continental League loomed as a bigger threat as Rickey began to put together impressive ownership groups in major cities.

In New York, Shea was quickly won over to the Continental camp, and he brought with him Joan Payson, who'd been a minority owner of the Giants and bitterly regretted their move to San Francisco. Her brother was publisher of the *New York Herald-Tribune* and US Ambassador to Great Britain. Other old money quickly joined. There was Dwight Davis Jr., whose father had funded tennis's Davis Cup, and George Herbert Walker (grandfather of eventual president George Herbert Walker Bush), a merchant banker with strong ties to the Harriman empire.

In Houston, it was all new money, but there was a lot of it. Craig Cullinan was Texaco. R.E. "Bob" Smith and "Bud" Adams had extensive oil and real estate interests in the Houston area. Roy Hofheinz was Smith's partner in many ventures and a former mayor of Houston. The Denver group was headed by Bob Howsam, owner of the minor league Denver Bears but with powerful political connections through his father-in-law, former Colorado governor and U.S. Senator Edwin C.

Johnson. In Toronto, it was media mogul Jack Kent Cooke. In Minneapolis, Rickey rounded up members of the Dayton-Hudson department stores and Hamms Brewing families, as well as George Pillsbury.

Rickey's Continental League would leave several legacies. It had coalesced viable ownership groups and educated them about dealing with the major leagues. And it had scared major league baseball.

In Washington, DC, Edwin C. Johnson's connections had brought about legislation to limit the number of players major league teams could keep under contract, and he had aided New York Representative Emanuel Celler's antitrust hearings on baseball. In Houston, Bud Adams had struck fear into the hearts of the owners. In addition to his baseball interests, Adams was a major player in the creation of the American Football League. In 1960, his Houston Oilers drafted the Heisman Trophy winner from LSU—Billy Cannon. The Los Angeles Rams of the National Football League had offered Cannon $10,000. Adams offered $110,000. The idea of competing for amateur talent with that kind of money reverberated through major league baseball.[1]

In August 1960, the National League announced it would absorb up to four teams from the Continental League. That killed Rickey's dream but woke up Del Webb, now chairman of the AL's expansion committee. The American League began its reactive spasms.

On October 10, Webb pushed the American League's somnolent Expansion Committee into going after Houston.[2] The next day, O'Malley announced the Houston Continental League group had applied for membership in the National League. Six days later, President Warren Giles announced Houston and New York, with its Continental League ownership group, would join the National League for the 1962 season.[3]

The 1960 census would soon show that the markets underserved by major league baseball were New York, Los Angeles, and Houston. The National League was now in all three, the American in one. But American League sources were sounding confident about the Dallas-Ft. Worth market, another growth area.[4]

A few days later, the American League revealed Calvin Griffith would be allowed to move his Washington Senators to Minneapolis–St. Paul and two expansion teams would be created in cities to be named.[5] To one-up the National League, Webb said it might add another two teams by 1964 and that its expansion teams would start play in 1961, a year before the National League. These teams had no general managers, no managers, no players, no ticket sales department, and a spring training that would begin in four months.

On November 17, 1960, American League president Joe Cronin announced that one of its expansion teams would replace the Senators in Washington and that it would petition major league baseball to be allowed into the Los Angeles area.[6] The promising market of Dallas–Ft. Worth fell out of the saddle. Cronin set the expansion draft for November 25. In those eight days, including a weekend and the Thanksgiving holiday, the league would have to resolve the Los Angeles situation. The Washington team would have eight days to prepare for the draft. The Los Angeles team, whose ownership group was not known, would have less.

November 25 passed with no resolution of the Los Angeles situation and no expansion draft. On November 28, the Senators lurched into life by taking Ray Semproch and John Gabler in the major league draft. The Los Angeles team didn't participate because it didn't exist yet.

By December 6, the AL had negotiated hastily with Walter O'Malley to get into Los Angeles and slapped together an ownership group headed by former country music star and radio/tv entrepreneur Gene Autry. Autry's organization would have eight days to prepare for the December 14 draft and less than three months before spring training.

For the draft, the Los Angeles team would be aided by several factors. Autry quickly hired former Braves manager Fred Haney as general manager and recently dismissed Giants manager Bill Rigney as field manager. Both were familiar with many major league players, although more heavily in the National League. Walter O'Malley ordered his staff to turn over the Dodgers' scouting reports on American League minor leaguers. But the big prize was Los Angeles-area resident Casey Stengel, recently fired as New York Yankees manager and very miffed about it. Stengel gave Haney and Rigney a full rundown on Yankees minor leaguers.

So, on the chilly morning of December 14, Haney and Rigney from the Angels as well as manager Mickey Vernon, general manager Ed Doherty, and farm director Hal Keller of the Senators climbed to the sixth floor of the IBM Building in Boston, where President Joe Cronin kept the American League's offices. Keeping the number of people in the room to six was designed to protect the secrecy of the players the existing eight teams had, or hadn't, protected.

Those teams had been required to expose 15 players from their 40-man rosters. Seven of those players had to come from the roster as of August 31, 1960, just before the September callups of minor leaguers. As would a different set of rules by the National League a year later, the process maximized protection for the existing franchises and minimized quality for the expansion teams. Each player selected would cost $75,000.

The league had created a complicated set of draft rules. Each team first had to select 10 pitchers, then two catchers, six infielders, four outfielders, and finally six players from those remaining. To make it even more complex, no existing team could lose more than seven players and no expansion team could take more than four players from any one existing team. Crucially, Bill Rigney recalled, the American League didn't inform drafting teams of this rule.[7]

The pitching and catching selections went smoothly enough, starting with the Angels choosing Eli Grba and the Senators taking Bobby Shantz, both from the Yankees. But, with the 27th pick, the Angels took infielder Coot Veal from the Tigers. They already had selected pitchers Bobby Sprout and Aubrey Gatewood, catcher Bob Rodgers, and third baseman Eddie Yost from Detroit. Four picks was the limit in the rules and Veal took them over.

Nobody at 540 Boylston Street raised a red flag. With the outfielder picks, things got really messy. With the 40th pick, the Angels took outfielder Ken Hunt from the Yankees, their fifth choice from New York. Four picks later, they took yet another Tiger—outfielder Neil Chrisley. Washington quickly joined the mess, taking Marty Keough and Jim King from Cleveland with the 41st and 43rd picks, giving them six picks from the Indians, in addition to the two taken by the Angels. The Indians and Tigers had now lost eight players and still nobody said, "Stop."

With the miscellaneous players, the situation got worse. The Angels took their fifth players from both the Red Sox and White Sox while the Senators took their fifth from Baltimore and Kansas City. Finally, Cronin stepped in after the Angels took Julio Becquer from the Twins with 55th and penultimate pick. He ordered Washington to drop catcher Red Wilson, one of their Indians' picks, and, because of the inflexibility of the rules, replace him with another catcher—Pete Daley of Kansas City. While reducing the Senators' Indians picks to five, this raised their Athletics selections to six. Cronin then had the Angels drop Neil Chrisley and take Faye Throneberry of the Twins. Then, Washington took its last regular pick, pitcher Rudy Hernandez from the Twins.

The scorecard now read Boston, Detroit, Chicago, and New York had lost seven players, but five each

were to the Angels; Boston and Cleveland had lost seven, but five to the Senators; Kansas City had lost seven but six were to Washington. Only the Twins losses were according to the rules.

Cronin now ordered trades to rectify the mistakes. To balance the Red Sox, the Senators sent pitcher Bob Davis of Kansas City to the Angels for Boston infielder Jim Mahoney. Cleveland and Detroit were evened out when the Angels shipped Coot Veal to the Senators for Cleveland infielder Ken Aspromonte. Kansas City, and New York's losses were brought into line with the rules when Washington traded infielders—Ken Hamlin to the Angels for Bud Zipfel.

One last trade was needed. The Senators had too many Orioles. The Angels had too many White Sox. Finally, with Cronin leaning in, the deal was struck. The Senators sent outfielder Joe Hicks to the Angels for a 19-year-old pitcher named Dean Chance who had spent the 1960 season at Fox Cities of the Three-I League. Hicks would have 389 more major league plate appearances, batting .221. Dean Chance would win 20 games twice and a Cy Young award.

Joe Cronin emerged from the draft and walked down Boylston Street to the Venetian Room of the Sheraton Plaza Hotel, where reporters awaited the results. He supplied each team's list of 28 choices and acknowledged one small glitch when they found the Indians had lost eight players. This was an oblique reference to replacing Red Wilson with Pete Daley. Cronin did not mention the Throneberry for Chrisley switch nor the four trades that made the picks conform to the draft rules. Neither of the expansion franchises would win a postseason game until 1979, nor a postseason series until 2002. ■

Sources
The material on the management of the expansion draft is available in the American League records at the National Baseball Hall of Fame and Museum and was confirmed by Hal Keller in a phone interview on October 30, 2010.

Notes
1. Shapiro, Michael. *Bottom of the Ninth.* New York: Times Books, 2009, 193–4.
2. Ibid., p. 240-1.
3. *Los Angeles Times,* 18 October 1960, Pt. IV, pl. 1.
4. King, Joe. "N.L. Opening Door for Houston—Dallas Likely A.L. Addition." *The Sporting News,* 19 October 1960, 6.
5. *Los Angeles Times,* 27 October 1960, Pt. IV, 1.
6. *Los Angeles Times,* 18 November 1960, Pt. IV, 1.
7. Kepner, Tyler. "Expansion the Hard Way by 1961 Angels." *The Press-Enterprise* (Riverside, CA) on 12 November 1997.

Table 1. Largest U.S. Cities and their MLB Franchises
The number in parentheses after the city name indicates the number of franchises in that city. The number at the bottom of the columns is the number of the 16 franchises which are in the top 10 cities. The American League lineup of 1903 is used to locate franchises.

	1900	1930	1950	1960
1.	New York (3)	New York (3)	New York (3)	New York (1)
2.	Chicago (2)	Chicago (2)	Chicago (2)	Chicago(2)
3.	Philadelphia (2)	Philadelphia (2)	Philadelphia (2)	Los Angeles (1)
4.	St. Louis (2)	Detroit (1)	Los Angeles	Philadelphia (1)
5.	Boston(2)	Los Angeles	Detroit (1)	Detroit (1)
6.	Baltimore	Cleveland (1)	Baltimore	Baltimore (1)
7.	Cleveland (1)	St. Louis (2)	Cleveland (1)	Houston
8.	Buffalo	Baltimore	St. Louis (2)	Cleveland (1)
9.	San Francisco	Boston (2)	Washington (1)	Washington (1)
10.	Cincinnati (1)	Pittsburgh (1)	Boston (2)	St. Louis (1)
11.	Pittsburgh (1)	14. Washington (1)	12. Pittsburgh	11. Milwaukee (1)
13.	Detroit (1)	17. Cincinnati (1)	18. Cincinnati	12. San Francisco (1)
15.	Washington (1)			13. Boston (1)
				16. Pittsburgh (1)
				21. Cincinnati (1)
				27. Kansas City (1)
	13	14	14	10

Table 2. After Outfielders

	Los Angeles	Washington	Total
Baltimore	1	2	3
Boston	4	2	6
Chicago	2	1	3
Cleveland	2	**6**	**8**
Detroit	**6**	2	**8**
Kansas City	1	4	5
Minnesota	1	3	4
New York	**5**	2	7

The Hidden Trades

- Washington traded Bob Davis (KCA) to Los Angeles for Jim Mahoney (Bos).

- Washington traded Ken Aspromonte (Cle) to Los Angeles for Coot Veal (Det).

- Washington traded Ken Hamlin (KCA) to Los Angeles for Bud Zipfel (NYY).

- Washington traded Dean Chance (Bal) to Los Angeles for Joe Hicks (Chi).

Table 3. After Adjustments

	Los Angeles	Washington	Total
Baltimore	2	**5**	7
Boston	**5**	2	7
Chicago	**5**	2	7
Cleveland	2	**5**	7
Detroit	**5**	2	7
Kansas City	1	**6**	7
Minnesota	3	4	7
New York	**5**	2	7

A Whole New Franchise

Creating the 1961 Los Angeles Angels in 120 Days

Roland Hemond

Roland Hemond has worked in Organized Baseball since 1951, when he was hired by the Hartford Chiefs, the Boston Braves' farm club (Class A-Eastern League) for a $28-a-week entry-level job. Along the way, Hemond has worked as an executive in the front offices of the Boston/Milwaukee Braves, Los Angeles/California Angels, Chicago White Sox (twice), the Commissioner's Office, Baltimore Orioles, and the Arizona Diamondbacks (twice). Since 2007 he has been special assistant to the President and CEO of the Diamondbacks. He is the recipient of the 2011 National Baseball Hall of Fame Buck O'Neil Lifetime Achievement Award. In this article Hemond reflects on a time 50 years ago, when a singing cowboy bought the rights to the new American League franchise in Los Angeles.[1]

In December 1960, I was at home in Milwaukee, prior to celebrating the holidays with my family, when the phone rang. Fred Haney, the newly appointed general manager of the Los Angeles Angels, was calling to offer me the job of scouting and farm director with the new franchise. I arrived at Los Angeles International Airport on January 3, 1961, with my wife Margo and our one-year-old daughter Susan (it was Susan's birthday) on a beautiful day. Florence Haney, Fred's wife, picked us up, and we were in awe of the warm climate, the palm trees, and the beauty of Southern California. We set up housekeeping temporarily in a motel in Hollywood before moving to an apartment. I reported to work at the Angels' office, which was on the second floor above a bar near Hollywood and Vine. Downstairs was an electrically operated massage chair that actually shook our office when it was in use. Next door, adjacent to my office, singing cowboys would come to practice their songs and play their guitars. A few weeks later we moved the front office to Wrigley Field. It was exciting to be part of a small staff, to launch such a challenge of putting together the foundation of a brand new major-league franchise. Spring training was beginning in about six weeks, and the Angels' inaugural baseball season on April 11.

I had known Fred since 1955, when he joined the Milwaukee Braves coaching staff under manager Charlie Grimm while I was working there as assistant farm and scouting director under John Mullen. When Fred resigned as manager of the Braves after the 1959 season, he returned to his hometown of Los Angeles and was working as a sportscaster when Gene Autry asked him to accompany him to the 1960 Winter Meetings in St. Louis. Autry owned the Golden West Broadcasting Company, and he wanted Fred's help in landing the radio broadcasting rights to the new American League franchise.

Bill Veeck and Hank Greenberg were applying for the Los Angeles franchise, and I was told that American League president Joe Cronin had approached Autry, encouraging him to throw his hat into the fray. Autry, a big baseball fan, was impressed with the idea of owning a major-league team, and on December 6 he was named the owner of the Los Angeles Angels. With Opening Day set for April 11, Autry had only a little over four months to pull an organization together. Even more immediate, he and the owners of the AL's other expansion team, the Washington Senators, had only eight days to select their players in the draft from the other clubs.

The American League had created the Angels franchise hastily to show some muscle, after the threat of the Continental League had led the National League to announce its expansion to ten teams in October 1960. (These two new NL franchises, the New York Mets and the Houston Colt .45s, would not begin play until 1962.) Naturally, the American League felt compelled to stay competitive, and the mass population of Southern California made it attractive despite the popularity of the Dodgers, who had moved from Brooklyn in 1958. Washington was an important replacement due to the move of the original Senators from that city to Minnesota and MLB's desire to have a presence in the nation's capital.

Autry immediately named Bob Reynolds as president and Fred Haney as general manager, and Bill Rigney was quickly hired as field manager. This proved to be vital in having two highly respected and knowledgeable baseball men in these important positions. Haney and Rigney were able to gather information about prospects from some of their friends in the industry. I heard that Casey Stengel recommended Eli Grba, a pitcher in the New York Yankees farm system. Rigney's friend with the San Francisco Giants, Chub Feeney, let Bill see his team's scouting reports. Jim Fregosi was a noted all-around high school athlete in Northern California, and Rigney, who lived in Walnut Creek, had heard of him. Jim had signed with the Boston Red Sox and in 1960 had played for their Alpine, Texas club in the Rookie Sophomore League. He was an outstanding pick for the Angels, as he quickly jumped to Triple A Dallas-Ft. Worth of the American Association in 1961 and on to the major-league club the latter part of the season.

BUILDING A FARM SYSTEM

It was exciting to come to work for the Angels, a fresh franchise in a new (to me) city. All of my career had been spent in the East and Midwest, so I really did not have many contacts in California when I arrived on the scene. Haney, however, had grown up in Los Angeles, and knew many local baseball men, so we were able to sign some very good California-based scouts, such as Ross "Rosey" Gilhousen, Tufie Hashem, Tom Downey, Bert Niehoff, Pep Lee, Joe Gordon, and Dolph Camilli. In addition to the West Coast scouts we signed, in the early stages I set out to hire scouts in other parts of the country who had worked for the Braves, such as Gil English in the Carolinas, Leo Labossiere in New England, and Nick Kamzic in the Midwest. The Braves were losing scouts due to their new regime, which was hiring scouts they knew better.

Since I did not get to Los Angeles until the first week of January 1961, there was very little time to prepare for spring training let alone line up a couple of farm clubs to send our expansion selections and new signings to. Virtually all the minor league clubs were affiliated with a major league club on a working agreement basis. The only lower classification city I could find that was looking for a major league parent club was Statesville, North Carolina, in the Class D Western Carolina League. We hooked up with Statesville, and by the end of spring training we had enough players to start the season.

The Angels also signed a joint Class AAA working agreement with Dallas-Ft. Worth, Texas, of the American Association. Ray Johnston, owner of the team, was a friend of mine, as he had worked in the concessions department for the Milwaukee Braves; Fred Haney also knew him well. We split the working agreement with the Minnesota Twins, as we would not have enough players to staff an entire Triple A club. Three of the best players on the Dallas-Ft. Worth club were shortstop Jim Fregosi, catcher Bob (Buck) Rodgers, and right-handed pitcher Dean Chance. Fregosi had only a half season of pro experience the previous year as a Boston Red Sox farmhand in Rookie ball. Bob Rodgers had played at Class AA Birmingham, Alabama, for the Detroit Tigers organization in 1960. Dean Chance was in the Class B Three-I League at Appleton, Wisconsin in 1960. After concluding their minor-league seasons, all three advanced to the Angels in 1961, and all went on to become major-league stars.

The 1961 Statesville Owls consisted of players signed at tryout camps in Southern California headed by scouts Ross "Rosey" Gilhousen, Tufie Hashen, Bert Niehoff, Pep Lee, and Tom Downey. Former major-league outfielder George Wilson managed the club. The club's future major leaguers were catcher Jack Hiatt, outfielder Dick Simpson, and right-handed pitcher Dick Wantz. After concluding his college career at the University of Southern California, first baseman Dan Ardell was sent to the Class D Artesia (New Mexico) Dodgers of the Sophomore League; he also made it to the majors with the Angels in 1961. Third baseman Tom Satriano, also a USC product, reported to the Angels upon signing in 1961. We assigned some of our players on loan to other clubs at different classifications that year. The Angels' Triple A Dallas-Ft.Worth club trained at Amerige Park in Fullerton, California in 1961, and lower classification players at La Palma Field in Anaheim.

You hear a lot about the organization's desire to "win one for the cowboy," but that really came up in the 1970s, after I had left in September 1970 to join the Chicago White Sox. When Harry Dalton became the general manager after the 1971 season and a bit later, when Buzzie Bavasi came along as Executive Vice President and GM after the 1977 season, the Angels did tend to go for major-league free agents, such as Reggie Jackson and Bobby Grich. But in the early 1960s we were working towards the building of the farm system. Tom Satriano and Dan Ardell were early signings out of the University of Southern California. They were given signing bonuses, but in general our budget was rather restricted. The Dodgers and other clubs had larger budgets for the scouting and signing of high school and college prospects. In 1964 the ownership and Fred Haney expanded the signing opportunities, resulting in the signing of highly sought outfielder Rick Reichardt of the University of Wisconsin as well as high school catcher Tom Egan.

Roland Hemond (*right*) with two University of Southern California bonus babies fresh from the 1961 College World Series championship, first baseman Dan Ardell (*far left*) and third baseman Tom Satriano (*near left*), whom he signed that July.

The two players showed fine promise but suffered physical setbacks. Reichardt was off to a great start in 1966 with 16 home runs by midseason, but a serious ailment (one of his kidneys had to be removed) put him out of action virtually the rest of the season. Pitchers Andy Messersmith, Clyde Wright, and Tom Murphy made it to the majors rather quickly after signing. (It's ironic that the signing of Reichardt for $205,000 led to the Draft Rule the next year and that Messersmith's challenge to the Reserve Clause led to the Major League Free Agent Rule upon the decision of arbitrator Peter Seitz after the challenge by Players' Association head Marvin Miller.)

It was amazing how well the 1962 club performed, as a second-year expansion team—the Angels stayed in the pennant race until early September. *The Sporting News* named GM Fred Haney the Executive of the Year and Bill Rigney the Manager of the Year. Rigney did a phenomenal job of instilling great spirit and made exceptional on-field decisions. Shortstop Jim Fregosi came up from Triple A to take over the position from veteran Joe Koppe, and Buck Rodgers became the everyday catcher, catching 150 games. Rigney recognized the baseball smarts of these two rookies,

mentoring them so well that they became young leaders and later fine major-league managers.

Outfielders Leon "Daddy Wags" Wagner and Lee Thomas led the hitting attack, with 37 home runs and 107 RBIs for Wagner and 26 home runs and 104 RBIs for Thomas. Fregosi hit .291 after taking over at shortstop, second baseman Bill Moran made the All-Star team; third baseman Felix Torres, a Rule 5 draft, played well in the field and had 74 RBIs. Center fielder Albie Pearson led the league with 115 runs scored. Right-hander Dean Chance was the ace of the staff with a 14–10 record, 2.96 ERA, and left-hander Bo Belinsky pitched an early season no-hitter against the Baltimore Orioles. Left-hander Ted Bowsfield went 9–8. Rigney was an expert in his use of bullpen veterans Art Fowler, Tom Morgan, Ryne Duren, Jack Spring, and Dan Osinski. It was incredible that a two-year expansion club could put together an 86–76 record. The other new franchises of the early 1960s didn't fare so well. The Washington Senators won 60 games and lost 101, finishing in tenth place (last) in the AL. The New York Mets, the loveable losers of their inaugural season of 1962, went 40–120, finishing last in the NL. And the Houston Colt .45s went 64-96, finishing eighth in the NL.

The Angels shared Dodger Stadium for the 1962–1965 seasons. But with the Dodgers drawing more than double our attendance, it was evident that the only way for the Angels to gain their own identity was to move to a city and a park of their own. Orange County was enticing due to it being a growing area in population and a chance to build our own fans. Long Beach had expressed some interest but Anaheim won out, as they were willing to build a fine ballpark, where the Angels have played since 1966. ∎

Notes

1. E-mails, Roland Hemond to Jean Hastings Ardell, March–July 2010.

Bo and Dean

A Lifetime of Fun and Friendship

Tom Nahigian

Every time I see his name on a lineup card, I feel like throwing up.
—Mickey Mantle [1]

Who was the pitcher who made the great Mickey Mantle not want to step into the batter's box? Why Dino of course, Wilmer Dean Chance. Mantle uttered his memorable quote during Chance's remarkable 1964 season. As sportswriter Phil Pepe said, "It's Chance, not CBS, who owns the New York Yankees. Lock, stock and barrel."[2] Chance pitched 50 innings against the Yankees that year, allowing only 14 hits and one run, a homer by Mantle. He started five games against the Bronx Bombers, threw four complete games and three shutouts, going 4–0 with a 0.18 ERA. For the record, Mantle went 13–53 against Chance over his career, a .245 average with a .403 OBP and a .415 slugging average, though he did homer three times off Chance.[3]

While Chance was a workhorse starter from 1962 though the 1968 season, it was his lasting friendship with bon vivant Bo Belinsky that most people remember him by. The two friends hit it off from the get-go and they are an important chapter in the early history of the Angels. Although Belinsky and Chance were teammates for only three seasons with the Angels, they had enough fun and adventure for several lifetimes.

Wilmer Dean Chance was born June 1, 1941 in the farming community of Wooster, Ohio, where his family owned a 166-acre dairy farm. When he wasn't milking cows, Chance was playing sports. As a gangly pitcher and basketball forward, he made his name at Northwestern High School. One report said that Chance pitched 18 no-hit games during high school and lost only once.[4] The Baltimore Orioles were growing their farm system in those days, and they signed Chance out of high school for $30,000.

Chance pitched for two seasons in the Orioles farm system, for the 1959 Bluefield Orioles of the Appalachian League, a short season Class D league, and and the 1960 Fox Cities Foxes of the Class B Illinois-Indiana-Iowa League, winning a total of 22 games.[5] But the Orioles considered Chance brash, so they decided to protect fellow pitcher Arne Thorsland from the draft instead. The Washington Senators selected Chance with the 48th pick during the AL Expansion draft on December 14, 1960. That same day the Senators traded Chance to their fellow expansion team, the Los Angeles Angels, for outfielder Joe Hicks. Thorsland, who later became the best man at Chance's wedding to Judy Larson on January 14, 1961,[6] hurt his arm the next spring and did not win another professional game.[7]

Chance started out the 1961 season with the Angels' Class AAA farm team, the Dallas-Fort Worth Rangers in the American Association. He was a teammate of future Angels' stars Jim Fregosi and Bob Rodgers. All three players would be called up to the Angels later that season.

Chance was 6-foot-3 and weighed 204 pounds. He has blue eyes and brown hair. His hobbies are bowling and basketball. He and Judy had a son, Brett in 1962. The couple later divorced.

———

When one thinks of Dean Chance, the name Bo Belinsky immediately comes up. The two life-long friends met for the first time in Clearwater, Florida, in 1959. When the Angels selected Belinsky from the Orioles in the Rule 5 Draft on November 27, 1961, the two became teammates and roomed together during the 1963 and 1964 seasons.

Belinsky was born in New York City December 7, 1936. He grew up poor in Trenton, New Jersey, becoming a pool hustler at a young age, but his strong left arm eventually got him into Organized Baseball. At 6-foot-2 and 191 pounds, Belinsky was movie-star handsome, with a winning personality and charm that made him irresistible to the opposite sex.

The Dodgers were the kings of baseball in Los Angeles in the early 1960s, and the Angels were a brand-new expansion team. Belinsky immediately made a splash by holding out for more money at a poolside press conference. He was soon big news, pushing Sandy Koufax and Don Drysdale off the front pages of the

Angels pitchers Ken McBride, Dean Chance, and Bo Belinsky at work in 1962.

sports section. On May 5, 1962, Belinsky pitched a no-hitter against the Orioles, winning 2–0. He made the acquaintance of gossip columnist Walter Winchell, who attended the game. This was front-page news around the country, making Belinsky a star and putting the Angels on the map. At one point Belinsky and Chance visited the FBI Building with J. Edgar Hoover.[8]

Belinsky was actually shy, but he trusted Chance from the beginning of their friendship. The two were often seen driving around town in Belinsky's candy-apple-red Cadillac, a gift from a car dealership after his no-hitter. Bo started the 1962 season 5–0 and finished with a 10–11 record.

"Dean and I were a marriage made in heaven or hell," Belinsky later said. "I saw Chance in spring training in 1962 with a wife and kid. Some guys belong with a wife and kid. Dean and me just didn't belong with a wife and kid, especially in Hollywood."[9]

Chance said of Belinsky, "Nobody made it with girls the way Bo did. I never learned his secret, but I enjoyed trying."[10]

Bo made the rounds in Hollywood, dating stars including Ann-Margret, Tina Louise, Juliet Prowse, and Connie Stevens. He had a much-publicized engagement with Mamie Van Doren, then broke it off. He married Jo Collins, Playboy's Playmate of the Year

in 1965. That marriage ended in divorce and later he married and divorced Weyerhaueser paper heiress Janie Weyerhaueser. The couple had twin daughters during their marriage.[11]

While Belinsky epitomized the baseball stereotype of a million-dollar arm and a ten-cent head, Chance went on to win the Cy Young Award in 1964. Chance was a workhorse, pitching over 200 innings a season for seven straight years, twice leading the American League in innings pitched. In his sensational 1964 season, he sported a 5–5 record on July 1. A blister contributed to his slow start.[12] Starting on July 11, he pitched three consecutive complete-game shutouts and never looked back, going 15–4 the rest of the year.[13] His first half ERA was 2.19; his second half ERA was 1.29. Of his 20 victories, five games were decided by 1–0 scores. At the time Chance was the youngest ever to win the Cy Young Award. From 1962 to 1966, a Los Angeles pitcher took the award: Don Drysdale in 1962, Sandy Koufax in 1963, 1965, and 1966, and Chance in 1964.[14]

The old gang of Belinsky and Chance broke up when Belinsky was traded to the Phillies after the 1964 season. An incident with sportswriter Braven Dyer led to his departure. Dyer was a 60-year-old sports editor for the Los Angeles Times. In Washington, DC an inebriated Dyer knocked on Belinsky and Chance's hotel room in the middle of the night and demanded to speak with Bo and then challenged him to a fight. Belinsky threw a glass of water into Dyer's face. Punches were thrown and Dyer was found unconscious on the floor with blood coming out of one ear. Dyer was friendly with Angels' General Manager Fred Haney and Bo was soon traded.[15] Chance left after the 1966 season when he was traded to the Minnesota Twins. Manager Bill Rigney said of the trade, "I'm not sure we'll find another arm like Dean's, but we had to do something about our first-base situation and overall hitting."[16]

Chance said, "I'm not surprised to be traded, but I am shocked that the Angels would trade me to an AL club. I'm shocked that they'd run the risk of letting me come back to haunt them."[17]

In 1967, Chance won 20 games for the second time in his career and was named the American League Comeback Player of the Year.[18] He started the final game of the 1967 season for the Twins against the Boston Red Sox and Jim Lonborg. At that point in the season Chance was 4–1 against Boston and Lonborg was 0–3 against the Twins. On August 6, Chance had beaten the Red Sox, 2–0, striking out four and pitching five perfect innings in a rain-shortened game. But on

Angels hurlers Dean Chance and Bo Belinsky out on the town with actress Mamie Van Doren, watching the Twist, April 5, 1963.

that October Sunday, the Twins led the Red Sox 2–0 heading into the bottom of the sixth inning. Red Sox pitcher Jim Lonborg bunted toward third and reached on an infield hit. Two more singles and a bases-loaded single by Carl Yastrzemski tied the game, 2–2. After a run-scoring fielder's choice, Chance was removed from the game and the Red Sox plated five runs that inning. The Twins rallied in the top of the eighth, but Yastrzemski threw out the Twins' Bobby Allison trying to stretch his run-scoring single into a double. The Red Sox won, 5–3.[19]

Chance threw a sinking fastball, a sweeping curve, and a slider. He had a good fastball and could also throw a changeup screwball.[20] During his delivery he turned his back to the hitter. Over his career, right-handed batters hit .223 and left-handed batters hit .248 against him.[21] He had particularly wonderful control against the Yankees. Author Arnold Hano said that Mickey Mantle had a hard time hitting him because Chance threw pitches low and outside at the knee. At that point in his career, Mantle could not get under the ball. Chance had a swing arm motion, a three-quarters delivery. With his bent-body posture, he never threw pitches above the waist.[22]

During the 1968 season, a *SPORT* magazine piece called Giants ace Juan Marichal and Dean Chance the shutout kings. Over their careers, Marichal was 243–142, with 52 shutouts in 457 games started. Chance was 128–115, with 33 shutouts in 294 career starts.[23] As of 1967, eight active 100-game starters had been able to average at least one shutout for every 10 starts, led by Marichal with 32 shutouts in 246 starts (.130) and Chance with 26 shutouts in 207 starts (.126).[24] Chance also started two All-Star games.[25]

Superman had his Kryptonite and Chance had his share of failure. He led the league in pitcher errors four times, in 1963, 1967, 1968, and 1971.[26] He was also unproductive as a hitter. For pitchers who had at least 500 plate appearances during their career, Chance has the lowest batting average at .066. In 662 at bats, he struck out 420 times. He had two doubles in his 44 hits. He did have 61 sacrifice bunts.[27]

After the 1968 season, Chance hurt his back rushing himself into shape and was never the same pitcher again.[28] He finished his career pitching for the Indians, Mets, and Tigers. He was released by the Tigers on October 6, 1971.[29] Since his retirement from baseball, Chance has tended to his real estate holdings, worked in a carnival, worked with a poster company, and managed boxer Ernie Shavers. He is president of the International Boxing Association. He is also a world-class gin rummy player.[30]

Belinsky and Chance remained lifelong friends. Chance refused to attend an autograph show unless Belinsky was invited. In a 1991 interview, Belinsky said that he was at a benefit with Hall of Fame pitcher Steve Carlton when two kids came up and asked for an autograph. "Carlton reached out to sign and one of the kids says, 'No, my dad said to get Mr. Belinsky's autograph.' I told Steve that he did it the easy way, by winning 300 games. You just try to get all this notoriety on 28 victories. Now that takes a lot of work."[31]

Through the years, both Chance and Belinsky made peace with God. Belinsky remarked a year before his

Bo Belinsky, circa 1985, feeling the toll of the years.

death, "Can you imagine? I had to come to Las Vegas to discover Jesus Christ." Belinsky worked for the Findlay Management Group and played golf with clients. He was active in the Trinity Life Church. His friend Rich Abajian, a general manager at the car dealership where Belinsky worked, said, "He found Christ, he was active in the church, he read the Bible. He was content."[32]

After Belinsky's death in 2001, Chance observed, "We made mistakes, tried not to hurt anyone. We were kids in a different time, pitching in a great city. It was like feeling that you had the world at your feet, like it would never end, and I think about those good times a lot and often talked with Bo about them. I can also tell you that if I had a dollar for every time somebody asked me where Bo was and what he was doing, I'd be a wealthy man. Everybody remembered him and I'm just glad he got his life straightened out and he knew in his last year where he was going."[33]

Chance arranged a memorial service for Belinsky in Dodger Stadium. He also handled the arrangements for his burial in Las Vegas. "Bo was a one-of-a-kind guy and there won't be another one like him," said Chance at the memorial. "He was full of cancer, his heart was bad and his hip was hurting him terribly at the end. He had slipped and fallen and it was really tough on him. But he made his peace with the Lord and he is probably better off today than he was last week. He's not suffering terribly any more."[34]

The memory of Bo and Dean will live forever in the hearts of Angels fans. They ushered in an era of fun that continued with free spirits Jay Johnstone and Jimmy Piersall. Johnstone later authored three books of humorous baseball anecdotes and Piersall's life story was told in a best-selling book, *Fear Strikes Out*, which later became a movie in 1957 starring Anthony Perkins and Karl Malden. ■

Notes

1. Maury Allen, *Bo: Pitching and Wooing*, the Dial Press, 1973, 104.
2. Robert Goldman, *Once They Were Angels*, Sports Publishing LLC, 2006.
3. Retrosheet.org.
4. Ray Robinson, *Baseball Stars of 1965*, Pyramid Books, 1965.
5. Baseball-reference.com.
6. *The Sporting News*, Baseball Register, 1966.
7. *Baseball Digest*, May 1967, 86.
8. *New York Times*, 27 November 2001.
9. *Los Angeles Times*, Sunday, 25 November 2001.
10. Ross Newhan, *The Anaheim Angels—A Complete History*, Hyperion, 2000.
11. *New York Times*, 27 November 2001.
12. Robert Goldman, *Once They Were Angels*, Sports Publishing LLC, 2006.
13. Retrosheet.org.
14. http://en.wikipedia.org/wiki/Dean_Chance
15. Robert Goldman, *Once They Were Angels*, Sports Publishing LLC, 2006.
16. Ross Newhan, *The Anaheim Angels—A Complete History*, Hyperion, 2000.
17. Ross Newhan, *The Anaheim Angels—A Complete History*, Hyperion, 2000.
18. Ray Robinson, *Baseball Stars of 1968*, Pyramid Books, 1968.
19. Retrosheet.org.
20. Rob Neyer and Bill James, *The Neyer-James Guide to Pitchers*, Fireside 2004.
21. Retrosheet.org.
22. Phone call with author Arnold Hano, 10 February 2010.
23. Pete Palmer and Gary Gillette, *The 2005 ESPN Baseball Encyclopedia*.
24. Allan Roth, *Sport Magazine*, Inside Facts July 1968.
25. *The Sporting News*, Baseball Register, 1972.
26. Baseball-reference.com.
27. Baseball-reference.com.
28. Maury Allen, *Bo, Pitching and Wooing*, the Dial Press, 1973.
29. *The Sporting News*, Baseball Register, 1972.
30. Robert Goldman, *Once They Were Angels*, Sports Publishing LLC, 2006.
31. *Los Angeles Times*, Sunday, 25 November 2001.
32. *Los Angeles Times*, Sunday, 25 November 2001.
33. *Los Angeles Times*, Sunday, 25 November 2001.
34. Associated Press, 25 November 2001.

Of Witches, Hexes, and Plain Bad Luck

The Reputed Curse of the Los Angeles Angels of Anaheim

Stephen Roney

From the mid-1970s until the Angels won the World Series in 2002, frequent stories of an Angels "curse" or "jinx" appeared in the local and national media. Typically blamed on a rumor that Anaheim Stadium was built on a Native American burial ground, the curse persists to the present day despite the fact that several of the victims of the curse predated the move to Anaheim in 1966. Tim Mead, the Angels' media relations director, researched the claim in the 1990s and found no evidence indicating a burial ground.[1]

The first reference to the Angels jinx in *The Sporting News* was an article by Dick Miller in March 1976, spurred by Nolan Ryan's arm troubles, which had limited him to 28 starts in 1975.[2] The curse had not been mentioned at all when Bruce Heinbechner became the third Angels player to die in March 1974, but when Mike Miley died in January 1977, Harry Dalton, then the Angels' general manager, said it was "the first thing I thought of," placing the first mention of the curse in this time frame.[3]

The deaths have always been the cornerstone of the Angels curse. Since 1960, 32 major-league players have died while on a major-league roster or within a year of their last game. The Angels are typically linked with seven of those deaths (five of those by 1978), more than 20 percent of the total. The only other team to have lost even three players in that time frame is the Cleveland Indians with three, and two of those died in the same boating accident in Florida in 1993. The Angels have lost three players in midseason and another late in spring training.

Naturally the curse was extended to include the postseason, when the Angels became the first team to blow a 2–0 lead in a best-of-five series in 1982, losing the last three games to the Milwaukee Brewers. In game five of the 1986 ALCS against the Boston Red Sox, the Angels were one pitch away from their first World Series appearance, up three games to one, with a 5–4 lead with two outs in the ninth, when Dave Henderson hit a 2–2 pitch to put the Sox on top with a two-run shot. The Sox went on to win that game and the next two to take the series before succumbing to their own curse and losing the World Series.

The Angels have also suffered numerous late-season collapses, the most devastating coming in 1995, when the Angels had to win their last five games to force a one-game playoff (which they lost) after holding an 11-game lead for the division as late as August 9 and a 10-game lead for the wild card on August 3.

The curse has even been extended to players who previously played for the Angels. Despite playing four years with the Reds after leaving the Angels, Jim McGlothlin, who died of cancer at 32 in 1975, is almost always mentioned. Even Ed Kirkpatrick, who was paralyzed in a car accident in 1981, is frequently mentioned, despite playing his last game with the Angels in 1968 and spending the bulk of his career with the Royals and Pirates before leaving the majors in 1977. Yet Fritz Brickell, who was the Angels' starting shortstop on Opening Day in 1961 and died of cancer at 30 in 1965, is never mentioned in an Angels curse article (until now).

Angels' family members are also mentioned. Ina Autry, wife of owner Gene Autry, met her unexpected death in 1980.[4] John Candelaria's son died in 1985 after a swimming pool accident left him in a coma for 11 months.[5] In 1996 Rod Carew's 18-year-old daughter lost her battle with leukemia.[6]

Attempts have been made to counter the curse. During a team slump in 1977, Dick Miller, a reporter for the *Los Angeles Herald-Examiner*, called Louise Huebner, "head of the Magic Circle of 4,000 witches nationwide, the largest coven in America."[7] She gave Magic Circle medals to owner Gene Autry, general manager Dalton, and the players just before they played the Yankees on August 3.

The Angels won six straight games before Huebner had a change of heart, saying, "Some of the players were very insulting. I wasn't too thrilled being involved with them. I felt I shouldn't have used the energy of the Magic Circle, because the Angels were not sincere and honest. They didn't participate or give anything back. I'm not Mary Poppins. I don't have to help anybody. So I just pulled out. I put the Curse back on."[8]

Around 2000, "two shamanistic women" gave little figurines to the players to protect them.[9] And late in the 2002 season, the *Press-Enterprise* of Riverside, California, reported that a local tribe had "blessed the ballpark themselves before this season began."[10] When the Angels won the World Series that year, the stories of an Angels curse or jinx pretty much disappeared. But the deaths of pitcher Nick Adenhart and veteran coach and scout Preston Gomez in 2009 and the 2010 freak injury to first baseman Kendrys Morales, have resurrected those stories. Many web sites offered curse chronologies after Adenhart's death, and the *Los Angeles Times* and *Orange County Register* have both revisited the club's unusual history of calamities. Over time, some of the stories have grown beyond their original incidents. A single mistake in one story will propagate over time. The following represent—and clarify and correct errors in—the most prominent and unusual injuries in Angels history.

The earliest named victim of the curse is usually Johnny James, acquired by the Angels on May 8, 1961. In his 1976 article Miller wrote, "James tried to break off a sharp curve one night at Wrigley Field and heard a bone in his arm crack. INCREDIBLY, his arm had been broken making the pitch and his career was over."[11] The mention of Wrigley Field (Los Angeles) places the incident in 1961, while other references to James have usually pegged the injury to his last pitching appearance in 1961 in Chicago.[12] James did not pitch the last two weeks of the season, though he did pinch run twice, and teammate Dan Ardell does not recall any word of James breaking his arm. Early 1962 articles show James in spring training and trying to

make the team. The April 4 issue of *The Sporting News* reported, "Jim Donohue and Johnny James have looked particularly sharp on the hill. The latter was laid up a few days with arm trouble but is all right again."[13] There are references to further injuries, but no broken arm. James pitched 21 games in the minors in 1962. In 1963 *Baseball Digest* reported, "Before a sore arm last year prompted his demotion and posed a threat to his future, Johnny James, the Angels' ex-Yankee, was one of the brightest pitching prospects."[14]

Outfielder Ken Hunt broke his collarbone while swinging a bat in the on-deck circle late in spring training in 1962.[15] Originally diagnosed with a strained arm, Hunt continued to play through part of spring training.[16] He was not placed on the disabled list until May, playing six games, three as a pinch hitter (striking out twice) and three as a pinch runner. He returned to action in September, playing three games at first and pinch-hitting three times.[17]

During batting practice in August 1962, veteran pitcher Art Fowler was hit by a line drive while in left field, leaving a four-inch cut running "above and to the side of the eye" and requiring eight stitches.[18] He gradually lost most of the sight in his left eye.[19]

Ken McBride missed much of the last six weeks of the 1962 season after discovering that he had cracked a rib from a bout of pleurisy.[20] McBride was an All-Star pitcher in 1963, but according to Miller, McBride was later in an automobile accident and suffered whiplash injuries, causing him to lose effectiveness in 1964.[21] This condition was not diagnosed until years later.

While not mentioned in curse articles, reliever Bob Lee's superb rookie season ended prematurely on September 11, 1964, when he broke two bones in his hand slugging a heckling sailor who reached into the

Dick Wantz, died 1965.

Bruce Heinbechner, died 1974.

Mike Miley, died 1977.

bullpen at Fenway Park.[22] The incident did not seem to have a lasting effect, perhaps saving Lee from being a part of normal curse lore.

In 1964, the Angels signed "two of the most highly sought-after players in the country."[23] But outfielder Rick Reichardt suffered kidney failure and had one kidney removed in 1966, while catcher Tom Egan lost some of the sight in his left eye when Earl Wilson beaned him in 1969.

The first Angels player to die while on the active roster was rookie Dick Wantz, who had pitched one inning for the Angels in April 1965, when he went on the disabled list, suffering from headaches. First diagnosed as a virus, a brain tumor was then discovered. Wantz did not survive the operation to remove the tumor, dying on May 13.[24]

Pitcher Jack Hamilton cracked a rib wrestling with George Brunet before a game in late 1968, according to Miller.[25] Contemporary accounts have him pulling a muscle in his side in May, with X-rays negative. He was outrighted to Seattle in early July.

Minnie Rojas was a top reliever for the club in 1966-1968, with a record of 23–16, 43 saves, and a 3.00 ERA. Many curse-related articles, starting with Dick Miller's *The Sporting News* obituary of Mike Miley (see below), have reported that Rojas was paralyzed in a car crash in 1968; however, he appeared in 12 Triple-A games in 1969. The crash actually occurred on April 1, 1970. Accounts of the crash said Rojas was "reported to have been trying to re-enter baseball" after having his career "cut short by arm trouble."[26] He was listed as 31 in the news article about the crash, but is currently listed as being five years older than originally reported.

Infielder Chico Ruiz died in a car accident in February 1972 after playing for the Angels in 1971. Usually credited as an Angels curse victim, he had signed with the Kansas City Royals prior to his death.[27]

Shortstop Bobby Valentine suffered a compound fracture of his right leg when he crashed into the outfield wall while filling in for Ken Berry in center field on May 17, 1973.[28]

Reliever Bruce Heinbechner never played in a regular season game in the majors, but had apparently made the opening day roster when he was killed in a two-car crash while returning to the Angels' spring training hotel in Palm Springs on March 10, 1974.[29]

In 1974, Rudy May threw four shutouts in his first six starts. According to Miller's 1976 curse article, one night, "[while] walking in the dark and carrying a tray, he tripped over his pet dog. May's and the Angels' season were ruined by a broken wrist and dislocated elbow."[30] There are inconsistencies in this story.[31] May threw four shutouts in his first six starts the year before, in 1973. However, his longest distance between starts in that season was 14 days, at the end of June and early July (spanning the All-Star break). His ERA continued to rise after that, but there is no time gap consistent with a broken wrist.[32] The following season he was used primarily in relief until he was traded to the Yankees in midseason, also with no large gaps in service.

Shortstop Mike Miley received $80,000 as the Angels' top pick in the 1974 amateur draft, passing up his senior year as quarterback at LSU in the process. He died in a single-car automobile accident on January 6, 1977.[33]

Newly signed infielder Bobby Grich herniated a disk in his back while lifting an air-conditioning unit at his apartment on February 14, 1977, causing him to miss most of spring training and eventually leading to season-ending back surgery in July.[34] A more conventional injury to Joe Rudi, signed during the same offseason, is often lumped in with this one.

Outfielder Lyman Bostock signed with the Angels in 1977 as a free agent after hitting .336 for the Minnesota Twins. On August 23, 1978, as he rode in a car in Chicago, he was shot and killed by the estranged husband of one of the passengers in the car.[35]

Pitcher Jim Barr broke his hand punching a toilet at a party

Lyman Bostock, died 1978.

Nick Adenhart, died 2009.

COURTESY OF ANGELS BASEBALL

celebrating the Angels' first division championship in 1979, causing him to miss the playoffs.[36]

First baseman Wally Joyner missed the end of the 1986 Championship Series with a staph infection in his leg.[37]

In 1989 reliever Donnie Moore had been released by the Angels and the Royals and was out of baseball when he committed suicide after shooting his wife, who survived.[38] He is almost always mentioned as an Angels curse victim, partially because the suicide is usually traced to the Dave Henderson home run he gave up in the 1986 playoffs.

On March 16, 1992, pitcher Matt Keough was sitting on the bench at Scottsdale Memorial Stadium when a foul ball off the bat of the first batter of the game hit him in the head. The injury ended his attempted comeback and nearly his life.[39]

Coach Deron Johnson died of lung cancer at the age of 53 on April 23, 1992.[40]

On May 21, 1992, an Angels team bus crashed in New Jersey during a road trip. Several members of the team were injured.[41] Infielder Bobby Rose was the only player placed on the disabled list, with a sprained ankle. First baseman Alvin Davis bruised a kidney, and first baseman Lee Stevens had some soreness in his arms and ribs.[42] Among those hospitalized were Davis, athletic trainer Ned Bergert, with a minor concussion and bruised kidney, and traveling secretary Frank Sims, with bruised ribs. Bullpen coach Rick Turner required 26 stitches for a cut below his left armpit.[43]

Nick Adenhart's death hours after he had pitched his first game of the 2009 season prompted a spontaneous memorial on the pitcher's mound of the diamond at the entry to Angel Stadium. All season long grieving fans left mementos, T-shirts, baseball gloves, photos, and flowers while pausing to reflect on the tragedy.

Manager Buck Rodgers was also hospitalized with elbow, knee, and rib injuries, causing him to miss more than half the season.

Infielder Rex Hudler was 16-for-30, with 3 homers in his last 9 games in May 1994, raising his average to .406, when he was injured during batting practice. Manager Marcel Lachemann and Hudler "were gathering balls in the outfield when they saw one lone ball in between them. They looked at one another, and took off running for it. Hudler was there first, and when he reached to pick the ball up, Lachemann jokingly lunged at it with his fungo bat. The bat bounced off the turf and hit Hudler's right ankle. Hudler then dove to avoid the bat, tumbled onto the turf, and landed on his right shoulder."[44] Returning after seventeen days on the disabled list, he went 11-for-60 the rest of the season, ending at .298.

Shortstop Gary DiSarcina tore a ligament in his thumb while sliding into second base on August 3, 1995, causing him to miss most of the rest of the season and the Angels' historic collapse.[45]

Pitcher Chuck Finley opened the 1997 season on the disabled list after a flung bat broke an orbital bone during spring training; later that season Finley went on the DL again when he slipped and injured his wrist while backing up home plate.[46]

DiSarcina missed half of the 1999 season after breaking his arm when a fungo bat swung by coach George Hendrick accidentally hit him.[47] He hit .229 in 81 games after his return, his lowest average since becoming a regular, and then played 12 games in 2000 before having rotator cuff surgery, which ultimately ended his career at the age of 32.[48]

Newly signed free agent first baseman Mo Vaughn slipped and fell trying to catch a pop fly in the visitors' dugout in his first regular season game with the Angels in 1999, wrenching his ankle.[49] While he only missed the minimum 15 days, Vaughn was never the player the Angels originally expected, though some of that may have been park effect. More conventional injuries to Jim Edmonds and Tim Salmon followed shortly.

In May 2000 in the second inning of a game against the Texas Rangers, pitcher Kent Mercker suffered a cerebral hemorrhage on the mound at Edison Field in Anaheim.[50] He returned in August, but that season and the following one were largely lost. He came back and had several fine seasons, starting with Colorado in 2002, last pitching in the majors with Cincinnati in 2008.

Outfielder Garret Anderson was limited to three games in the 2007 American League Division Series against the Red Sox due to pink eye. He was 2-for-9.[51]

Preston Gomez, assistant to the general manager, special assignment scout, and spring training instructor, died at age 86 on January 13, 2009 from injuries suffered when he was hit by a truck at a Blythe, California gas station nine months earlier.[52]

Hours after pitching six scoreless innings against the Oakland A's in his first start of the season on April 8, 2009, young pitcher Nick Adenhart was a passenger in a car hit by an alleged drunk driver. He and two companions were killed, prompting the creation of a memorial shrine in front of the stadium, which remained for the entire season.

Announcer Rory Markas died suddenly January 4, 2010, at the age of 54. He had been a radio announcer with the Angels for eight years and was going to move to the television booth for the upcoming season.

First baseman and clean-up hitter Kendrys Morales hit a walk-off grand slam on May 29, 2010, but broke his leg jumping into the crowd of players at home plate, causing him to miss the rest of the season and all of 2011. He was hitting .290 with 11 homers in 51 games.

So the Angels have had more than their share of deaths and perhaps more of their share of unusual injuries, along with a normal share of "normal" injuries. This has caused a fair amount of embellishment by the media over the years, and while the discussion has calmed down, a couple more weird injuries like Morales's may prompt more stories in the Southern California press about the Angels' curse. ∎

Notes

1. Bradley, Mickey and Gordon, Dan, *Haunted Baseball*, Lyons Press, 2007, 253.
2. Dick Miller, "Angels' Pitchers Seem Hexed; Long History of Staff Jinxes," *The Sporting News*, 27 March 1976, 36.
3. Dick Miller, "Death Robs Miley of Great Dream," *The Sporting News*, 29 January 1977.
4. Gallagher, Danny, *Angels' Halo Haunted*, Scoop Press, 1998, 31.
5. Gallagher, Danny, *Angels' Halo Haunted*, Scoop Press, 1998, 31.
6. Gallagher, Danny, *Angels' Halo Haunted*, Scoop Press, 1998, 32.
7. John B. Holway, "The Angels' Witch," adapted from *Baseball Astrologer and Other Weird Tales*, 2000. http://baseballguru.com/jholway/analysisjholway33.html.
8. John B. Holway, "The Angels' Witch," adapted from *Baseball Astrologer and Other Weird Tales*, 2000. http://baseballguru.com/jholway/analysisjholway33.html.
9. Bradley, Mickey and Gordon, Dan, *Haunted Baseball*, Lyons Press, 2007, 254.
10. Chris Suellentrop, "The Anaheim Angels: The worst team you've never heard of," 18 October 2002, www.slate.com/id/2072685.
11. Dick Miller, "Angels' Pitchers Seem Hexed; Long History of Staff Jinxes," *The Sporting News*, 27 March 1976, 36.
12. Retrosheet.org.
13. "Angel Dyer-y," *The Sporting News*, 4 April 1962, 30.
14. Libby, Bill, "Why Not Batters as Hitting Coaches?" *Baseball Digest*, March 1963, 78.
15. Bradley, Mickey and Gordon, Dan, *Haunted Baseball*, Lyons Press, 2007, 254.
16. Newhan, Ross, "'Mystery Injury' Hits Hunt," *Long Beach Press-Telegram*, 2 April 1962, C-2.
17. Retrosheet.org.
18. Newhan, Ross, "Fly-in-Eye Injured Fowler OK," *Long Beach Press-Telegram*, 7 August 1962, C-1.
19. Newhan, Ross, *The Anaheim Angels: A Complete History*, Hyperion, 2000, 63–4.
20. Newhan, Ross, *The Anaheim Angels: A Complete History*, Hyperion, 2000, 64.
21. Dick Miller, "Angels' Pitchers Seem Hexed; Long History of Staff Jinxes," *The Sporting News*, 27 March 1976, 36.
22. Snyder, John, *Angels Journal*, Clerisy Press, 2010, 88.
23. Dick Miller, "Angels' Pitchers Seem Hexed; Long History of Staff Jinxes," *The Sporting News*, 27 March 1976, 36.
24. "Angels' Dick Wantz Succumbs to Brain Tumor," *Los Angeles Times*, 15 May 1965, A1.
25. Dick Miller, "Angels' Pitchers Seem Hexed; Long History of Staff Jinxes," *The Sporting News*, March 27, 1976, 36.
26. "Minnie Rojas Injured, 2 Children Die in Crash," *The Sporting News*, 18 April 1970, 38.
27. Snyder, John, *Angels Journal*, Clerisy Press, 2010, 88.
28. Dick Miller, "Angels' Pitchers Seem Hexed; Long History of Staff Jinxes," *The Sporting News*, 27 March 1976, 36.
29. "A pitcher lost, but hardly forgotten," *Long Beach Press-Telegram*, 12 March 1974.
30. Dick Miller, "Angels' Pitchers Seem Hexed; Long History of Staff Jinxes," *The Sporting News*, 27 March 1976, 36.
31. "Minnie Rojas Injured, 2 Children Die in Crash," *The Sporting News*, 18 April 1970, 38.
32. Retrosheet.org.
33. Dick Miller, "Death Robs Miley of Great Dream," *The Sporting News*, 29 January 1977.
34. Newhan, Ross, *The Anaheim Angels: A Complete History*, Hyperion, 2000, 163–4.
35. Gallagher, Danny, *Angels' Halo Haunted*, Scoop Press, 1998, 8–11.
36. Gallagher, Danny, *Angels' Halo Haunted*, Scoop Press, 1998, 30.
37. Dufresne, Chris, "The Hex Files," *Los Angeles Times*, 27 May 1999.
38. Gallagher, Danny, *Angels' Halo Haunted*, Scoop Press, 1998, 1–7.
39. Gallagher, Danny, *Angels' Halo Haunted*, Scoop Press, 1998, 27.
40. Snyder, John, *Angels Journal*, Clerisy Press, 2010, 220.
41. Snyder, John, *Angels Journal*, Clerisy Press, 2010, 221.
42. Elliott, Helene, "Young Angels Growing Up Fast," *Los Angeles Times*, 26 May 1992, C-1.
43. Gallagher, Danny, *Angels' Halo Haunted*, Scoop Press, 1998, 17–20.
44. Nightengale, Bob, "Loss Isn't Their Only Setback," *Los Angeles Times*, 31 May 1994, C-1.
45. Weyler, John, "DiSarcina Is Angels' Biggest Loss," *Los Angeles Times*, 5 August 1995, C-1.
46. Dufresne, Chris, "The Hex Files," *Los Angeles Times*, 27 May 1999.
47. Bradley, Mickey and Gordon, Dan, *Haunted Baseball*, Lyons Press, 2007, 252.
48. DiGiovanna, Mike, "DiSarcina's Agent Optimistic After Meeting," *Los Angeles Times*, 14 September 2000, D-1.
49. Dufresne, Chris, "The Hex Files," *Los Angeles Times*, 27 May 1999.
50. Bradley, Mickey and Gordon, Dan, *Haunted Baseball*, Lyons Press, 2007, 252.
51. Woke, Dan, "The unlucky history of the Angels," *Orange County Register*, 3 June 2010, http://www.ocregister.com/sports/history-251698-angels-unlucky.html?pic=3.
52. DiGiovanna, Mike, "Preston Gomez, 1922–2009; Angels consultant spent 64 years in pro baseball," *Los Angeles Times*, 14 January 2009, B-6.

Buck Rodgers

On the Road to Anaheim

Maxwell Kates

Millions of Californians were not born here but chose the Golden State as the center of their career and family lives. Two of them, London's Bob Hope and Tacoma's Bing Crosby, won fame and glory in Hollywood with a series of "road" movies. The subject of this article, however, is a baseball personality whose life has followed a unique road from the heartland of America to the state of California.

Even as a rookie with the 1961 Los Angeles Angels, Buck Rodgers demonstrated leadership qualities and the ability to motivate his teammates. After injuries prevented him from reaching his full potential as a player, Rodgers was frequently mentioned as a possible Angels manager. After a coaching and managing odyssey that took him to Minnesota, San Francisco, Milwaukee, and Montreal, he achieved that goal. Rodgers described himself as "a teacher, a motivator, someone who's fair but who will never take fairness for weakness."[1]

His openness, honesty, and willingness to communicate made him a popular figure with the fans and the media despite periodic clashes with some of his players and general managers. The road that Rodgers traveled, however, was not always a safe one, and on more than one occasion, it proved calamitous for the Rodgers family.

Rex and Winifred Rodgers of Delaware County, Ohio welcomed a son, Robert Leroy, on August 16, 1938. A naturally gifted athlete who was nicknamed Buck, Rodgers won letters in basketball and track as well as baseball at Prospect High School, where he pitched six no-hitters in addition to catching.[2] He also played American Legion baseball in nearby Marion, Ohio before he signed as a free agent with the Detroit Tigers in 1956. Rodgers soon found himself caught in a logjam of catchers, including Dick Brown, Mike Roarke, and rising star Bill Freehan. The Tigers deemed him expendable, and he was selected by the Los Angeles Angels in the 1960 expansion draft. Years later, Rodgers credited Angels owner Gene Autry with saving him "from having to find a real job."[3] Meanwhile, Rodgers had married his high school sweetheart, the former Judy Long, on January 18, 1958.

Rodgers, a 6-foot-2, 195-pound switch hitter, played for Walker Cooper at Dallas-Ft. Worth, where he was honored by *Look* magazine as the American Association's top catcher of 1961. A scouting report describes him as having "excellent speed for a catcher, good accurate arm, line drive power, [and being a] fine handler of pitchers."[4] That September, the Angels brought him up, where he batted .321 in 16 games, including a grand slam home run off the Indians' Barry Latman.

After watching that performance, manager Bill Rigney lauded Rodgers as "an imaginative catcher who can go on to become one of the game's best."[5] Meanwhile, Rodgers was learning from Rigney that "the competitive edge lay in guile, cunning, and courage to make the right moves at the right time."[6] Cerebral and bumptious, Rigney was constantly challenged by both his young catcher and his shortstop Jim Fregosi. In reference to Rodgers and Fregosi, Rigney noted that "you wouldn't have had to look very far" in predicting future big league managers on the team.[7]

A country image fused with urban charm served Buck Rodgers well in Tinseltown. As Daniel Okrent described him in *Nine Innings*, "Rodgers was a tall man, broad shoulders, blessed with bright eyes and a movie star's face. He wore cowboy boots, well cut sports coats, and open collared shirts…he had chewed tobacco all of his adult life, yet always took care to use whitening drops on his teeth to combat the inevitable staining. *Playgirl* magazine even featured Rodgers in an article on baseball's sexiest men."[8]

The season of 1962 was a banner year for both the fledgling Angels and Rodgers. Rodgers disappointed nobody in an early season contest in Minnesota when he drove in five runs in a 12–5 victory over the Twins.[9] A month later, on May 5, he caught Bo Belinsky's no-hitter at Chavez Ravine. After sweeping the Washington Senators in a July Fourth doubleheader, the Angels led the American League, in this, their sophomore season. On August 28, Rodgers hit one of three consecutive fourth-inning home runs as part of a 10–5 victory at Kansas City, and went on to hit .440 during a two-week span in September. Although the

Angels finished the season in third place, their young catcher shattered the record for games caught by a rookie with 150 while turning a club record 14 double plays.[10] He displayed marksmanship with his bat, leading the Angels with 8 sacrifice flies and 34 doubles while tying Albie Pearson with 6 triples. Rodgers finished second to Tom Tresh as Rookie of the Year.

The 1962 offseason marked the first of several in which Rodgers's name was suggested by the Angels in trades. One winter rumor had him going to Chicago, the next winter he was headed for Baltimore, and the third time, he and Bob Lee were to be packaged to Minnesota for Jimmie Hall and Earl Battey. Rodgers was candid in telling sportswriter Ross Newhan, "[I]f I worried every time I heard my name involved in a trade, I'd be a nervous wreck." General manager Fred Haney routinely tried to ease Rodgers's apprehensions by declaring that his catcher was "not for sale."[11]

A finger injury curtailed Rodgers's effectiveness in 1963, but he continued to show flashes of brilliance.[12] He matched his record of 14 double plays in 1964, batted .342 during the club's 11-game winning streak in June, and touched Dick Radatz for an inside the park home run in September. An ankle injury among other ailments limited Rodgers to a .209 average and 32 RBIs in 1965. After a stellar defensive season in 1966, Rodgers was developing a reputation as one of the better callers of pitches in the game. He complimented pitchers George Brunet and Marcelino Lopez on "never having better control of [their] breaking stuff" in spring training 1967. Of course, there was no love lost with pitchers who ignored his advice—he once called Dean Chance "the dumbest I've caught." As the vice president of Pacific Bus Lines, Rodgers was only too pleased to offer Dean Chance a one-way ticket to Minnesota when traded to the Twins. Chance "shook him off" and rode Greyhound.[13]

Another injury in 1967 and a lingering blood infection limited Rodgers to 6 home runs with 41 RBI in 139 games.[14] Having recovered by August 18, he caught Jack Hamilton the night Red Sox outfielder Tony Conigliaro was beaned. Rodgers compared the horrific incident to "taking a bat to a pumpkin."[15] By the end of the decade, Rodgers moved his family, including daughters Lori, Lisa, and twins Jan and Jill, from his home state of Ohio to Yorba Linda, California.

The Angels released Rodgers in 1969, the year Rigney was fired. In 1970, he followed Rigney to Minnesota as one of his coaches (Dean Chance had since been traded to Cleveland). Sandwiched around another Rigney coaching assignment in San Francisco were two managerial postings in the Angels' organization:

Buck Rodgers as a rookie in Tiger Stadium in 1961, the first of his 15 seasons in the Angels' system as a player and manager.

Salinas in 1975 and El Paso in 1977. By now, the name "Buck Rodgers" was synonymous with "Angels manager of the future"—but it would prove a circuitous route for Rodgers's return to Anaheim.

After the Milwaukee Brewers hired Angels general manager Harry Dalton, other Angels personnel moved to new positions with the Brewers in 1978, among them Milwaukee's new third-base coach Buck Rodgers. Two years later, he was promoted to replace the ailing George Bamberger as manager. Rodgers won a division title in 1981 but a slow start in 1982 could not save his job. After a successful campaign managing Indianapolis in 1984, he was hired to manage the Montreal Expos beginning in 1985. During most of his tenure in Montreal, he kept the Expos in contention despite operating on a shoestring budget. The apex of his career occurred in 1987 when his club won 91 games and he was honored as Manager of the Year. Falling out of favor with a new regime in Montreal, he accepted his release early in the 1991 season.

Meanwhile, the Angels were imploding under manager Doug Rader. Was it time for a change? General manager Whitey Herzog thought so and brought Rodgers back to Anaheim. The Angels did not improve in the standings under Rodgers, finishing in last place in 1991 despite a .500 record. Off the field, Rodgers endured the fright of his life on May 21, 1992, when the Angels' team bus crashed into a ravine alongside the New Jersey Turnpike. Rodgers recalled the incident a few years later. "I saw a big tree limb coming and I ducked. Fortunately I missed it because it would have taken my head off. Then I got hit in the right side of the head.... My right ribs were hit by the trees that crashed into the right side of the bus and I had a crushed elbow."[16] After a long convalescence—he also had a broken leg—Rodgers returned to the Angels' dugout on August 28. Piloted in his absence by interim managers John Wathan and Marcel Lachemann, the Angels ended the 1992 season with a losing record. The following year, the Halos won only 71 games in 1993 and after butting heads with new general manager Bill Bavasi, Rodgers knew the team had to contend in 1994 in order for him to keep his job. The team did not, and after calling Angels' President Rich Brown a "cancer," he was fired from his final managing position.[17]

Rodgers went to work for his friend Jim Fregosi as a West Coast scout for the Philadelphia Phillies.[18] In 1997 he was hired as the manager and director of baseball operations for the Mission Viejo Vigilantes, a team that represented Orange County in the independent Western Baseball League. But Rodgers's 1997 season ended suddenly in June when his family was rocked by another highway tragedy. His mother Winifred was killed and his father seriously injured in a car accident in Ohio.[19] Rex Rodgers died from injury-related illness six months later.[20] After returning to Mission Viejo in 1998, Rodgers was able to retire that year when he was awarded an insurance settlement of approximately $1 million from the 1992 bus accident.[21] After many years in Yorba Linda, Buck and Judy Rodgers moved to the seaside village of Corona Del Mar, where they reside today, 20 miles from Angel Stadium. He remains active in the community, conducting golf tournaments and other charitable events with Mike Witt and other Angels alumni. In the half century he has spent here, Buck Rodgers has represented Southern California well. Those who have followed his career closely would agree with his family in recognizing him as "a man, a gentleman, and a baseball manager—in that order."[22] ∎

Sources

Los Angeles Angels 1962 Year Book. Los Angeles: The Los Angeles Angels, 1962.

Los Angeles Angels 1963 Year Book. Los Angeles: The Los Angeles Angels, 1963.

"Mother of Vigilantes' Rodgers Dies in Crash" in *Los Angeles Times*: 8 pars. [Journal Online]. Available from http://articles.latimes.com/1997-06-08/sports/sp-1491_1_ohio-state-highway-patrol. Accessed 24 May 2010.

"Rex Rodgers" in Social Security Death Index: retrieved 7 June 2009.

Halofan, Rev. "Top 100 Angels: Bob Rodgers #46" on *Halos Heaven*: 7 pars. [Journal Online]. Available from www.halosheaven.com/2009/1/11/716939/top-100-angels-bob-rodgers. Accessed 24 May 2010.

Dyer, Braven. "Rig Raids Bullpen for Seraph Starters" in *The Sporting News*: 1 June 1963.

Gallagher, Danny. *Angels' Halo Haunted: Baseball Tragedies Revisited.* Toronto: Scoop Press, 1998.

Goodale, George, and Irv Kaze. *Los Angeles Angels 1965 Yearbook.* Los Angeles: Petersen Publishing Company, 1965.

Newhan, Ross. "'Dean Dumbest Pitcher I've Caught' Says Rodgers" in *The Sporting News*: 8 April 1967.

Newhan, Ross. "Rodgers Wrecks 'For Sale' Tag – He's Avenging Angels with a Bat" in *The Sporting News*: 28 May 1966.

Okrent, Daniel. *Nine Innings: The Anatomy of a Baseball Game.* New York: Ticknor & Fields, 1985.

Notes

1. Brian Schecter, ed., *Les Expos, Nos Amours*, English ed., (Montreal: TV Labatt, 1989).
2. *Los Angeles Angels 1962 Year Book*, (Los Angeles: The Los Angeles Angels, 1962), 19.
3. Daniel Okrent, *Nine Innings: The Anatomy of a Baseball Game*, (New York: Ticknor & Fields, 1985), 6.
4. *Angels 1962 Year Book*, 19.
5. *Los Angeles Angels 1963 Year Book*, (Los Angeles: The Los Angeles Angels, 1963), 23.
6. Okrent, 115.
7. Okrent, 6.
8. Okrent, 5.
9. *Angels 1963 Year Book*, 3.
10. *Angels 1963 Year Book*, 23.
11. Ross Newhan, "Rodgers Wrecks 'For Sale' Tag—He's Avenging Angel with a Bat," in *The Sporting News* (28 May 1966), 17.
12. Braven Dyer, "Rig Raids Bullpen for Seraph Starters" in *The Sporting News* (1 June 1963), 23.
13. Ross Newhan, "'Dean Dumbest Pitcher I've Caught' Says Rodgers" in *The Sporting News*: (8 April 1967): 12.
14. Newhan (1967): 12
15. Danny Gallagher, *Angels' Halo Haunted: Baseball Tragedies Revisited*, (Toronto: Scoop Press, 1998), 26.
16. Gallagher, 16.
17. Rev Halofan, "Top 100 Angels: Bob Rodgers #46" on *Halos Heaven*: par 5; [journal online]; available from www.halosheaven.com/2009/1/11/716939/top-100-angels-bob-rodgers; Accessed 24 May 2010.
18. Gallagher, 25.
19. "Mother of Vigilantes' Rodgers Dies in Crash" in *Los Angeles Times*: par 3; [journal online]; available from http://articles.latimes.com/1997-06-08/sports/sp-1491_1_ohio-state-highway-patrol; accessed 24 May 2010.
20. "Rex Rodgers" in Social Security Death Index: retrieved 7 June 2009.
21. Gallagher, 24.
22. Schecter, "Les Expos, Nos Amours"

Buster Keaton, Baseball Player

Rob Edelman

Across the decades, Hollywood stars from Bob Hope and Bing Crosby to Bill Murray and Billy Crystal have been baseball fans. But few were physically adept at playing the game at a high-quality level. One such aficionado-athlete was a comedy legend of the silent cinema, Buster Keaton.

Keaton, who was born Joseph Francis Keaton Jr. in Piqua, Kansas in 1895, spent his youth touring with his family in vaudeville, appearing in a comic-acrobatic act in which his father tossed him around the stage. The physicality required for the act blended right in with young Buster's offstage athleticism.

"As far back as I can remember," he wrote in his autobiography, "baseball has been my favorite sport. I started playing the game as soon as I was old enough to handle a glove. A sand lot [sic] where baseball was being played was the first thing I looked for whenever The Three Keatons played a new town."[1] Upon completion of the vaudeville season, Keaton spent tranquil summers at a house his father purchased on Michigan's Lake Muskegon, and it was here where he really honed his baseball skills.[2] In fact, present-day Muskegon visitors may play on the same field where, a century earlier, Keaton swung a bat and shagged flies.

By the mid-1920s, Keaton had emerged as one of the screen's top comic actors, a status that allowed him to oversee the creation of his films. During pre-production, he would ask potential cast members two questions: "Can you act?" and "Can you play baseball?"

"The Keaton Production Company was in fact an ever-ready baseball team, prepared to start a game on a moment's notice," reported Tom Dardis, a Keaton biographer. "That moment would often come whenever a production problem arose that seemed to defy immediate solution. Buster would officially declare that a game was in order. If someone had an inspiration halfway through it, the shooting would resume."[3]

While filming at MGM in the late 1920s,

Keaton often concluded his lunch break with an impromptu ballgame on a field constructed on the lot. "Half the crew went with him," recalled Willard Sheldon, an assistant director, "and there were usually problems afterward getting everybody back on the set." Reportedly, Louis B. Mayer, top man at the studio, considered adding a "no-baseball clause" to Keaton's next contract.[4]

"Each September," Keaton wrote in his autobiography, "I did my best to finish my fall picture in time to go to New York for the World Series."[5]

Whenever he could, Keaton took his baseball act on the road. While shooting *The General* (1927), a Civil War-era comedy, in Cottage Grove, Oregon, Buster paid for the leveling of the turf and the building of a new backstop behind home plate in the town ballyard. To raise funds for the purchase of playground equipment, he played third base for the local Lions club in a game against the Kiwanis.[6]

Given Keaton's love of the game, it is not surprising that he occasionally incorporated baseball into his films—most famously in *College* (1927) and *The Cameraman* (1928). In *College*, Keaton offers a comic takeoff on the game's basics; *The Cameraman* features

In "College," Buster Keaton goes out for the baseball team, despite a lack of experience and a history of despising sports, to win the heart of a co-ed.

Buster Keaton demonstrates his baseball skills in this publicity shot.

an affecting pantomime of every baseball fan's dream of standing on the mound or in the batter's box of a major league stadium.

Keaton stars in *College* as Ronald, the top scholar in his high school class. At his graduation, he delivers a valedictory speech on the "Curse of Athletics" (which is an inside joke, given Keaton's real-life baseball obsession). "The student who wastes his time on athletics rather than study shows only ignorance," Ronald proclaims. Of course, he is not to be taken seriously, as he concludes his sermon by noting, "What have Ty Ruth and Babe Dempsey done for science?"

Upon arriving at Clayton College, Ronald realizes he will have to alter his thinking to win the sports-loving girl he adores. He appears at his school's ball field and is told to play third base, which he mans garbed in catching attire. The game begins, and a batter hits a grounder that rolls between Ronald's legs. He avoids a line drive hit his way as if dodging a bullet. A runner tries to steal third base; Ronald misses the ball thrown by the catcher, and is knocked over by the sliding runner. Another grounder is hit to Ronald, which he picks up and holds helplessly. And so the sequence unfolds.

Eventually, Ronald comes to the plate. He tries to limber up by swinging three bats at once, but only succeeds in conking himself in the noggin. As this part of the sequence plays itself out, Ronald eventually is hit in the behind by a pitch. He leaps into the catcher's arms, toppling the

backstop over. After taking first base, he attempts to steal second but promptly trips. The next batter pops up, but Ronald dashes around the bases, past the runners in front of him. He somersaults into home plate, only to be informed by the umpire that he "forced two men out and you're out, too." So ends Ronald's baseball career. Even though the character is supposed to be athletically inept, what makes the comedy work is Keaton's very real physical dexterity—most noticeably as he rolls into home plate.

In *The Cameraman*, Keaton plays Buster, a klutz who is a would-be newsreel cameraman. At one point, he trudges out to Yankee Stadium to photograph Babe Ruth and company. But on that day they are playing in St. Louis. What to do? Buster sets his camera down by the pitcher's mound and pantomimes a hurler about to go into a windup, acknowledging the sign from his catcher, attempting to pick off a runner, shifting his infielders, and handling a double-play ball. He also pantomimes a batter who is almost hit by a pitch, and who then smacks an inside-the-park dinger. He slides headfirst into home plate and waves his hat at the fans, who exist only in his mind.

The closest Keaton came to making a "pure" baseball movie was *One Run Elmer* (1935), a two-reel comedy released when Keaton was past his prime as an A-list Hollywood commodity. While *One Run Elmer* is a talking picture, most of its gags are visual. Buster plays a hapless gas station owner who practices ballplaying with a rival. Elmer's pitches are promptly hit through the windows and walls of his rickety

Keaton takes a baseball break with his wife, Natalie Talmadge, handling the bat.

station. When it is his turn to bat, he misses the first pitch, which further destroys his building; he connects on the next toss, which smashes the window of a car whose owner will umpire the following day's game. Similar slapstick bits follow once that contest starts.

During his time in Southern California, Keaton was at the center of the local baseball scene. His earliest films were one- and two-reel comedies featuring rotund Roscoe "Fatty" Arbuckle. In 1919 Arbuckle purchased a controlling interest in the Vernon Tigers, the Pacific Coast League team that later became the Hollywood Stars. On that first opening day, Arbuckle, Keaton, and other screen comics staged a mock mini-game using a plaster ball and bat. Arbuckle pitched. Al St. John was the batter. Keaton was the catcher. Rube Miller umpired—and a fun time was had by all.[7]

Keaton and Joe E. Brown—another ballplaying actor who starred in three Warner Bros. baseball comedies, *Fireman, Save My Child* (1932), *Elmer the Great* (1933), and *Alibi Ike* (1935)—regularly formed their own teams and sought out competition. Both also employed their love of the sport in fundraising ventures. In February 1932 both were involved in a charity benefit for the upcoming Los Angeles Olympics. Over 8,500 fans packed Wrigley Field to watch the Joe E. Browns best the Buster Keatons by a 10–3 score. Their rosters were lined with major leaguers: Rogers Hornsby, Gabby Hartnett, Paul Waner, Lloyd Waner, Sam Crawford, Billy Jurges, Stan Hack, Tris Speaker, Dave Bancroft, Carl Hubbell, Charlie Root, Pat Malone,

Johnny Moore, and Pie Traynor, among others.[8] Keaton also played in the industry's annual Comedians-Leading Men contests.

Keaton often employed big leaguers in his films. Sam Crawford plays a baseball coach in *College*. Mike Donlin appears as a Union general in *The General*. Jim Thorpe has a bit as a ballplayer in *One Run Elmer*. Byron Houck photographed a number of Keaton features, while Ernie Orsatti worked for Keaton as a prop man.

While there is no doubt that Keaton was adept at ballplaying, a question arises: Was he good enough to play pro ball? Might he even have made the majors? While there is no definitive answer here, one point is indisputable. "Throughout his life," observed Marion Meade, another Keaton biographer, "baseball would be his religion."[9] ∎

Notes

1. Buster Keaton with Charles Samuels. *My Wonderful World of Slapstick*. New York: Doubleday, 1960. 154.
2. Tom Dardis. *Keaton: The Man Who Wouldn't Lie Down*. New York: Charles Scribner's Sons, 1979. 8.
3. Dardis, 79.
4. Marion Meade. *Buster Keaton: Cut to the Chase*. New York: HarperCollins, 2004. 205.
5. Keaton, 154.
6. Edward McPherson. *Buster Keaton: Tempest in a Flat Hat*. London: Faber and Faber, 2004. 183.
7. Keaton, 154.
8. Rob Edelman. "Joe E. Brown: A Clown Prince of Baseball." *The National Pastime: A Review of Baseball History*. Cleveland: The Society for American Baseball Research, 2007. 127–131.
9. Meade, 205.

Relocation, Descent, and Rejuvenation

Patterns are observed during each baseball season—
In weather, on the field, and in individuals' play;
But few transitions compare in scope, import or reason
With the Dodgers' unique move to LA.

When O'Malley took his team west in '58,
A bond with Brooklyn was lost;
But in his mind the fruits of the Golden State
Justified the sentimental cost.

The owner's decision affected so many people
And changed the image of the franchise so much;
Chavez Ravine, once built, would seem almost regal
As young players instilled a fresh touch.

At first, games were played in the huge Coliseum
Which to purists was simply obscene;
Its dimensions affected many a game's outcome
For in short left stood a 40-foot screen.

Wally Moon would take advantage of the Coliseum's design
'Til Dodger Stadium's construction was through;
Not known as a slugger, Moon did refine
The skill of popping "cheap" homers on cue.

Clearing the other fences took a great poke,
Power hitters returned to the dugout mad;
Duke Snider was one who, despite a powerful stroke,
Missed dearly his old launching pad.

The first Dodgers team in the "City of Angels" was weak,
Falling four spots from the previous year;
After a third-place finish in '57, seventh place seemed quite bleak,
Enthused fans found little to cheer.

What factors played into the club's decline?
Surely more than just the vast venue…
Perhaps in moving from snug Ebbets to a football shrine,
"Dem Bums" stumbled upon an altered lifestyle, too.

For Hollywood is not Brooklyn, the first lives for "The Show,"
The two are direct opposites in fact;
With the culture out west so unlike the Borough,
Some players were slow to adapt.

Or was age the true culprit? Old Father Time!
Had the heroes of Brooklyn grown old?
Clearly several of them were passing their prime
And were soon to be traded or sold.

Even before a dramatic changing of the guard
Came Roy Campanella's tragic wreck;
The catcher, who for a glorious decade had starred,
Was paralyzed beneath his very strong neck.

Following that crippling emotional blow,
The magic of earlier days seemed to cease;
Declines plagued Erskine, Hodges, the battling Furillo,
"The Duke" and long-time captain, Pee Wee Reese.

Former ace Newcombe, no exception to the rule,
Was sent to the Reds with a sore arm;
Without "Newk" and "Oisk", Walt Alston had a new mound pool
Of Koufax, Drysdale, and Stan Williams (from the farm).

Three years before, Johnny Podres had seemed like a babe
In producing World Series elation;
Now, as a relative graybeard yet to fade,
He was the veteran in a youthful rotation.

Jim Gilliam, another fixture in Ebbets Field,
Was displaced from second base;
Bumped from the keystone spot by rookie Charlie Neal,
He landed in a different place.

He moved to left field and then the hot corner,
Becoming a reminder of "franchise past";
That was far better than being a benchwarmer
Or no longer part of the cast.

The personnel wheel continued to spin
As budding players mixed with the old;
But the team would bounce back and once again win—
In '59, O'Malley *and* Alston struck gold!

Zimmer soon followed his pals on their way out,
John Roseboro assumed Campanella's former role;
Frank Howard created a new definition of "clout,"
Tommy and Willie Davis joined the fly-chasing patrol.

With the quickness of one of Maury Wills' many steals,
The fresh generation ascended;
"Double D" and Sandy produced hitting ordeals,
Ensuring that past glories were extended.

While Campy's plight illustrated the uncertain nature of life,
"His team" confirmed an inspiring fact:
When advancing age or fate strike like a knife,
Reactions *do* have an impact.

Deep feelings displayed, on a May night in '59,
Expressed much more than the crowd realized;
Candles in the Coliseum were lit, Vin Scully urged prayers most divine,
Affirming that bodies—not hope—are paralyzed.

The light from those candles, so resplendent and bright,
Reflected the fate of the catcher's ball club as well,
For the dawn of a new era, inspired by O'Malley's long flight,
Would provide Scully wondrous tales to tell!

—Francis Kinlaw

"There's No Crying in Baseball"

Balls, Bats, and Women in Baseball Movies

Rob Edelman

Baseball is not just a game for boys. This was never more apparent than when *A League of Their Own* came to movie theaters in 1992.

Granted, the primary purpose of *A League of Their Own* is to entertain audiences and rake in profits for its makers. But in offering a fictionalized history of the first season of the All-American Girls' Professional Baseball League, which Chicago Cubs owner Philip K. Wrigley initiated after scores of major leaguers exchanged their flannels for khakis during World War II, the film casts a welcome spotlight on the AAGPBL's then-long forgotten participants.

The two primary characters in *A League of Their Own* may be fictional ballplaying sisters, but they are very real products of their era. Dottie Hinson (Geena Davis) yearns for her husband's return from the war and has no sense of the importance of the AAGPBL. Conversely, playing in the league allows Kit Keller (Lori Petty) a freedom for which she yearns but otherwise could not enjoy, given her gender and the prevailing culture. The film's impact is summed up by film critic Roger Ebert, who observed, "Until seeing [it], I had no idea that an organization named the All-American Girls' Professional Baseball League ever flourished in this country, even though I was 12 when it closed up shop [in 1954]....[Director Penny] Marshall shows her women characters in a tug-of-war between new images and old values, and so her movie is about transition—about how it felt as a woman suddenly to have new roles and freedom."[1]

Almost two decades after its release, *A League of Their Own* remains memorable as much for rescuing the AAGPBL from oblivion as for its now-iconic line, spoken by Rockford Peaches skipper Jimmy Dugan (Tom Hanks), an alcoholic ex-major leaguer who is an amalgam of Jimmy Foxx and Hack Wilson. After berating player Evelyn Gardner (Bitty Schram)—as any manager might—Dugan is aghast when Evelyn begins to cry. "Are you crying?" he asks, rhetorically. And he continues: "Are you crying? *Are you crying?* There's no crying! *There's no crying in baseball!*"

A League of Their Own is not the only film that spotlights females swinging bats and fielding grounders. But it easily is the best-known. Coming in a close second is the original (and best) version of *The Bad News Bears* (1976), in which Amanda Whurlitzer (Tatum O'Neal), a 12-year-old with a whale of a pitching arm, rescues an inept Little League nine. While stressing that the purpose of Little League is to have fun, the scenario emphasizes that a girl can play ball as well as a boy. Almost three decades later, a dumbed-down remake was released. Here, a girl who is the Pedro Martinez of Little League uplifts the Bears, but all the adult female characters are *Playboy* Playmate-like bimbos or caricatures of humorless, type-A personality 21st-century businesswomen. In the 2005 *Bad News Bears*, there is even product placement for Hooters.

If *A League of Their Own* shows how women once played pro ball in a league of their own, the point of *Blue Skies Again* (1983), a little-seen baseball fairy tale, is that a woman just might be able to compete *alongside* men. The one desire of Paula Fradkin

In *Girls Can Play* (1937), a young Rita Hayworth serves as catcher for a women's softball team run by a crook who eventually poisons her with bad liquor.

(Robyn Barto), the film's heroine, is "to play second base for the [major league Denver] Devils." While by no means a great film, *Blue Skies Again* insightfully examines the struggles of women who attempt to upend the male establishment. At Paula's first tryout, a white ballplayer tells a black counterpart, "I can't see [team owner Sandy] Mendenhall being the one to integrate baseball." When the black man glares at him, the white man begins to sputter. "You know what I mean…" he says, and "integrate" soon is replaced by a word not found in any dictionary, "interfeminate."

An additional feature spotlighting women ballplayers is *Girls Can Play* (1937), which despite its proactive title is no ode to sexual equality. It is the tale of an ex-racketeer who organizes a girls' softball team as a front for selling watered-down liquor. Eventually, he fatally poisons his girlfriend, the team's catcher, because she "knows too much." The "girls" of the title are cast primarily for their attractiveness, and are passive sex objects and victims. The film is of note only for the presence of young Rita Hayworth, playing the murder victim, who then was serving an apprenticeship as a Columbia Pictures B-film player.

Various short subjects highlight women baseballers. A typical title is *Gracie at the Bat* (1937), a comedy whose working title was *Slide, Nellie, Slide*. "Fireball Gracie," the featured character, pitches for the Fillies, a girls' softball team. Gracie has the oddest wind-up, but she literally throws smoke at an opposing batter. Unlike The Mighty Casey, she belts a game-winning homer. But her teammates are a temperamental lot who peruse romance magazines and powder their noses in the dugout.

Similarly, in *Fancy Curves* (1932), an entry in the "Play Ball with Babe Ruth" series, the Bambino agrees to coach a sorority squad that has challenged a fraternity to a ballgame. "I've often wondered why girls haven't played more baseball," the Babe observes, adding, "It's no more difficult than any other sport they take part in." Nonetheless, his charges are tired stereotypes. After singling, one of the women produces a pocket mirror and powders her face while on first base. The girls inflict damage on the boys only when the Babe dons a wig, swishes up to home plate, and pinch hits a homer. This denouement also is employed in the animated *Casey Bats Again* (1953), in which a father or-

ganizes his daughters into a girls' team and dresses in drag to enter the game and drive in the winning run.

Some high-profile on-screen baseball aficionados have been women. Easily the most celebrated is Annie Savoy (Susan Sarandon) in *Bull Durham* (1988), who memorably expresses her belief in the "church of baseball." But Annie's idea of baseball worship is not only spiritual. She is highly sexed, and readily sleeps with her ballplayers of choice. An altogether different female fan is *Aunt Mary* (1979), the fact-based account of a Baltimore spinster and die-hard baseball devotee (Jean Stapleton) who coaches a sandlot ball club. The story of Mary Dobkin shows how the unlikeliest of women can do a "man's job" and function in her own modest way as an activist. Conversely, Gloria Thorpe (Rae Allen), a nosy female sportswriter, is a villain in *Damn Yankees* (1958). Gloria is determined to unravel the mystery of Joe Hardy, savior of the Washington Senators, and her snoopiness implies that women have no business in the press box.

Across the decades, bats, balls, and women have mixed in non-baseball films. An instant-classic baseball moniker is found in *Whip It* (2009), the saga of female roller derby players who are known to their fans by nicknames. The lead character (Ellen Page) chooses one that a baseball-lover will embrace: Babe Ruthless!

Then there is Katie O'Hara (Ginger Rogers), the heroine of *Once Upon a Honeymoon* (1942), an American who finds herself in Paris just before France falls to the Nazis. Upon being asked where she was born, Katie proudly replies, "Parkside Avenue, Brooklyn."

In an iconic moment from *A League of Their Own* (1992), Manager Jimmy Dugan (Tom Hanks) asks Evelyn Gardner (Bitty Schram), "Are you crying? *Are you crying?* There's no crying! *There's no crying in baseball!*"

NATIONAL BASEBALL HALL OF FAME LIBRARY, COOPERSTOWN, N.Y.

Marjorie Winfield (Doris Day) wants to play with the boys (for a while at least) in 1951's *On Moonlight Bay*.

"Near Ebbets Field?" is the response.

"Foul balls used to light in my backyard," Katie quips, before sighing, "Dem lovely bums."

In *Woman of the Year* (1942), all it takes is an afternoon at Yankee Stadium to transform highfaluting, baseball-ignorant political columnist Tess Harding (Katharine Hepburn) into an ardent rooter.

One of the most fascinating portrayals of a distinctly pre-feminist woman ballplayer is found in *On Moonlight Bay* (1951). Doris Day plays Marjorie Winfield, a tomboy jock. In a game in which her teammates and opponents are boys, she promptly bashes a triple. Then she steals home. But Marjorie's athleticism is treated as a passing phase of her young life. One look at the handsome boy-next-door (Gordon MacRae) and Marjorie readily exchanges her mud-stained flannels for a frilly dress. Her mother shows her how to enhance her bosom, telling her, "Sometimes nature needs a little help." As their first date concludes, the lad calls her "the most beautiful and the most *feminine* girl I've ever met." As they kiss goodnight, Marjorie's white-gloved left hand pushes aside forever the cap and ball that are resting on the table beside her.

Thankfully, not all pre-feminist women were so easily swayed away from sports. Leave it to Lucy—as in pre-*I Love Lucy* Lucille Ball—to play a 1940s woman who oozes spunk and swings a mean bat. In *The Dark Corner* (1946), Lucy is Kathleen Stewart, the newly-hired secretary of a troubled private detective (Mark Stevens). One evening, the pair visits a penny arcade. After swatting at pitches in a batting cage, Kathleen explains her prowess by noting, "My father was a major league umpire." When her boss makes a pass at her, she quips, "I haven't worked for you very long, Mr. Galt, but I know when you're pitching a curve at me—and I always carry a catcher's mitt." He defends himself by noting, "No offense. A guy's gotta try to score, doesn't he?" She responds, "Not in my league."

In Hollywood movies across the decades, baseball often has symbolized wholesome, mom's-apple-pie Americana. This representation radiates from *Cass Timberlane* (1947), based on a Sinclair Lewis novel, which charts the evolving relationship between the title character, a widowed, middle-aged, small-town Minnesota judge (Spencer Tracy) and Virginia Marshland (Lana Turner), a much younger woman from the proverbial other side of the tracks. Clearly, the judge is respectable. But how do we know that the same can be said for Virginia? Because, early on, we see her immersed in a spirited softball game.

Despite the prevailing post-World War II culture, in which men were expected to rule the family and women to embrace femininity while staying home and baking cookies, an enlightened male still could be supportive of a female athlete. Virginia and Cass eventually marry. As Cass nervously awaits the birth of their child, he and a nurse peer through a hospital window at eight newborns. "You need one more for a baseball team," Cass declares. "Ah, save that spot in the outfield for young Timberlane, will ya!"

The nurse poses a question: "Supposing the baby's a little girl?"

"Oh, that's so much the better," Cass responds. "Mrs. Timberlane's a very fine ballplayer herself." ∎

Notes

1. Ebert, Roger. "A League of Their Own." *Chicago Sun-Times,* 1 July 1992.

Bibliography

Edelman, Rob. "Baseball at the Movies." *culturefront,* vol. 8, no 3 & 4 (Fall, 1999): 49–52.

———. "Baseball's Cinematic Presence Mirrors America's National Spirit." *Memories & Dreams,* vol. 25, no. 2 (Spring, 2003): 5–8.

Wood, Stephen C. and J. David Pincus. *Reel Baseball.* Jefferson, NC and London: McFarland & Company, 2002.

Home Run Derby

A Tale of Baseball and Hollywood

Don Zminda

It was just the top of the first, and Willie Mays hit four home runs before Mickey Mantle could even step to the plate. Decades before it invaded the All-Star game, *Home Run Derby* sprouted in the fertile soil of Hollywood.

Home Run Derby was filmed at L.A.'s Wrigley Field, former home of the Pacific Coast League Los Angeles Angels and soon to become the first-year home of the expansion L.A. Angels of the American League. But to fans unfamiliar with PCL baseball, the park was a mystery. The show's host, Mark Scott, never mentioned the name of the park or its Southern California location. And that seems curious, because *Home Run Derby* was an L.A.—and Hollywood—production through and through.

Mark Scott was more than just the host of *Home Run Derby*; he was one of the creators of the show. Born in Chicago in 1915, Scott excelled in track, baseball, and basketball, but a knee injury suffered playing football at the University of Illinois ended his athletic career. He began working in broadcasting and landed his first baseball play-by-play gig in Norfolk, Virginia, where he did re-creations of major league games by day and live minor league games at night. In Virginia, Scott met his wife, Dorothy, and on a late honeymoon in Havana, Cuba in 1951, he ran into J.G. Taylor Spink, publisher of *The Sporting News*. Scott was looking for a higher-level announcing job, and Spink suggested he contact Bob Cobb, owner of the Hollywood Stars of the Pacific Coast League (and also owner of Hollywood's famous Brown Derby Restaurants). Scott landed a job as the Stars' play-by-play announcer beginning in 1952.[1]

Scott quickly became a well-known figure in the Hollywood/Los Angeles scene. He did Stars games and was sports director at radio station KFWB, announcing boxing matches, horse and dog races, and hosting a daily 15-minute radio show, "Mark Scott's Pressbox." When the Dodgers brought major league baseball to Los Angeles in 1958, Scott became host of the "Meet the Dodgers" television show.[2]

This being Hollywood, Scott became friends with many people in the entertainment business, and before long he was supplementing his broadcasting career with occasional acting gigs, usually appearing as a broadcaster or narrator. Among his film credits were *The Kid From Left Field*, *Killers from Space*, *The Harder They Fall*, and a cameo role in *Somebody Up There Likes Me*, a sports bio-pic with Paul Newman as boxer Rocky Graziano.[3] The cast of *Somebody Up There Likes Me* also included a young ballplayer-turned-actor named Michael Dante, who had played for several years in the minor leagues under his given name of Ralph Vitti. Scott and Dante became good friends.[4]

Another of Scott's entertainment-industry colleagues was Hollywood veteran Lou Breslow. A writer, producer, and director with a long history in both movies and television, Breslow had worked on films featuring the Marx Brothers, Laurel and Hardy, Abbott and Costello, and the Three Stooges, among others. While he had mostly worked in comedy, Breslow had also dabbled in sports films. In the 1930s he wrote several short films that featured Babe Ruth.[5]

By the late 1950s, Breslow was working mainly in television, and during that time, he came up with the idea for *Home Run Derby*.[6] The premise of the show was simple. Each week, two major-league sluggers would face off in a home run hitting contest that would last nine "innings." A home run counted as a run, but any batted ball that failed to reach the seats, as well as any taken pitch that was called a strike by the umpire, was considered an out. With that format, each contest could easily be completed in a half hour.

Breslow shared his idea with Scott and a few TV production people, and the group formed a company, Homer Productions. Breslow would be the show's producer, with Scott serving as host as well as helping do much of the work needed to bring their brainchild to the screen.[7]

While *Home Run Derby* seemed like a promising idea, it wasn't the kind of show likely to appear on one of the three major television networks. So Breslow, Scott, and their colleagues turned to Ziv

Mark Scott, producer and emcee of *Home Run Derby*, and earlier the voice of the Hollywood Stars, poses with the Mark Scott Gold Cup Award which his station, KFWB, awarded annually to the outstanding high school football player in the Los Angeles area.

Television Productions, a company which specialized in distributing weekly first-run shows to local stations across the country. At its peak in the mid-1950s, Ziv was producing more than 250 half-hour television episodes annually.[8]

Ziv shows were known for tight production schedules and modest budgets,[9] and Breslow, Scott, and company did their best to make *Home Run Derby* an economical operation. Prize money for the ballplayers consisted of $2,000 for the winner of each show and $1,000 for the loser, with a $500 bonus for any player who hit three straight home runs without making an out. That was pretty good money in those days as the World Series winner's share in 1960 came to $8,417.94.[10] But, it wasn't overly generous by TV standards, and Homer Productions found other ways to keep their costs down. Apart from a small production and camera crew, the show featured only Scott, a plate umpire and two foul-line umps, two pitchers, a catcher, and a few people to shag balls in the outfield. Costs for use of Wrigley Field were held down by filming two episodes a day. Contestants were usually flown into Los Angeles the day prior to an episode,

then flown back home the night of the shooting unless the player was a returning champion.[11]

Scott used his personal contacts to line up the pitchers, catchers, and umpires who worked on the show. One of the pitchers was Tom Saffell, a former major league outfielder who had played for the Hollywood Stars during Scott's term as the club's broadcaster. Behind the plate was Eddie Malone, who had caught for Hollywood 1952–54.[12] Art Passarella, the plate umpire, was a former American League arbiter (1941–42, 1945–53), who, like Scott, dabbled in acting. Passarella had appeared in the movie version of the Broadway hit *Damn Yankees* and the Ziv-produced television show *Sea Hunt*.[13] He would go on to numerous acting roles in the years following his umpiring stint on *Home Run Derby*—most notably as Sergeant Sekulavich in the Karl Malden/Michael Douglas police show, *The Streets of San Francisco*.[14]

Scott proved remarkably successful at lining up the contestants. Of the 20 players who had hit 25 or more home runs during the 1959 major league season, all but four (Joe Adcock, Orlando Cepeda, Woodie Held, and Charlie Maxwell) would appear on *Home Run Derby*. Fifteen of the 16 major league teams were represented. The missing club, the American League champion Chicago White Sox, had no players with more than 22 home runs in 1959. Nine of the 19 competitors would be elected to the Baseball Hall of Fame.[15]

Home Run Derby began filming in December. Working on its two-episodes-a-day schedule, the 26 contests were completed in a three-week period.[16] Scott would open each episode by describing the rules of the game and introducing the players. "Gentlemen, today you're going for the big money," he would say. While one competitor took his licks, the other would sit behind the plate engaged in conversation with Scott, who also described the action. Controversy was religiously avoided. When one of the more flamboyant players of the era, Dick Stuart, appeared on the show, Scott made a point of saying, "Dick, you know and I know differently, but a reputation got out that you were somewhat of a pop-off guy. It's enlightening for people to see you here and see that you're like any other ballplayer—you like your base hits, but you're not a braggart." Stuart responded by admitting that "a few years ago I did say a few offbeat things, but I learned the hard way."[17]

But if the commentary could be a little bland, the contests themselves were usually entertaining. In the series-opening clash, Mays led 8–2 after the top of the sixth inning, but Mantle—batting right-handed

Table 1. Home Run Derby Weekly Results

Game 1
Willie Mays   402 110 000 – 8
Mickey Mantle   110 001 321 – 9

Game 2
Ernie Banks   100 000 101 – 3
Mickey Mantle   001 120 10X – 5

Game 3
Jackie Jensen   100 010 000 – 2
Mickey Mantle   220 320 00X – 9

Game 4
Harmon Killebrew   011 010 213 – 9
Mickey Mantle   022 102 001 – 8

Game 5
Rocky Colavito   000 004 001 0 – 5
Harmon Killebrew   100 101 101 1 – 6

Game 6
Ken Boyer   000 101 001 – 3
Harmon Killebrew   100 010 000 – 2

Game 7
Henry Aaron   200 011 230 – 9
Harmon Killebrew   201 120 000 – 6

Game 8
Jim Lemon   000 010 003 – 4
Henry Aaron   101 010 30X – 6

Game 9
Ed Mathews   100 001 001 – 3
Henry Aaron   001 010 011 – 4

Game 10
Al Kaline   000 100 000 – 1
Henry Aaron   000 103 10X – 5

Game 11
Duke Snider   000 001 000 – 1
Henry Aaron   001 101 00X – 3

Game 12
Bob Allison   000 011 000 – 2
Henry Aaron   000 101 10X – 3

Game 13
Wally Post   120 031 000 – 7
Henry Aaron   001 110 001 – 4

Game 14
Dick Stuart   002 005 020 2 – 11
Wally Post   200 005 020 0 – 9

Game 15
Gus Triandos   000 000 100 – 1
Dick Stuart   300 001 12X – 7

Game 16
Frank Robinson   100 100 121 – 6
Dick Stuart   010 100 001 – 3

Game 17
Bob Cerv   101 101 022 – 8
Frank Robinson   001 004 101 – 7

Game 18
Bob Allison   000 001 021 – 4
Bob Cerv   011 000 010 – 3

Game 19
Willie Mays   013 020 014 – 11
Bob Allison   010 000 011 – 3

Game 20
Harmon Killebrew   110 102 010 – 6
Willie Mays   110 010 301 – 7

Game 21
Jim Lemon   001 020 000 – 3
Willie Mays   102 012 00X – 6

Game 22
Gil Hodges   002 200 110 – 6
Willie Mays   000 011 010 – 3

Game 23
Ernie Banks   220 002 032 – 11
Gil Hodges   100 011 301 – 7

Game 24
Jackie Jensen   331 021 310 – 14
Ernie Banks   011 141 201 – 11

Game 25
Rocky Colavito   000 000 110 – 2
Jackie Jensen   000 102 00X – 3

Game 26
Mickey Mantle   012 240 112 – 13
Jackie Jensen   020 611 000 – 10

Table 2. Home Run Derby Player Stats

Player	W–L	HR	HR/Game	3-4-5*	Earnings
Hank Aaron	6-1	34	4.86	1-0-0	$13,500
Mickey Mantle	4-1	44	8.80	2-0-0	10,000
Dick Stuart	2-1	21	7.00	2-0-0	6,000
Willie Mays	3-2	35	7.00	0-0-0	8,000
Jackie Jensen	2-2	29	7.25	1-0-1	8,500
Harmon Killebrew	2-2	23	5.75	0-0-0	6,000
Wally Post	1-1	16	8.00	0-0-0	3,000
Frank Robinson	1-1	13	6.50	1-0-0	3,500
Gil Hodges	1-1	13	6.50	0-0-0	3,000
Bob Cerv	1-1	11	5.50	0-0-0	3,000
Ken Boyer	1-1	9	4.50	0-0-0	3,000
Ernie Banks	1-2	25	8.33	1-0-0	4,500
Bob Allison	1-2	9	3.00	0-0-0	4,000
Eddie Mathews	0-1	3	3.00	0-0-0	1,000
Al Kaline	0-1	1	1.00	0-0-0	1,000
Duke Snider	0-1	1	1.00	0-0-0	1,000
Gus Triandos	0-1	1	1.00	0-0-0	1,000
Rocky Colavito	0-2	7	3.50	1-0-0	2,500
Jim Lemon	0-2	7	3.50	0-0-0	2,000

* Number of times player hit 3, 4, or 5 consecutive HR.

despite the fact that he was facing a right-handed pitcher—fought back to win the game, 9–8, with a homer in the bottom of the ninth. Mantle would go on to defend his crown by defeating Ernie Banks and Jackie Jensen before losing episode four, 9–8, to Harmon Killebrew.[18]

Home Run Derby hit the airwaves in April 1960, coinciding with the start of the major league season.[19] While Scott had his share of critics,[20] his simple approach would, for many, become one of the show's charms. As David Gough wrote many years later, "When we watch the program today … we can still sense Scott's enthusiasm for the game and his desire to infect his listeners and viewers with a similar appreciation."[21] The show proved popular with fans, and there seemed little reason to doubt that Ziv would bring back *Home Run Derby* for a second season in 1961.

But it was not to be. Tragically, Mark Scott died of a heart attack in Burbank, California on July 13, 1960—about halfway through the syndicated run of the show's first season. He was only 45 years old.[22] Without its host and driving force, the show was not renewed for a second season, and *Home Run Derby* disappeared from the airwaves.

Remarkably, *Home Run Derby* would return to television nearly 30 years later—and become, if anything, more popular than ever. In 1988, ESPN acquired the rights to the show, and the contests featuring legendary sluggers of the past—along with the occasional Wally Posts and Jim Lemons—found a whole new audience. The show had another successful run several years later on the Classic Sports Network. The entire 26-episode run was made available on DVD by MGM Home Entertainment in 2007.[23]

One of the people who reconnected with *Home Run Derby* when it returned to the airwaves was Mark Scott's daughter, Mary Jane, who had been only eight years old when her father passed away in 1960. "One day in November of 1988, my mother called and told me that ESPN was broadcasting a show called *Home Run Derby* at 1:30 A.M.," Mary Jane related. So early the next morning, Mary Jane turned on ESPN, "and there's my dad, just like I remembered him. It was like an episode of *The Twilight Zone*. It was just mind-blowing." Mary Jane subsequently got in touch with Larry Stewart, who had written a *Los Angeles Times* article about the return of the show, and Stewart invited her to a meeting of the Southern California Sports Broadcasters Association, which was honoring *Home Run Derby*.[24]

Mary Jane began attending SCSBA meetings on a regular basis, and a few years later, she and her mother attended a meeting of the organization whose theme was "Athletes to Actors." Many of the guests at the "Athletes to Actors" meeting had been friends and colleagues of Mark Scott. Dorothy Scott was especially pleased to reconnect with Chuck Connors, who had been one of her husband's closest friends during the 1950s.[25]

In the course of their conversation with Connors, Chuck introduced Mary Jane to Michael Dante – the actor and former minor league ballplayer who had befriended Mark Scott after working with him in *Somebody Up There Likes Me*. On this occasion, somebody down here liked Mary Jane—Michael Dante. The feeling was mutual. The two exchanged phone numbers, began dating, and a couple of years later, Mary Jane and her father's old friend were married. A true Hollywood ending.[26]

"It was my dad who introduced me to Michael, through Chuck Connors," Mary Jane Dante says. "My whole life changed through the return of *Home Run Derby*. It's a miracle … my dad is alive and well. He is my guardian angel."[27] ■

Notes

1. Interview with Mary Jane and Michael Dante, 1 April 2010.
2. Ibid.
3. IMDB.com, filmography of Mark Scott.
4. Dante interview.
5. IMBD.com, filmography of Lou Breslow.
6. Richard Hoffer, "Original Home Run Derby was a television show back in 1959," si.com, 30 June 2010.
7. Dante interview.
8. www.museum.tv, "Ziv Television Programs, Inc."
9. Ibid.
10. J.G. Taylor Spink, etc., *Baseball Guide and Record Book 1961* (Charles C. Spink & Son, 1961), p. 151.
11. David Gough, "Home Run Derby: Looking back at a television sports legend," *The National Pastime* #17, 1996, pp. 111–116.
12. Correspondence with Tom Saffell, March 2010.
13. IMDB.com, filmography of Art Passarella.
14. "Art Passarella, Ex-Umpire, Later Acted in Films and TV," obituary, *New York Times*, 16 October 1981.
15. *STATS Pass* (STATS LLC MLB database).
16. Gough, p.112.
17. "*Home Run Derby*, Volumes 1–3," MGM Video, 2007.
18. Ibid.
19. Joe King, "Sluggers Swing for Heavy Sugar in TV Home Run Derby, *The Sporting News*, 2 March 1960.
20. Don Page, "Sandy Is Dandy on Baseball Commentary" (includes review of *Home Run Derby*), *Los Angeles Times*, 11 June 1960.
21. Gough, p.116.
22. Mark Scott obituary, *The Sporting News*, 20 July 1960.
23. Gough, 116.
24. Dante interview.
25. Ibid.
26. Ibid.
27. Ibid.

Everybody's a Star
The Dodgers Go Hollywood

Jeff Katz

In a scene from the Marx Brothers' Animal Crackers, *Chico and Harpo attempt to switch a priceless painting with a copy. After the usual mayhem, the duo turns to exit, stage left. When they open the French doors, there's a caterwauling of thunder, with lightning and sheets of rain. The pair close the doors, head toward the opposite side of the room, and open the portals. Outside the birds are twittering; it's beautiful and sunny.*

"Ha, ha, California!" exclaims Chico joyfully.[1]

Prior to the 1958 season, the Dodgers took a similar journey west, leaving the grime and decay of Brooklyn for the balmier environs of Southern California. Happily ensconced under the sun, they were quickly embraced not only by fans starved for major league baseball but also by the entertainment world. The motion picture industry had been centered in Hollywood for decades, and the burgeoning television industry had recently switched coasts, leaving the advertising-centric world of New York City for the glamour and studio life of Los Angeles.

After the Dodgers' arrival, a marriage was made. Stars and starlets became a staple at Dodgers home games, and ballplayers were eagerly sought to appear in television episodes and movies. The late 1950s was an innocent time of simple athletic hero worship; a Dodger star on screen was sure to attract a bigger audience.

Jerry Lewis's *The Geisha Boy* (1958) marks the first credited appearance of the new Los Angeles Dodgers. Film's greatest idiot, Lewis had a soft spot for baseball dating to his youth, when his hero was the New York Giants' future Hall of Famer, first baseman Bill Terry. In this film, Jerry carries on as the quintessential fan, yelling and mugging as he watches the Dodgers visit a Japanese team. Lewis would turn to the Dodgers often, featuring coach Leo Durocher in *The Errand Boy* (1961) and casting speedy centerfielder Willie Davis in a major part in *Which Way to the Front?* (1970), with Davis, in army togs adorned with an incongruous peace symbol, playing a member of Lewis's private army.

In his 1959 acting debut in the television series *Colt .45*, Koufax brings a different kind of heat as a Civil War cavalryman. Koufax is shown here with actress Dorothy Provine.

Much to the chagrin of Brooklyn fans who had waited decades for their first World Series victory in 1955, the Los Angeles Bums won it all in their second season. After defeating the Chicago White Sox in the 1959 World Series, many on the team were offered TV roles. Duke Snider menacingly rode into town on *The Rifleman*. Wally Moon, after a season in which he turned the Dodgers' homer-friendly Coliseum into a launching pad for his "Moon shots," brought his dark looks and heavy eyebrows to perfect use as a Western hero in an episode of *Wagon Train*. Another fall star, outfielder Chuck Essegian, appeared in yet another oater, *Sugarfoot*. And, of course, there were Koufax and Drysdale.

MARQUEE STARS

As if divine talent weren't enough, Sandy Koufax had the looks of a matinee idol: dark, slender and Jewish, more Robert Taylor than Robert Redford. Hollywood came calling after Sandy gave a sneak preview of his future brilliance in the 1959 World Series. Koufax appeared in three television programs in 11 days. He first played a policeman in "Ten Cents a Death," on the trailblazing series *77 Sunset Strip* (January 29, 1960). Two days later, amid much press coverage, Sandy appeared in an episode entitled "Impasse" on *Colt .45*. (Koufax dies in the opening scene, before critics could get a handle on his acting chops. Pleased that he didn't "have to ride a horse, just die," the quick-witted Koufax remarked, "I've gone out quicker in some games."[2]) He then returned as a doorman in the detective series *Bourbon Street Beat*.

Hollywood couldn't get enough of California native Don Drysdale. Tall, handsome, and the ace of the pitching staff—at least until Koufax hit his stride—"Big D" showed up on the small screen in an episode entitled "The Hardcase," (January 31, 1960) on *The Lawman*. A Western was the natural beginning to the acting career of Drysdale, who had been described as "a handsome giant in the John Wayne tradition."[3] He followed up that year with another character role, that of Eddie Cano in an installment ("Millionaire Larry Maxwell") of *The Millionaire*.

As the decade progressed, the team became more Californian, their Brooklyn ancestry more remote. On the field, the Dodgers were the class of the National League, winning two more world championships (1963 and 1965) and garnering two second-place finishes before record numbers of devoted fans. They were truly hometown Los Angeles, and the appearance on the screen of their stars was losing its novelty. Only the most telegenic and famous Dodgers would continue to get the call from Tinseltown.

Coach Leo Durocher brought west his own show business resume, a failed marriage to movie star Laraine Day and friendships with screen stars Spencer Tracy and George Raft. "The Lip," famous in baseball since his playing days in the 1920s, was cast as himself in the aforementioned *The Errand Boy* and in memorable TV segments of *The Beverly Hillbillies*, *The Munsters*, and *Mister Ed* (this last rated by *TV Guide* as the 73rd best episode in television history). Besides Durocher, Koufax and Drysdale were the two most often solicited by Hollywood to boost a show's profile.

However, the most fascinating appearance on television during the first half of the 1960s is that of Dodgers owner Walter O'Malley in a parable of the Brooklyn Dodgers story for a 1965 episode of Chuck Connors's *Branded*. In "The Bar Sinister," with O'Malley cast as a crusty doctor, the town mayor is willing to rip a beloved boy (read Dodgers) from his rightful guardian, his Native American mother (read Brooklyn). Why? To acquire land and riches, an allusion to the controversial transfer of Chavez Ravine and its environs by the City of Los Angeles that enticed O'Malley westward—parallels that made Walter O'Malley the perfect choice for the role.

THE STUDIO VERSUS THE BALLPARK

O'Malley was not the only Dodger to arrive in film land thanks to Chuck Connors. Connors, an ex-Brooklyn first baseman, had become a television star with *The Rifleman*, *Branded*, and the short-lived *Cowboy in Africa*. Through his starring vehicles, several Dodgers—Roy Gleason, Ron Perranoski, Duke Snider, and Don Drysdale—got their TV breaks, but the former first sacker's biggest role came in the most important Dodger story of the mid-1960s, the Great Holdout. This significant convergence of baseball and show business took place after the Dodgers' 1965 world championship as both industries competed for the services of the two marquee stars, Koufax and Drysdale, who had notched a combined 49 wins that season. While stars like Willie Mays and Mickey Mantle had reached the lofty standard of $100,000 in salary, no pitcher had been able to attain that plateau. In late October, at their first meeting with Dodgers general manager Buzzie Bavasi, the two

Former Dodger Chuck Connors (*left*) and Don Drysdale share an off-screen moment during the shooting of The Rifleman. In this episode, "Big D" is hauled away by the local sheriff—one too many beanballs?

hurlers presented a seven-figure proposal they would split down the middle over the next three years. Bavasi laughed and offered Koufax $100,000 for 1966 and Drysdale $90,000. The pitchers had formed a players union of two; one would not sign without the other. They turned him down.

Advising the Dodgers duo was agent/attorney Bill Hayes of Executive Business Management in Beverly Hills. In February 1966, as spring training began, Hayes announced that Drysdale and Koufax would have speaking roles in *Warning Shot*, a new film starring David Janssen. With Koufax playing a detective sergeant and Drysdale a television commentator, production was to start on April 4, eight days before the defending champs were to play their home opener. Said Director Buzz Kulik, envisioning sports page headlines translating into boffo box office receipts, "They're hot properties."[4]

Said Bavasi, "Good luck in the movies, boys!"[5]

Dodgers teammates and fans grew more concerned as publicity stills for *Warning Shot* began circulating. Riding in to save the day was Chuck Connors, who knew two things: Bavasi had quietly arrived back in California from Florida, and Koufax and Drysdale were itching to get back on the mound. Towards the end of March, Connors called Bavasi and said, "These fellas are ready to sign."[6] He then called Drysdale and told him he should give the Dodgers GM a ring. A meeting was arranged at Nicola's, a restaurant near Dodger Stadium, and terms were hammered out, Drysdale acting with Koufax's blessing. The holdout was over: Koufax signed for one year at $125,000, Drysdale for one year at $110,000.

As the 1960s wore on, the wholesome appeal of a Dodger in uniform lost its luster. And by the post-*Ball Four* era of the 1970s, as ballplayers were transformed in the public eye into money-hungry, drug-using, sex-driven, self-absorbed divas, the appearance of a pampered superstar could turn off as many people as it could turn on. Once reporters had covered up the personality quirks and foibles of the average athlete; now their mission was to expose their every gaffe and misdeed. The day when viewers welcomed two-dimensional sports figures into their living rooms as the kind of men their sons could safely revere and their daughters could pine over without threat was over.

Today, as fans deal with loving the game of baseball while remaining ambivalent about its players, it's unlikely that TV shows and movies will ever return to the days when Gil Hodges looks on in wonder as Jerry Lewis takes a pitch to the mouth, Sandy Koufax pitches to a grocery store owner on a sandlot, or Don Drysdale chats with The Beaver on a long distance call. Perhaps this is why the Dodgers-Hollywood connection and the players' performances of the 1950s and early 1960s resonate with the sweetness of that time. A refreshing lack of cynicism and self-awareness make this a wonderful time to revisit. It was an era when we could still look forward to seeing our athletes as supermen without the character failings that we mortals suffer through. And isn't that what Hollywood dreams are made of? ■

Notes

1. Marx, Chico. *Animal Crackers.* Directed by Victor Heerman. Los Angeles: Paramount Pictures, 1930.
2. Finnegan, Joe. "Pitcher Koufax, Hit in Acting Debut, Relieved After first inning Collapse." National Baseball Hall of Fame Library.
3. "The Drysdales in Showbiz." *Los Angeles Herald Examiner*, 25 March 1966, D2. National Baseball Hall of Fame Library.
4. Mitchell, Jerry. *Sandy Koufax.* New York: Grosset & Dunlap, 1966, 189.
5. Gruver, Edward. *Koufax.* Dallas: Taylor Publishing Company, 2000, 200.
6. Ibid.

The (Movie) Hollywood Stars Game

By Mark Langill

Long before the Dodgers spied the bright lights and greener pastures of the West Coast, baseball and Hollywood brought together ballplayers and actors gladly willing to exchange hats.

The "Hollywood Stars" game was the brainchild of Danny Goodman, who had taken charge of concessions and promotions for the Pacific Coast League Hollywood Stars when they opened Gilmore Field in 1938. The Stars' majority owner was Bob Cobb, inventor of the Cobb Salad and owner of the Brown Derby restaurant chain. Several Hollywood Stars of the movie variety—Bing Crosby, Gary Cooper, Cecil B. DeMille, Gene Autry, Barbara Stanwyck, George Raft, Robert Taylor, William Powell, and both George Burns and Grace Allen—were minority owners of the team. Goodman suggested a promotion of having the movie people play in a game and the tradition began.

When the Dodgers moved to Los Angeles, Walter O'Malley brought most of his executive team with him. Goodman was one of the few local people hired. Goodman's malapropisms were as famous as those Joe Garagiola would later attribute to Yogi Berra.

When he proposed to O'Malley that the Hollywood Stars game promotion be continued, the owner asked, "Will you be able to get the stars?"

"Are you kidding?" Goodman replied. "I'll get you stars you've never heard of!"

Goodman's longtime association with the Friar's Club in Beverly Hills as entertainment committee chairman padded the Hollywood Stars rosters. While the Brooklyn Dodgers were winning their first championship in 1955, Goodman had been the first "layman" honored with a roast. The toastmaster was Ronald Reagan and the dais included Jack Benny, George Burns, Phil Silvers, Dean Martin, Leo Durocher, Charlie Dressen, Red Sanders, Tom Harmon, Fred Haney, Casey Stengel, and Ty Cobb.

The Hollywood Stars game was a publicity bonanza for both sides and the talent roster through the 1960s continued to attract top Hollywood talent. The Dodgers roster was sprinkled with superstars such as Sandy Koufax, Don Drysdale, Maury Wills, and Tommy Davis. And the Dodgers employed a coach who carried a higher profile than manager Walter Alston in the entertainment world—Leo Durocher, who was married to actress Laraine Day and made several cameos on baseball-related episodes of *The Munsters*, *The Beverly Hillbillies*, and *Mister Ed*.

The large amount of foul territory at Dodger Stadium in those days allowed automobiles, along with other vehicles, to become props in whatever skit was needed for a particular Hollywood star playing in the game.

Kent McCord and Martin Milner, the TV stars of *Adam-12*, pulled onto the field in a squad car and "took away" the home plate umpire after a disputed call. Dean Martin arrived in a limo for his at-bat. Before the first pitch, he signaled to the car and a waitress jumped out and offered a martini on a silver tray. Martin took a sip and resumed his plate appearance.

After the photo-ops and planned routines, the stars actually played baseball. Their opponent usually was the winning team from a previous game—staged weeks earlier in a much emptier ballpark—pitting the local sportswriters versus the local sportscasters. Many stars were former athletes, including Chuck Connors, a former first baseman in the Brooklyn Dodger organization who was discovered by an MGM talent agent in 1952 while playing for the Los Angeles Angels, then a Chicago Cubs affiliate.

"The guy who impressed me was Dean Martin," said longtime Dodgers manager Tommy Lasorda. "I met him in the Hollywood game when I pitched for the Angels in 1957, along with other stars like Gordon MacRae, Forrest Tucker, and Soupy Sales. Dean was a great athlete."

For many of the Hollywood Stars, the game was just another opportunity for publicity. But for some it was a chance to fulfill every young man's dream of playing on a major league field before a large crowd.

In the 1970s Rob Reiner was starring as Michael "Meathead" Stivic on the Emmy-Award-winning comedy *All in the Family*. He'd played some in high school and was active in serious softball leagues. Now a 64-year-old director, Reiner's voice goes up a notch when he recalls his appearances and his memory pulls out details of at-bats and plays from nearly four decades ago. There was the single off Tom Niedenfuer (coyly announced as a reporter for a suburban newspaper). There was the night he hit a ball to the warning track and another off the 375 sign in left center and (he thinks) circled the bases while Walter Matthau (then in his 50s) tried to track down the ball.

There was the time he was playing left field and threw out a runner trying to score from second. Don Newcombe, pitching for the Stars, told him, "Thanks for saving my shutout," Reiner recalls with relish. "That was the biggest. There were maybe 48,000 people in the stands and they went nuts."

It was fun for Dodgers players as well. Wes Parker's favorite Hollywood Stars moment occurred as a rookie. "After the Hollywood game, Nat King Cole walked through the locker room," Parker said. "I went up to him and told him what a big fan I was and how I appreciated listening to his music in person at the Coconut Grove. He said, 'You're a fine young player and you have a bright future.' I'm glad I had a chance to tell him because he passed away the following spring."

"I remember my first Hollywood Stars game was about 1970," says Steve Garvey. "I walked into the dugout early that afternoon and there was Jack Benny, Walter Matthau, Jerry Lewis, and some young actors at the time who had just made their first movie and went on to become big stars. I got some autographs myself!"

"We've always had a tremendous following from Hollywood," said Ron Cey. "And it wasn't just for the Hollywood Stars game. They came around a lot. We had all sorts of walks of life here—Milton Berle, Billy Crystal, Tony Danza, Dean Martin, Kareem Abdul-Jabbar. I remember getting my picture taken with Jack Benny."

One of the enduring images of Hollywood Stars Night is Billy Barty and Kareem Abdul-Jabbar, polar opposites in terms of height, but who both brought unique athletic perspectives to the game. Barty founded Little People of America, which promoted the rights of others with dwarfism. Barty was a good athlete and even played football at Los Angeles City College.

Abdul-Jabbar took the "giant" role in stride. Usually in the middle of his plate appearance, time would be called and two stars would carry an oversized bat for Abdul-Jabbar to swing. But running around on the

Tommy Lasorda, Rob Reiner, and University of Southern California baseball coach Rod Dedeaux pose before a Hollywood Stars game.

Billy Barty was a perennial participant in the Hollywood Stars game.

The Hollywood Stars game drew celebrities from beyond movies and television. Here, basketball Hall of Famer Kareem Abdul-Jabbar, a Dodgers fan from Brooklyn days, joins Jack Lemmon and Tommy Lasorda hamming it up before the game.

Hollywood Stars Night at Dodger Stadium—Saturday, July 24th

From Jackie Gleason (*upper left*) to Dean Martin (*lower right*), this promotional piece reveals the range of stars who appeared during the 1960s.

field and playing first base, Kareem in his heart was enjoying playing baseball.

Born Lew Alcindor on April 16, 1947, the day after Jackie Robinson's historic debut, Abdul-Jabbar was a childhood fan of the Brooklyn Dodgers. When Duke Snider's uniform No. 4 was retired by the Dodgers during Old Timers Day ceremonies in 1980, Abdul-Jabbar showed up for the ceremony and talked his way onto the field as the reigning star of the Los Angeles Lakers. He carefully carried some black-and-white snapshots and told Snider, "I took these at Camera Day in 1956 when my mother took me to Ebbets Field. May I have your autograph?"

"Kareem was the crossover athlete people enjoyed seeing because of his height and presence," Garvey said.

In the 1970s Garvey struck a friendship with Ron Masak, the veteran actor and voiceover artist best known as the sheriff in *Murder, She Wrote* and who became a longtime catcher in the Stars game. Over the course of 30 years, Masak's favorite memories include comedian Jon Lovitz taking a turn at the microphone and overly praising Brandon Tartikoff to the point where the NBC president couldn't swing because he was laughing so hard.

"The first time I played, they had Jack Lemmon and Walter Matthau both playing center field as 'The Odd Couple,'" Masak said. "Jack Gilardi, one of the co-producers with Joe Siegman, said, 'Can anyone here catch?' No one answered, so I said, 'If no one is crazy enough, I will.' So they asked Steve Yeager to get me some catching gear and as we walked by Alston, Yeager said, 'You wearing a cup?' I said, 'Hell, I haven't even got a saucer.' Yeager said it was the biggest laugh he had ever seen from Alston.

"Every year in the clubhouse, we were just a bunch of guys ready to live out a dream and play on the same field used by great players like Koufax, Drysdale, and Garvey. It was better than Oscar night." ■

June 2009: Dodgers vs. Oakland A's

"He can't hit the curve! He can't hit the curve!" the guy
a few rows behind us shouts, as if the Dodger pitcher
can hear this news about the batter, Nomar Garciaparra,
all the way from these top deck seats, and then he'll send
an out-making curve ball to the plate. The truth is that

nobody, ever, down on the field, can hear what we know
so high up that birds can graze our heads. We want to help.
We want to say the magic words, solution to the puzzle
slowly solving itself between the Dodgers and the A's,
down there,

way down there, where the grass is as green as Oz when Judy Garland
steps from black and white into Technicolor. "Get the bat off your shoulder,
Kershaw!" the same guy yells when the Dodger pitcher stands at the plate,
ultimately striking out. He did move the bat; he swung hard, but not because
this guy told him to. Why do we try? Why am I screaming, "Charge!"
after the familiar fanfare. Why am I chanting, "Let's go, Dodgers, let's go!"

over and over? Eating a lukewarm Dodger dog, the doughy bun falling apart?
Because I need to be a fan, worshipping divinity of solid rules,
of constant practice, within which utter unpredictability and error hold sway.
The Game: The Quest. Not for The Grail, but for a batting average somewhere
beyond 300. Out of 1,000. A thousand would be perfect,

but baseball isn't perfect. It's just beautiful. Harry and I bring our aging bodies
to the stadium, the cheapest seats, closest to an evening sky, those birds
skimming everybody's bright blue Dodger cap. There are holy rituals:

A toddler with his dad and uncle, the baby wearing an expensive all-wool
Dodger jacket he'll outgrow in weeks, but he's an acolyte for now. The young
and gentle couple sitting in the row ahead of us, sharing Chinese stir-fry, nuzzling each other's
necks — consecrated, loving union. And now, Tommy Lasorda, long-time Dodger manager and
saint, waddles to the field, accepting adulation. The wonder of all this

as potent as it was the one time I went to Notre Dame Cathedral,
Paris, Ascension of the Virgin Mary being celebrated. Candles blazing. Incense
made me swoon. Now, after the 7th inning stretch, Harry says, "Let's leave,"

and I am grateful to escape intensity, the yelling and the push of 50,000 people.
We drive home, the game still on the radio; then, at home we watch the end —
my shoes are off. My head is steadying itself. Home: our safe retreat, as dear to us
as any home-run hitter's trot around the bases to the final one.

What's our batting average? Less than nothing in the stats. No baseball player
in the Major League would even know our names. Tommy Lasorda doesn't care
if we're in Dodger Stadium or not — thousands of other people are.
I care, though. I like becoming the old lady who can tell somebody else
to "Charge," can urge our Dodgers to bring forth their youth and talent
for imperfect excellence. Error-filled beauty. Stunning strikeouts —

losses, in the truest scheme of things, as glorious as winning.
These men wrestle with The Game, their god, and we all come away,
no matter what the outcome, happily reborn and sanctified.

— Holly Prado

Walter O'Malley Was Right

Paul Hirsch

Few men in sports history have been vilified to the extent Walter O'Malley was when he moved the Brooklyn Dodgers to Los Angeles in 1957. Over recent decades, New York City Parks Commissioner Robert Moses has begun to share some, if not all, of the blame for the Dodgers' move. Countless trees have died supporting the contention that either O'Malley ripped the franchise from the bosom of a borough that has never recovered its identity or self esteem, or that Moses did not understand the value of keeping the Dodgers in Brooklyn and was unnecessarily obstinate when it came to reaching a mutually satisfactory agreement with O'Malley to keep the team in the city. The purpose of this article is to provide a more dispassionate account without the assigning of blame and arrive at some conclusions regarding what choices O'Malley had to make when he brought major league baseball to Southern California.

From 1946 through 1957 the Brooklyn Dodgers won more games than any other franchise in the National League[1] and were arguably the loop's most exciting team. Only the Yankees won more. The Dodgers were loaded with diverse and interesting personalities who immersed themselves in the community, and the core players were virtually constant over that entire period. A decade or more of success with basically the same crew meant one thing; on-field personnel were getting too old to maintain a championship level of play. By 1957 Pee Wee Reese was 38, Roy Campanella 35, Carl Furillo 35, Sal Maglie 39, Gil Hodges 33, and even the relative youngsters, Duke Snider, Carl Erskine, and Don Newcombe, were past 30.[2]

In early 1957 Sandy Koufax and Don Drysdale were nothing more than promising youngsters; Johnny Podres was in the Navy; Maury Wills, John Roseboro, and Tommy Davis were minor leaguers; Wally Moon was a Cardinal; Ron Fairly and Frank Howard were in college; and Willie Davis hadn't finished high school. With all due respect to Brooklyn's regular second baseman Jim Gilliam, he was hardly a cornerstone franchise player. No one could have known that this

group would dominate the National League from 1962 through 1966.

It's one thing to lose games and quite another to struggle with the balance sheet when baseball is the family business. In Brooklyn, the history was either contention or bankruptcy. When the team went twenty years between pennants before 1941, it landed in receivership and major decisions were being made or influenced by The Brooklyn Trust Company.[3] Attendance dipped under 500,000 five times during this period.[4]

Walter O'Malley was also justified in considering a move from Ebbets Field. By 1957 the right field screen hung in tatters, the bathroom odors were stifling, and parking was available for only 700 cars.[5] In 2003 Buzzie Bavasi wrote, "Ebbets Field was a great place to watch a game if you were sitting in the first 12 rows between the bases. Otherwise, we had narrow seats, narrow aisles, and a lot of obstructed views."

Mid-1950s attendance compared with the Dodgers' primary rivals of that time was also disturbing. From a high of 1.8 million in 1947,[6] as the team won five more pennants and finished second three other times, Dodger attendance dwindled. When the Boston Braves moved to Milwaukee before the 1953 season, a worrisome situation grew dire.

Table 1. Dodger Attendance vs. Top Competitors

Year	Brooklyn	Milwaukee	Yankees
1953	1,163,419	1,826,397	1,537,811
1954	1,020,531	2,131,388	1,475,171
1955	1,033,589	2,005,836	1,490,138
1956	1,213,562	2,046,331	1,491,784
1957	1,028,258	2,215,404	1,497,134
Total	5,459,359	10,225,356	7,492,038[7]

Lower attendance compared with the primary competition meant fewer concessions sold, less money available for player procurement and development, and was perhaps a sign of waning interest. On the last Wednesday of the 1956 season, with the defending World Champions one-half game out of first place, the day after Maglie had thrown a no-hitter, the Dodgers drew 7,847 to Ebbets Field.[8] Player procurement would be more important than ever as the team rebuilt, and O'Malley would have been justified in worrying that he wouldn't have the cash to compete.

But wait, O'Malley critics claim the Dodgers were profitable during this period. They are right, but the claim is not as straightforward as it might seem. In 1955, for example, the Dodgers earned $787,155 from WOR TV.[9] They accomplished that by televising all home games and twenty road games. Yet, in August 1955, Yankees owner Dan Topping was working hard to convince O'Malley and Giants owner Horace Stoneham to curtail or eliminate the practice of televising home games. O'Malley was receptive, in part because he believed the televising of home games cut into concession revenue, casting doubt on the net profit of the WOR deal.[10] That income was crucial to the franchise's profitability.[11] The importance O'Malley placed on concession revenue could be seen in his willingness to make every Saturday home date a Ladies' Day in 1956 and 1957, when female fans were admitted at no charge.[12] Brooklyn's net income from 1952–1956 ranged from a low of $209,979 in 1954 to a high of $487,462 in 1956 when Brooklyn hosted four World Series games.[13] With an aging, deteriorating team and ballpark, slipping attendance, and the TV revenue in question, there was plenty of cause for concern in the Dodgers business office.

Another element of the profitability question has to do with Walter O'Malley's vision for his franchise. He needed profits to help build a new ballpark, regardless of where it was located. A new ballpark was his best chance of continuing to compete well in a three- or even a two-team market given that fans were staying away from Ebbets Field despite the winning ways of the team on the field. If fewer games were made available to television, and ticket and concession revenue declines were not reversed, it was debatable how much longer the franchise would be viable playing at Ebbets Field.

O'Malley was a devout capitalist, and that no doubt drove him. Yet finances were not his only problem. To build a new stadium in Brooklyn, he needed a cooperative city government. That's where he ran up against Robert Moses. As the head of many public agencies, including the cash cow Triborough Bridge Authority, Moses was the most powerful public works administrator in New York City. By all accounts, his influence was far-reaching and abundant...and he and O'Malley did not see eye-to-eye on the Dodgers' needs.

Table 2. The O'Malley-Moses Stalemate

O'Malley Position	Moses Position
Privately financed stadium	Municipal stadium
Stadium in Brooklyn	Stadium in Queens
Condemn stadium land as public purpose	Brooklyn stadium not a public purpose
Baseball a civic centerpiece	Attendance/interest in decline
Custom baseball facility	Multi-purpose facility

In divorce court this dichotomy might be classified as "irreconcilable differences." Moses's influence was such that nothing as significant as a major league stadium could be built without his cooperation and approval. O'Malley owned the Dodgers, and his primary recourse was to move the franchise. Moses and Mayor Robert Wagner did not believe that the political fallout from losing National League baseball would be enough to cost them power. They were proved right about that. Wagner's opponent in the November 1957 mayoral election, held about six weeks after the Dodgers and Giants played their last games in New York and well after their exodus had been confirmed, received fewer votes than Wagner's 1953 opponent. Brooklyn voters, meanwhile, gave Wagner a plurality of more than 330,000 votes.[14] A reasonable person might wonder how much the typical Brooklyn resident cared about retaining the Dodgers. Moses did not face elections and retained enough influence to remain in power well into the next decade. The two had simply read the tea leaves and determined that there was no pressing need to keep the Dodgers and Giants in New York on anything other than the city's terms.

In *Twilight Teams*, his excellent accounting of postwar major league baseball franchise shifts through 1971, author Jeffrey Saint John Stuart makes the point that generally the new city made more attractive offers than the city from which a team was leaving. While Moses, Wagner, and other officials dithered in New York, Mayor

Dodgers owner Walter F. O'Malley, who led the team's move to Los Angeles.

LOS ANGELES DODGERS

LOS ANGELES DODGERS

Los Angeles City Councilwoman Rosalind Wyman, a strong Dodgers supporter throughout the maneuvering to bring the team to Los Angeles and build Dodger stadium, presents a commendation from the Beverly Hills B'nai B'rith to owner Walter O'Malley.

Norris Paulson, Supervisor Kenneth Hahn, and Councilwoman Rosalind Wyman put together an offer in Los Angeles that was too attractive for O'Malley to dismiss. Space limitations preclude a detailed accounting of that offer, but suffice to say that the Dodgers wound up in 1962 with a privately owned, 56,000-seat stadium at the confluence of several major freeways[15] surrounded by 16,000 parking spaces.[16] Dodger Stadium remains functional and attractive to this day. Moses's vision, which turned into Shea Stadium in 1964, "looked old the day it opened," according to New York sportswriter Leonard Koppett. Shea was closed after the 2008 season and torn down that winter.

Those who have complained the longest and the loudest about O'Malley (primarily Dick Young, Dave Anderson, and Roger Kahn) were New York sportswriters left with less to cover. Rumblings about a move out of Brooklyn had begun in 1953,[17] and Dodgers fans had responded by attending fewer games despite the team's success. New York officials were circumspect in their dealings with the Dodgers, while Los Angeles politicians were highly cooperative, if not downright accommodating. On top of all that, moving to Los Angeles meant that O'Malley would have the third largest city in the United States all to himself in terms of major league baseball.

If one views a baseball franchise as a public trust, then a case can be made that the Dodgers should have stayed in Brooklyn and taken what they could get in New York. If one views owning a baseball franchise as a competitive, profit-driven enterprise, then moving to Los Angeles was probably the best baseball-related gift O'Malley could give his family. In this case, at that time, for this author, the offer to move to Los Angeles made too much sense for O'Malley to ignore. The situation in Brooklyn was deteriorating and looked to get only worse, at least in the short term. It would have been an act of irresponsibility towards his stockholders and his family to remain in Brooklyn.

Despite all the finger-pointing over the past 54 years, it is very possible that there is no villain in the case of the Dodgers relocating to Southern California. It may be nothing more than reasonable people with understandable motivation responding rationally to a unique set of circumstances. ∎

Sources

The 1980 Baseball Dope Book. The Sporting News. 1980.
Brooklyn Dodger Yearbooks, 1956–1957.
D'Antonio, Michael. *Forever Blue.* Riverhead Books. 2009.
Fetter, Henry D. *Revising the Revisionists, Walter O'Malley, Robert Moses, and the End of the Brooklyn Dodgers,* New York History, Winter 2008.
Goldblatt, Andrew. *The Giants and the Dodgers.* McFarland & Co. 2003.
Golenbock, Peter. *Bums; An Oral History of the Brooklyn Dodgers.* Putnam. 1984.
Kahn, Roger. *The Boys of Summer.* Harper and Row. 1971.
Kahn, Roger and Al Helfer. *The Mutual Baseball Almanac.* Doubleday & Co. 1954.
Los Angeles Dodger Yearbooks, 1958–1962.
McGee, Bob. *The Greatest Ballpark Ever.* Rutgers University Press. 2005.
Moses, Robert. *The Battle of Brooklyn, Sports Illustrated.* 22 July 1957.
Murphy, Robert E., *After Many a Summer.* Union Square. 2009.
Schiffer, Don editor, *The Major League Baseball Handbook,* 1961. Thomas Nelson & Sons 1961.
Stuart, Jeffrey Saint John, *Twilight Teams.* Sark Publishing, 2000.
Sullivan, Neal, *The Dodgers Move West.* Oxford University Press, 1987.
www.baseball-reference.com.
www.retrosheet.org.
www.walteromalley.com.
Personal conversation with Leonard Koppett, 2002.
Email exchanges with Buzzie Bavasi, 2001–2008.

Notes

1. 1958 Los Angeles Dodger Yearbook, 43.
2. www.baseball-reference.com.
3. *Forever Blue,* 38.
4. *1980 Baseball Dope Book,* 71–72.
5. *After Many a Summer,* 66–67.
6. Ibid, 72.
7. Ibid, 72, 57, 39.
8. www.retrosheet.org.
9. *The Dodgers Move West,* 35.
10. *After Many a Summer,* 145.
11. *The Dodgers Move West,* 68.
12. Brooklyn Dodger Yearbooks, 1956, 48; 1957, 47.
13. *The Dodgers Move West,* 69.
14. *After Many a Summer,* 328.
15. Los Angeles Dodger Yearbook 1962, cover.
16. Ibid, 3.
17. *After Many a Summer,* 97.

A Home Like No Other

The Dodgers in L.A. Memorial Coliseum

By Don Zminda

With a seating capacity of over 90,000, the Los Angeles Memorial Coliseum was the largest ballpark ever to regularly host major league games.[1] It was also one of the strangest. Games at the Coliseum could contain 250-foot home runs to left, 440-foot flyouts to right, and fielders staggering to pick up the ball in the park's combination of single-decked seats, bright sunlight, and white-shirted fans (some of them movie and television stars). "It was weird, weird, weird playing in the Coliseum," said Dodgers infielder Randy Jackson, summing up the feelings of many players.[2] But in the four seasons the Dodgers called the Coliseum home (1958-61), the stands were often packed, and the games were seldom dull.

Consider the first regular-season game ever played at the Coliseum, on April 18, 1958. In front of 78,672 fans—at the time, a major league record crowd for a single game—the Dodgers took a 6–3 lead into the eighth inning, when 41-year-old Hank Sauer of the Giants became the first player to homer over the park's 40-foot-high screen in left field. In the ninth, the first three Giants batters doubled (Jim Davenport), tripled (Willie Kirkland), and singled (Willie Mays), plus the Dodgers committed an error … but the Giants scored just one run because Davenport had failed to touch third base on Kirkland's triple. The Dodgers hung on for a 6–5 win—not that everyone saw it clearly. "In the far reaches of the vast arena…" wrote Al Wolf in the *Los Angeles Times*, "the game resembled a pantomime. You couldn't follow the ball, but the actions of the players told you what was happening. Nobody complained."[3]

Or how about the *last* regular-season contest at the Coliseum, on September 20, 1961, played before only 12,068? Facing a Chicago Cubs lineup that included three future Hall of Famers (Richie Ashburn, Ernie Banks, and Billy Williams), Sandy Koufax struck out 15 batters in a 13-inning complete game before the Dodgers pulled out a 3–2 victory. According to statistics compiled by Alan Roth, Koufax threw a staggering 205 pitches in the game—allowing no hits after the eighth inning.[4]

LOS ANGELES DODGERS

With the move to the Coliseum, the Dodgers tried to compensate for the short distance to left field with a high screen and national park-like dimensions for right and right-center. This is the 1958 layout. The fences in right and right-center were pulled in for the next season and the left field screen probably took away as many home runs as the shorter-than-normal distance allowed.

When the Dodgers moved west from Brooklyn following the 1957 season, it took them several months to decide on a temporary home while a new stadium in Chavez Ravine was being constructed. As late as January 1958, the Dodgers expected to play in Pasadena's Rose Bowl, but when talks with Pasadena officials broke down, the club turned to the Coliseum, home of the NFL Los Angeles Rams and the collegiate USC and UCLA football teams.[5] The oval-shaped Coliseum was predictably difficult to configure for baseball, producing very short dimensions in left field (250 feet down the line, 320 to left-center) and distant fences in center (425 feet) and right-center fields (440).[6] The Dodgers erected the screen atop the left-field wall to help reduce the number of home runs, but many baseball people feared that Babe Ruth's single-season home run record was in jeopardy.[7]

Such fears proved unfounded. The park did produce some crazy moments during the L.A. Dodgers' inaugural season—such as a three-homer game on April 24 from the Cubs' Lee Walls, who had hit only six four-baggers during the entire 1957 season. But while the Coliseum yielded 193 home runs during the 1958 campaign, most in the majors, that total was actually lower than the MLB-high 219 four-baggers that were hit in Cincinnati's Crosley Field in 1957.[8] And in the four seasons that the Dodgers played in the Coliseum, no Dodger player hit more than 14 home runs at home in a single season.

That is not to say that the Coliseum was beloved by players—especially pitchers. San Francisco Giants pitcher Johnny Antonelli called the left-field wall "the biggest farce I ever heard of,"[9] and Dodger pitcher Don Drysdale commented, "It's nothing but a sideshow. Who feels like playing baseball in this place?"[10] Outfielders, meanwhile, often complained about being unable to see batted balls. "Those rows of seats go so high, it's awful hard to see anything but high flies," said Willie Mays. "Line drives, they are murder."[11]

For Dodgers players, the Coliseum could be heaven—or hell. Lefty-swinging Wally Moon, who joined the club prior to the 1959 season, reconfigured his swing to hit high flies ("Moon Shots") over the left-field screen,[12] hitting 37 home runs in the Coliseum from

1959–61, compared to only 12 on the road. Another lefty swinger, future Hall of Famer Duke Snider, struggled with the Coliseum's deep right field dimensions in 1958, hitting only six home runs at home all season. But Snider rebounded after the Dodgers shortened the right-field fence in 1959,[13] and actually hit more home runs in the Coliseum (32) than on the road (21) 1959–61.

Among Dodgers pitchers, no one was hampered by the Coliseum more than Sandy Koufax—despite some great individual games there. From 1958 through 1961 Koufax was 28–20 with a 3.57 ERA and 33 home runs allowed in Dodger road games; in the Coliseum, he was 17–23, 4.33 with 56 home runs allowed. Koufax did not fully blossom as a superstar pitcher until 1962, when he won the first of five straight ERA titles in the Dodgers' first season in Dodger Stadium.

The Dodgers themselves prospered when they moved from the Coliseum to Dodger Stadium in 1962, increasing their season attendance by more than 900,000 the first year.[14] But the team's four seasons in the Coliseum had included an All-Star game (1959), the club's first World Series championship on the West Coast (1959), and numerous memorable games, many featuring record-breaking attendance. What follows are a few highlights.

May 7, 1959. 93,103 fans—at the time, a record crowd for an organized baseball game in the United States—pack the Coliseum for Roy Campanella Night, a Dodgers-Yankees exhibition game held to benefit

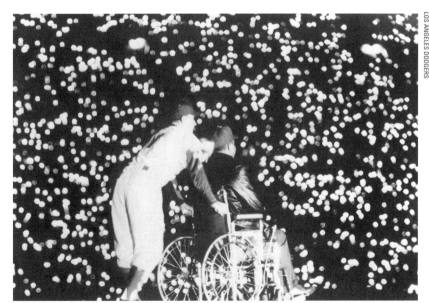

Pee Wee Reese wheels Roy Campanella onto the Coliseum's playing field as fans wave matches and lighters in honor of the All-Star catcher who had been injured in a car accident. The May 7, 1959 game pitted the Dodgers against the Yankees, setting the attendance record for an exhibition game at 93,103, with an estimated 15,000 turned away.

the former Brooklyn catcher who had been permanently disabled in an auto accident. An estimated 15,000 fans are turned away from the sellout.[15]

August 3, 1959. In the first All-Star Game played west of St. Louis, the American League All-Stars defeat the National League, 5–3, before 55,105 fans. The game is the second of two All-Star games played that year; Don Drysdale, who had started the first All-Star Game in Pittsburgh on July 7, becomes the first and only pitcher to start two All-Star Games in the same year.[16]

August 31, 1959. Before a paid crowd of 60,194—82,974 including charity and non-paid admissions—Sandy Koufax sets a modern National League single-game strikeout record and ties Bob Feller's 1938 modern major league mark (since 1900; both records later broken) by fanning 18 San Francisco Giants in a 5–2 Dodger victory. Koufax records strikeouts on 15 of the last 17 outs and strikes out the side in the ninth on 10 pitches.[17]

October 4–6, 1959. Three record crowds over 90,000—including an all-time World Series record 92,706 in Game Five—watch the Dodgers defeat the Chicago White Sox in Games Three and Four of the World Series, before losing Game Five, 1–0. The Dodgers go on to wrap up the Series in Game Six in Chicago, with the World Series record six-game attendance of 420,784.[18]

August 16, 1961. The Dodgers drop out of first place by losing twice to the Cincinnati Reds, 6–0 and 8–0, but the Wednesday night twin bill sets a National League record for attendance in a doubleheader (72,140).[19]

March 29, 2008. In an exhibition game celebrating the Dodgers' 50th anniversary in Los Angeles, the Dodgers lose to the Red Sox, 7–4, before 115,300 at the Coliseum—setting a new world record for attendance at a baseball game. Because of renovations on the Coliseum's running track and football field, the left-field wall is only 201 feet from home plate at the foul line, and the left-field screen is 60 feet high.[20] ■

Notes

1. Based on seating capacities listed in Philip J. Lowry's *Green Cathedrals* (Addison-Wesley Publishing Co., Inc., 1992).
2. Danny Peary, editor, *We Played the Game: 65 Players Remember Baseball's Greatest Era 1947–1964* (Hyperion, 1994), 391.
3. Al Wolf, "Players Complain but Fans Happy," *Los Angeles Times,* 19 April 1958, A1.
4. Sandy Koufax with Ed Linn, *Koufax* (The Viking Press, 1966), 158.
5. Neil Sullivan, *The Dodgers Move West* (Oxford University Press, 1987), 139–40.
6. Lowry, 169.
7. Norm Nevard, "Joke or Jonah? That 250-Foot Los Angeles Fence," *Baseball Digest,* April 1958, 27.
8. *Official Baseball Guide and Record Book 1959* (*The Sporting News,* 1959), 100.
9. Rube Samuelson, "250-Ft. Foul Line Sparks Hot Debate," *The Sporting News,* 29 January 1958, 5.
10. Don Drysdale with Bob Verdi, *Once a Bum, Always a Dodger* (St. Martin's Press, 1990), 71.
11. Wolf, A5.
12. Jerry Holtzman, "Home Runs by Moon-Light," *Baseball Digest,* July 1961, 23–29.
13. Lowry, 168.
14. "Los Angeles Dodgers Attendance Data," baseball-almanac.com.
15. "Record 93,103 Hail Campanella at L.A." *The Sporting News,* 20 May 1959, 5.
16. David Vincent, Lyle Spatz and David Smith, *The Midsummer Classic* (University of Nebraska Press, 2001), 170–73.
17. "K-Man Koufax Joins L.A. Comeback Kids," *The Sporting News,* 9 September 1959, 2.
18. Steve Gietschier, *The Complete Baseball Record and Fact Book 2006* (Sporting News Books, 2006), 391.
19. Ibid., p. 85; record verfied through 2010 using STATS LLC database
20. Bill Shaikin, "Baseball from another dimension," *Los Angeles Times,* March 30, 2008.

Statistical breakdowns and game box scores/play-by-plays from www.retrosheet.org.

Vin Scully

Greatest Southpaw in Dodgers History

An Appreciation by Greg King

Chances are if one were to poll SABR members about the greatest left-hander in the 121-year history of the Dodgers franchise, the most frequent response would be, "Sandy Koufax." But they would be incorrect. Without a doubt, the honor of greatest southpaw in organizational history belongs to Vincent E. Scully.

Since the emergence of radio-broadcast baseball, America's love and fascination with the sport has been amplified by the play-by-play announcers who describe and interpret the strategies and resulting action with their own unique conversational style and insider baseball knowledge. On the surface it seems simple enough. The broadcaster watches the game from a booth overlooking the diamond and speaks into a microphone headset reporting the game. But it is much more than that.

The principal announcer, the team's "voice," is the embodiment of the link between the team and its loyal fans. No one is a better illustration of that nexus than the Dodgers' Vin Scully, whose professional work for the organization has spanned two coasts and over sixty consecutive years. Scully's remarkable career with the Dodgers began in 1950, eight years before the team pulled up stakes in Brooklyn and headed west. No one has called the play-by-play for one team longer. Only two major league stadiums remain from his rookie year. A full six decades? It is likely we'll witness Joe DiMaggio's 56-game hitting streak surpassed or Cal Ripken's consecutive games tally streak shattered before the one Scully established is matched.

Scully's constant presence in the tapestry of Dodgers baseball history extends into the various eras and themes that run through its history. Scully was there, of course, to call the seasons that saw the Dodgers capture five National League pennants in the 1950s, and three more with Sandy Koufax-Don Drysdale-Maury Wills in the span between 1963 and 1966. He covered the swinging '70s with the likes of the record-setting infield of Ron Cey, Bill Russell, Davey Lopes, and Steve Garvey, who brought three additional National League Championships to Los Angeles; he helped shepherd in Fernandomania and a World Championship in 1981, and he was up in the booth in 1988 when Orel Hershiser and Kirk Gibson led their team to the last Dodgers' Series crown. He was there throughout the half-century of the O'Malley family ownership, the complete managerial careers of Walt Alston and Tommy Lasorda (totaling 43 seasons), the seasons of the 12 Dodgers who have won the National League Rookie of the Year Award in Los Angeles. He was there through the debacle of the Fox ownership of the Dodgers. When current Dodgers owner Frank McCourt wants to introduce change, his message is more palatable to the public when the words come from Scully's mouth.

Despite being away from NBC weekly Saturday afternoon broadcasts since 1989 and CBS radio postseason broadcasts since 1997, Scully may still have the most recognizable voice in baseball, thanks largely to the universal availability of out-of-town games through DirecTV and via game broadcasts on the MLB.com website. His signature is an easy-going, golden-throated delivery, displaying a great command of the English language, deployed in a manner that has been called nothing short of an art form. *USA Today* called him "the poet laureate of baseball."[1]

For over 50 years, Vin Scully has provided the soundtrack for the Southland summer—not to mention a good part of spring and a sprinkle of fall. To say that he has a sizable following in Southern California would be an understatement. The elongated announcement by Scully at the start of every Dodgers television broadcast, "It's time for Dodger baseball," as it has been for decade after decade, is as familiar to Angelenos as the Hollywood sign. Yet, despite his long association with the Dodgers, he is not viewed as a "homer" by fans—a term used in reference to those sportscasters who openly root for the team whose games they cover. Scully reports the plays objectively, regardless which team made the spectacular catch, or conversely, failed to hit the cut-off man. It is for this reputation that the *Los Angeles Times Sunday Magazine* ran a long feature piece on Scully with the banner, "The Most Trusted Man in L.A."[2]

Broadcaster Jerry Doggett, Scully's sidekick for the Dodgers' first three decades in Los Angeles.

Scully has always credited his honed objectivity in reporting the game to two primary factors. First, he got his start when greater New York City sported the Dodgers, Giants, and Yankees. "I was very conscious of other fans listening to the ballgame," he said. Second, he was teamed with Red Barber, who "had the greatest influence on my working life. He impressed upon me that I should be reporting and not cheerleading. Actually, it helped me because I was inclined to feel the emotion. But I have learned to withhold it, up to a point. Objectivity is a habit."[3]

Scully's love of sports broadcasting traces back to his childhood when he would shoehorn himself under the oversized cabinet radio in his Bronx apartment. He enjoyed listening to the sports broadcasting giants of the era, Byrum Saam, Ted Husing, and especially Bill Stern. The sound waves carrying crowds raucously cheering for a goal line stand, or a ball hit in the alley with men on base, washed over him like an ocean wave and induced chills. When asked by a teacher at age eight what he wanted to be when he grew up, Scully simply wrote in his composition, "sports announcer." He practiced aloud while playing stickball with his chums in the streets of New York.[4]

The broadcaster of Irish descent was born in the Bronx near the Grand Concourse not far from Yankee Stadium in the storied year of 1927, but he became a fan of the Giants. An 18–4 drubbing at the hands of the Yankees in the second game of the 1936 World Series had Scully feeling sorry for the men in black and orange, and he immediately adopted them as his own.[5] The redheaded youngster received complimentary game tickets to the Polo Grounds from the Catholic Youth Organization or Police Athletic League, or he would scrape up enough change from selling newspapers or returning soda pop bottles to buy bleacher tickets to see the afternoon games. "I saw a complete home stand once," remembered Scully fondly. But he couldn't stop himself from adding in his characteristic good humor, "That was just shortly after the discovery of fire."[6]

He especially idolized the Giants' southpaw slugger Mel Ott. "I just thought he was the cat's meow," he recalled, dropping in a popular phrase of a bygone era. Scully went so far as emulating Ott's unorthodox batting style: elevating his right leg up high prior to swinging the bat and moving into the pitch, a technique that gave Ott 512 career home runs. "It didn't help me," said Scully, who played outfield on varsity baseball squads in high school and college.[7]

Educated at Fordham University, with a short break for service in the U.S. Navy toward the tail end of World War II, he became a member of the initial class of students admitted to the new radio communications program. There, Scully received hands-on experience working at radio station WFUV, handling college football, basketball, and baseball games, as well as many other programming and station responsibilities.

Following graduation in June 1949, he accepted a summer internship with CBS affiliate WTOP in Washington D.C., where a combination of dedication, hard work, natural communication abilities, and warm personality were in ample evidence. That fall, he adeptly covered a key Boston University-Maryland match for the nationally aired CBS Radio Football Roundup in an emergency pinch role when an announcer became ill. Despite adverse working conditions [covering the game from the roof of Fenway Park on a bone-chilling November afternoon], he made a favorable impression on the "ol' Redhead," Red Barber, the network's sports director, who doubled as the Dodgers broadcaster. A few weeks later, after an unexpected opening came up on the Dodgers broadcasting team—Ernie Harwell had jumped ship to the Giants for more air time and a salary bump—Scully was recommended by Barber to Dodgers' President Branch Rickey, who hired him to become the third man behind Barber and Connie Desmond. The young redhead had just turned 22.[8]

In his first broadcast stint for the Dodgers, an exhibition game in spring 1950, Scully called a triple play, and in hindsight, more importantly, had the opportunity to meet the legendary Philadelphia A's manager of fifty years. "I was overwhelmed to meet Connie Mack," he remarked over the airwaves in 2010. In his first year in the booth he saw the Dodgers lose in heartbreak fashion to the "Whiz Kid" Phillies on the last day of the season. He could already understand firsthand the Brooklyn fan's refrain, "Wait 'Til Next Year." But the 1951 season with the crushing defeat of the Dodgers at the hands of the Giants and Bobby Thomson certainly topped it.[9]

What was it like for Scully in those early years of broadcasting? "You had the Southern gentleman, the father (Barber), the good-natured Irishman, the older brother with the big sweeping baritone everyone loved (Desmond), and I was the kid off the streets of New York," was how Scully characterized the trio.[10] They quickly formed a cohesive partnership.

"Connie and I trained him, loved him, teased him, and rejoiced in his remarkable development," Barber wrote.[11] Scully, who handled the third and seventh innings, rapidly demonstrated both an understanding of baseball and an acute ability to communicate this knowledge to listeners in a naturally powerful and rich voice. Scully valued Barber's instructions and explained, "Red Barber taught me to get to the park early, to do my homework, to be prepared, and to be accurate. He was a stickler for that. He cared."[12]

When Barber balked at covering the 1953 Dodgers-Yankees World Series, the plum television broadcasting assignment was offered to Scully, with his mentor's blessing. The credible job he did [paired with Mel Allen] had viewers and the sporting press taking notice.[13] Barber soon ended his fifteen-year tenure with the Dodgers and went crosstown to the Yankees while Desmond became increasingly unreliable from periodic bouts of alcoholism. Scully was elevated to the top spot following the 1954 season.

The Sporting News wrote about Scully in 1955, "He has a clear voice and a casual, friendly manner that projects comfortably over the air. He stays alert and displays an unmistakable grasp of his subject."[14] Nothing in the intervening decades would change that assessment written some 55 years ago.

Though he has called thousands of games for the Dodgers, when I asked Scully many years ago what his most memorable baseball broadcast was, he responded without a moment's hesitation: "The 1955 World Championship. But I have to preface it by saying I was younger and more impressionable then. The Dodgers had a background of frustration that you have to be aware of and I certainly was, growing up in New York. The Dodgers played the Yankees in the World Series in 1941, '47, '49, '52, and '53, and they always lost. The 1955 Dodgers club had a lot of fellows who were there when I started. It was sort of like my graduating class. I knew their frustration of getting so close and not making it. I was empathetic."[15]

Players like Pee Wee Reese, Jackie Robinson, Duke Snider, Roy Campanella, Gil Hodges, and Don Newcombe had long been excluded from the champagne drenching that accompanied the celebration and crowning of baseball World Champs. The 1955 Fall Classic went down to the seventh game, with Johnny Podres shutting out the Yankees, 2–0.

"On the last out of the game in the finale, I said, 'Ladies and gentlemen, the Brooklyn Dodgers are the champions of the world.' Then I stopped and didn't say another thing. All winter long people asked me, 'How could you have stayed so calm?' Well, the truth is, I was so emotionally overwhelmed by it all that if I had to say another word I think I would have cried."[16]

When the Dodgers moved to Los Angeles following the 1957 season there were those within the organization who believed Scully should adjust his style to better promote the relocated team to its new audience. And strong consideration was given to replacing Jerry Doggett (who had joined the Dodgers broadcast team in September 1956) with a local announcer already familiar to Southern California listeners. This was to be a new start. Scully made the case to Walter O'Malley for Doggett to remain his sidekick and eschewed openly rooting for the Dodgers. Doggett remained in the booth together with Scully for nearly a third of a century, each calling his own innings.

Dodgers fans picked up the knack of bringing their transistor radios, as revolutionary in their day as when iPhones were introduced, to the cavernous Memorial Coliseum almost immediately. East Coast critics of the transplanted team, ever ready to lambaste the Hollywood crowds, claimed the pocket radios were proof the fans were so genuinely ignorant of the sport that the game had to be explained to them as they watched. No doubt there was some truth to this assertion, for there were obviously those in attendance who knew little about baseball. What such commentators conveniently ignored, of course, was that a high caliber of baseball in the form of the Pacific Coast League had long been played in Southern California.[17]

There was another reason fans felt compelled to bring their portable radios to the ballpark: Vin Scully instantly captivated the Southland. Then, as now, his Irish lilt made baseball what it was supposed to be— entertaining. It was natural for Angelenos to wonder beyond the mere statistics: just who were these guys?

The Dodgers' most valuable lefty keeps score as he broadcasts a Dodgers-Mets game at Dodger Stadium in the 1960s.

"Although people were aware of some of the superstars, they weren't aware of the rank-and-file ballplayers," said Scully. "So they brought their radios to hear me tell them about the players."[18] Scully adeptly sketched their personal histories and provided color to go along with the game's action, something in which he particularly excelled. Moreover, with the exception of road games in San Francisco against the Giants, no Dodgers games were shown on local television. For many years, from the late 1950s through the 1960s, radio would be king in Los Angeles. Another contributor was that the expansive region was dominated by cars and traffic jams. When the Dodgers played on the road against anyone but the Giants, the time zone difference meant the games were beginning as drivers headed home from work on the area freeways. Factors such as these helped cement the relationship between Scully and his listeners.

"More than anyone, Scully made the Dodgers successful in Los Angeles," Dodgers GM Buzzie Bavasi wrote in his memoirs, *Off the Record*. "He was the biggest asset we had coming to California."[19] Immediately fueling Scully's popularity was that the Dodgers, following a seventh place finish in 1958, snared a World Championship trophy in only their second year in Los Angeles, which Scully found "thrilling because it was so unexpected."[20] A record album, *Dodgers '59*, was promptly produced following the season by the Dodgers and their flagship station KMPC, featuring nothing but Scully's notable calls during the magical year.

The custom of the transistor-laden fan entering turnstiles intensified when the Dodgers moved into

their new ballpark in 1962, as major league season attendance records were shattered. A cacophony of Scully's voice over the airwaves could be heard wafting through the Stadium crowd when he was calling the innings of any game.[21] During the middle innings (Doggett's time) batteries were generally conserved. The tradition of fans leaving the game early may have been more than just an effort to beat the traffic, as listening to Scully on the car radio was just as much fun, or better, than being at the game itself.

When Scully was announced as the recipient of the Ford C. Frick Award for broadcasting excellence in 1982, in the fifth year of the award's existence, he already was marking his 33rd season as a Dodgers team broadcaster, roughly 25 of those years as its main voice. Perhaps what is most remarkable in hindsight is that up to that point he had been on the national television stage for baseball only during the occasional Dodgers World Series appearances or to call sporadic All-Star games. His tenure as host of the NBC Saturday Game of the Week was still ahead of him, as were his many years behind the mike for CBS Radio Network coverage of the World Series. However, he already had a monopoly over much of the West by virtue of Dodgers flagship station KFI 640, which carried its clear 50,000-watt signal across the mountains and deserts and as far away as Des Moines and Denver.

Scully was appreciated even in the enemy territory of the San Francisco Bay area where future Giants and ESPN broadcaster Jon Miller was within earshot of Scully's distinctive baritone voice. Miller learned to mimic him. The Giants announcer remembered listening as a teenager to Scully's call of Koufax's perfect game in 1965. "That alone should have put him in the Hall of Fame," Miller said.[22] A word-for-word transcription of Scully's ninth-inning call became a part of a classic anthology, Charles Einstein's book, *The Baseball Reader*. As Einstein wrote as a preface to Scully's play-by-play, "And as you read Scully's spontaneous description, it will become hard to believe that this wasn't written, but indeed the unrehearsed spoken word instead."[23]

In early 1969, Scully agreed to emcee a daytime game show on NBC, *It Takes Two*. He even ventured into hosting a short-lived 30-minute daytime variety show on CBS, *The Vin Scully Show*, in 1973, where he was able to perform some stand-up humor, act in skits, conduct celebrity interviews, and occasionally sing. "I was sandwiched around the soap operas and actually nobody knew it was on and nobody really knew when it was off."[24] When asked what he would have liked to have done had he not become a sports broadcaster, he answers "a song and dance man—perhaps a combination Danny Kaye and Gene Kelly."[25]

Not only do few remember Scully's ventures into daytime television, his work as the primary CBS weekend sportscaster for championship tennis, golf tournaments, and pro football between 1975 and 1982 has now been overshadowed by his long and constant association with the Dodgers. At the time he signed his CBS contract, some sports media pundits questioned whether Scully could readily transfer his baseball broadcasting style and techniques to a non-baseball venue. *The Sporting News* soon gave Scully the ringing endorsement, "He seems proficient in describing tennis, golf, and other sports as he is in baseball."[26] He became the highest paid sportscaster in the nation at the time.

When CBS Sports reneged on a promise to have Scully cover the 1982 Super Bowl, he rejected their new ten-year contract deal.[27] NBC acted fast to sign him to broadcast *The Baseball Game of the Week*. For seven seasons, from 1983 through 1989, until NBC was outbid for baseball, Scully greeted television viewers with his friendly invitation, "Pull up a chair and spend part of Saturday with us." Fans across the country were finally treated on a weekly basis to arguably the best baseball broadcaster in the business.

"There is only one thing that guaranteed Scully's success," said the late Leonard Koppett, who toiled for several New York papers—"Talent!"[28] Revered by his peers, Scully remains a master of the art of baseball broadcasting and the English language. In the grand Irish tradition, Scully is a consummate storyteller. Does Scully trace his own communication talents to his family's Gaelic roots? "I think there might have been a horse thief and a poet in the tribe," Scully joked.[29]

Vin Scully's choice of words is a delight, the language fresh, witty, and original. A change-up "squirts out like a wet bar of soap." A batted ball "squirts foul." The ball springing off a broken bat sounds like it was "hit with a morning newspaper." A pitcher unable to find the strike zone is "wild as anything this side of Barnum & Bailey." The two pitchers in a scoreless duel "are like two bucks with their antlers locking." The lanky, pencil-thin pitcher standing on the mound with his arms close to his chest "looks like six o'clock." A breaking ball left up in the strike zone to a menacing batter, who clobbers it for a home run, came in "like a letter from home." Arizona's relief pitcher is "built like a 2-iron." When two Dodgers in their white uniforms fall down going after a base hit,

Scully remarks, "It looks like a bowling alley out there!" The first baseman stretching his reach for the ball with his foot on the bag "opened up like a pair of scissors."

Yet, as colorful as these descriptions might be, to conclude Scully's popularity is due solely to his command of language would certainly miss the boat. The secret behind Scully's broadcast is that he loves people and finds them interesting. Added to it is a sense of compassion that could not be feigned. Scully is invariably intrigued by any ballplayer who has overcome difficult personal circumstances and he will masterfully weave these personal narratives into the play-by-play without missing a pitch. They are the vignettes of players who toil for years in the minors but do not give up their dream to find a way to the big leagues. They are the stories of players who were considered washed up but whose careers are revived by another big league club. They are the accounts of players who grew up amid poverty in Third World countries. In listening to Scully's broadcasts, and without being entirely conscious of it, a fan cannot help but be moved to have a larger appreciation of the human dimension. These are not just men with bats and gloves—and in recent years, lots of money—but people with their own personal life stories.

Although he has kept pace with technology and conducts prodigious research before each game via the Internet, Scully has never abandoned his instincts as a reporter to gather information on opposing players from the visiting press or lifelong contacts including coaches and scouts he knows with virtually every team the Dodgers play. Nevertheless, in many ways he would have to be considered old-school. When he walks into a broadcast booth he usually is decked out in an elegant suit from which a handkerchief spills on a front pocket, and he always sports a tie—for no more than about a minute of face time per televised game. He does this as a consummate professional who wants to be reminded when he is in the broadcast booth he is all about business. Not that he thinks of broadcasting baseball as work. "Learn to do something you love, and you won't have to work a day in your life," Scully has said from time to time.[30] He is the rarest of broadcasters; he prefers to work alone, speaking to the audience in a one-on-one conversation, and not in reaction to a color man's comment. He covers each inning of all the locally televised Dodgers home games and travels with the team on road trips to Denver and all points west, sitting behind the television mike between 110 and 120 games a year. He is heard on radio as part of a simulcast for the first three innings.

The television contract is too lucrative and sponsors too demanding to share Scully more than that.

You never know what Scully will say next. There is his journalist's innate curiosity about most anything. That unpredictability makes each and every broadcast unique. He might incorporate the lyrics from a classic show tune, or a recent country ballad, or a verse from a poem, if it seems to fit the occasion. For example, when Chipper Jones was approaching Dale Murphy's Atlanta team records, Scully remarked, "As the great Pearl Bailey sang, that 'ain't no bad crowd to hang around with!'"[31]

On one occasion he might discuss the connection between Wrigley Field and Mexican General Santa Anna of the Battle of the Alamo (hint: gum) and on another describe outfielders climbing the terrace at Cincinnati's Crosley Field or the Gashouse Gang rolling around in the dirt in old Sportsman's Park in St. Louis. He might discuss a current book he is reading, such as David Maraniss's biography of Roberto Clemente, or ask whether listeners are familiar with the writer James Lee Burke and his descriptions of New Orleans as a player hailing from Bayou Country made an appearance on the mound. He can dust off a Winston Churchill quote in World War II speaking of Europe's "soft underbelly" and smoothly transition to say, "Well, the 'soft underbelly' for Colorado is its pitching." Miss this story or that observation expressed in a creative fashion—and told within the context of this particular game—and you might never hear it again.[32]

Is there any broadcaster better at weaving baseball's past in with the present? Something might remind Scully during one game of a story involving Preacher Roe throwing his equipment into the crowd. Harkening back to the play of Jackie Robinson, Stan Musial, Henry Aaron, and Willie Mays, or the lesser known likes of Ron Hunt, Chico Ruiz, and Bob Friend, or any of thousands of other players he has observed, Scully is well aware that the simple demographics of those tuned into the broadcast will necessarily mean most were born after these players had long called it a career. Scully may not consciously believe he carries some responsibility to convey to today's fans some of the game's history. He obviously feels that by connecting to the past the game becomes more enjoyable for the fan and provides a context for watching or listening to today's game. Regardless, it never seems forced when the story involves players or other references to earlier eras.

For example, in one game not long ago a demonstration of timely hitting by an opposition player got

Scully interviews 1959 World Series hero Larry Sherry after the team returns from a Game Six triumph over the Chicago White Sox.

Scully pondering great past hitters. "I'll always remember meeting Paul Waner," Scully explained during the game's lull. "He had very intense, bright blue eyes." Scully called a pitch. "I would look at his eyes and think of a fighter pilot." A ball was fouled off. Scully then went on to relate a story concerning the longtime outfielder for the Pirates; Waner had a small flask in his hip pocket as he stood in the on-deck circle. "He took a nip. And a second one. Umpire Bill Klem chastised him, 'Young man, you're a disgrace to this game!' Waner replied something to the effect, 'oh yeah?' and proceeded to set a record that day for most doubles, or some such," Scully told listeners. "Boy, he could reeaalllly hit." Scully then laughed.[33]

Since 1950, Scully has been getting behind the mike to not just call the play-by-play, but to provide word pictures to make each game truly entertaining, regardless of the score and team standings. He is endowed with several gifts that have put him at the top of his profession, including a great voice, a rich imagination which enables him to incorporate seemingly perfect similes into the broadcast, a contagious enthusiasm for intelligent ball-playing regardless of uniforms, and an ability to speak to listeners as if he were merely an old friend. Despite his rise to prominence, having received virtually every national sports broadcasting award possible, including having the press box at Dodger Stadium named in his honor, Scully has remarked many times that he is not special.

He has never taken himself too seriously, as illustrated in the following short recollection told over the air in 2010. "Wilver Stargell hit the first ball out of Dodger Stadium in 1969 off Alan Foster," Scully recalled before asking his audience, "Who called it?" Scully would then answer his own quesion with the confession, "Jerry Doggett—bless his heart. I was in the rest room."[34] His is just a simple story of a kid with a hole in his pocket growing up in the Bronx—who was able to realize his boyhood dreams. ∎

Notes

1. http://officialvinscully.com/biography.php.
2. *Los Angeles Times Magazine*, 26 April 1998; Remarked during Dodgers broadcast, 15 June 2007.
3. Interview with Vin Scully, 17 September 1991.
4. *Los Angeles Times*, 1 June 1966; Curt Smith, *Pull Up a Chair*, Washington D.C.: Potomac Books, 2009, 4–5.
5. *Los Angeles Times*, 1 June 1966 .
6. Remarked during Dodgers broadcast, 29 April 1995.
7. Interview with Vin Scully, 17 September 1991.
8. *The Sporting News*, 15 June 1955; 24 July 1989; *Christian Science Monitor*, 10 November 1986.
9. Remarked during Dodgers broadcast 3 October 2010; *The Sporting News*, 15 June 1955.
10. *The Sporting News*, 24 July 1989.
11. Red Barber, *The Broadcasters,* New York: The Dial Press, 1970, 187.
12. *The Sporting News*, 23 January 1982.
13. See Red Barber, *The Broadcasters,* New York: The Dial Press, 1970, 185–188. While broadcasting the 1996 World Series for radio, Scully reflected back to his first fall classic and working with Mel Allen. "I remember how extra kind he was," Scully said. CBS Radio Broadcast, 20 October 1996.
14. *The Sporting News*, 3 August 1955.
15. Interview with Vin Scully, 17 September 1991.
16. Interview with Vin Scully, 17 September 1991.
17. Robert Creamer, "The Transistor Kid," *Sports Illustrated*. 4 May 1964.
18. Curt Smith, *Voices of the Game*. South Bend: Diamond Communications, Inc., 1987, 492.
19. Buzzie Bavasi. *Off The Record*. Chicago: Contemporary Books: 1987, 194.
20. Interview with Vin Scully, 17 September 1991.
21. The Dodgers even requested fans to turn down their radios at one point. See *Los Angeles Times*, 4 August 1973.
22. Interview with Jon Miller, 27 June 1998. Miller said that he had listened to Scully on CBS Radio in his car during the previous World Series (1997) and found his broadcast "exciting as he regaled listeners with stories."
23. Charles Einstein, ed., *The Baseball Reader*. New York: McGraw-Hill, 1980, 273.
24. Binghamton, NY, *Sun-Bulletin*, 27 January 1975.
25. Interview with Vin Scully, 17 September 1991.
26. *Los Angeles Times*, 14 January 1975; The Sporting News, 3 May 1975.
27. *Washington Post*, 27 May 1982; TV Guide, 12 June 1982.
28. Interview with Leonard Koppett, 8 November 1997.
29. Interview with Vin Scully, 17 September 1991.
30. *Baseball Weekly*, 8–14 March 1995.
31. Remarked during Dodgers broadcast, 2 April 1997.
32. Remarked during Dodgers broadcasts on: 17 August 2003; 24 June 2006; 16 April 1996; 18 September 2004.
33. Remarked during Dodgers broadcast, 23 June 1998.
34. Remarked during Dodgers broadcast 29 April 2010.

Fernandomania

Vic Wilson

Jaime Jarrin, the Dodgers Hall of Fame Spanish-language broadcaster, tells the story that Walter O'Malley wanted to tap the growing Latino market in Southern California by finding a Mexican Sandy Koufax. O'Malley was not alive to see his dream realized when Fernando Valenzuela broke in with the Dodgers in late 1980.[1] Valenzuela's two wins, one save, and 17⅔ scoreless innings gave a glimpse of what the future was to bring.

April 9, 1981 saw the birth of Fernandomania. Valenzuela, at the time the No. 3 starter, was moved up to pitch the opener due to an injury to Jerry Reuss. His five-hit shutout of the defending division champion Houston Astros caught everybody's attention. What Fernando did in his first 8 starts was a streak for the ages: 8 wins, 7 complete games, 5 shutouts and 4 earned runs surrendered in his first 72 innings. In streaks of over 80 innings, only Bob Gibson's 3 earned runs in 103 innings in 1968 was better than Fernando's 4 earned runs in 89⅔ innings dating back to 1980.[2]

He was to become the biggest story in baseball on the field in the first half of the 1980s.

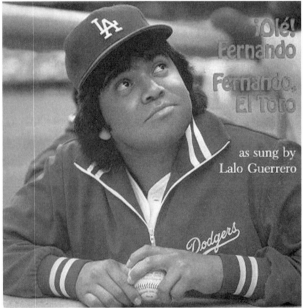

Mexican American artist Lalo Guerrero wrote a song dedicated to Fernando, or El Toro, the bull.

In the 1981 strike-shortened season, Fernando became the first player ever to win the Rookie of the Year and Cy Young awards in the same season. Valenzuela beat out Tom Seaver in a close race (70 to 67 votes). Numbers that undoubtedly swayed the judges included more innings (192 to 166), shutouts (8 to 1), complete games (11 to 6), strikeouts (180 to 87), and a slightly better earned run average than Seaver (2.48 to 2.54). He also won the Silver Slugger award as the best hitter at his position.

Fernando's reputation was enhanced with wins in both the 1981 division and league championship series. His Game Three win in the World Series—a gut-wrenching 147-pitch, 5–4 victory—was the turning point as the Dodgers began a four-game win streak to beat the Yankees.

Upon receipt of the Cy Young Award in November 1981, Fernando was asked by the press if he knew who Cy Young was. His answer: "I do not know who he was, but a trophy carries his name so he must be someone very special to baseball."[3]

Fernando's journey from the barren, dry lands of northern Mexico to the heights of baseball royalty made him the toast of two countries. Meeting with presidents, dealing with the press and a multitude of fans, Fernando always kept his bearings, saying, "I knew I was representing Mexico to many people."[4] Fernando had become a cultural icon, much larger than his performance on the field.

Fans flocked to Dodgers games at home and on the road. Eleven of Fernando's 12 starts at Dodger Stadium in 1981 were sellouts. On the road during his first two years, Valenzuela's starts drew more than 13,000 more people than other Dodger starters. Prior to 1981, the Dodgers had only broken the 3 million mark in attendance twice. From 1982 to 1986, home attendance was over 3 million every season. The Dodgers broke the major league attendance record in 1982 with 3.6 million fans and slipped only slightly to 3.5 million in 1983.

While many excellent pitchers over history had brought extra people to the ball park, Fernandomania was different. What Fernando did that was unique is best summed up by Jaime Jarrin: "I truly believe that there is no other player in major league history who created more new fans than Fernando Valenzuela. Sandy Koufax, Don Drysdale, Joe DiMaggio, even Babe Ruth did not. Fernando turned so many people from Mexico, Central America, South America into fans. He created interest in baseball among people who did not care about baseball."[5]

Latinos from California to halfway to Antarctica had found a new hero. Fernando's games were broadcast on television in Mexico City, a city twice the size of Los Angeles and bigger than New York City. The number of radio stations broadcasting Dodgers games in Mexico jumped from 3 to 17. At the height of Fernandomania, the Spanish broadcasts had more than twice the listening audience of Vin Scully.

The Dodgers had been the first major league team to broadcast in Spanish but Latino attendance remained relatively low—8 percent of the total in a region where the Spanish-speaking population was growing. Fernandomania brought that percentage up to close to 30 percent in the mid-eighties. More importantly, Fernando had changed the "face of Dodger Stadium" attendance. In 2005, Jaime Jarrin said 42 percent of Dodgers' attendance was Latinos.[6] The legacy of Fernandomania still lives.

Fernando became the most important Mexican player in major league baseball history. Only Bobby Avila, with an American League batting championship in 1954, was of any previous note. Before Fernando, most of the Latino stars had come from the Caribbean, such as Roberto Clemente of Puerto Rico and Juan Marichal of the Dominican Republic.

Fernando Valenzuela went on to pitch 11 years for the Dodgers (1980–1990). He won 141 games (8th in franchise history). He was also a six-time All Star (1981–1986) and third in the Cy Young voting in 1982 with 19 wins and second in 1986 when he led the league in wins with 21. In five appearances in All-Star Games (7⅔ innings), Fernando did not give up a run. In the 1986 All-Star Game, he struck out 5 batters in a row to tie the record of another screwballer, Carl Hubbell, who did it in the 1934 All-Star Game. His overall postseason record was 5–1 with a 1.98 earned run average. From 1981 to 1987 Fernando won more games than any other National League starter and had the second-best ERA of NL pitchers with 1,000 innings during that period (second to Nolan Ryan). Fernando

Valenzuela was a magnet for drawing Latino, especially Mexican American, fans to Dodger Stadium. His return to the team as a color commentator for Spanish-language broadcasts in 2003 was cheered nightly when he was introduced from the booth.

Fernando Valenzuela: Attendance vs. other Dodger games*

Year	Home Games	Increase*	Road Games	Increase*
1981	48,431	7,519	33,273	14,292
1982–83	47,703	4,453	33,274	7,588
1984–86	43,198	5,567	27,763	3,694
1987–90	37,913	2,118	27,108	3,266
Total	39,979	5,492	29,334	4,384
Games	157			164

Note on the attendance: Fernando's games are compared to other Dodger games so that the product is equal and the only difference is who was pitching. Remember that the Los Angeles Dodgers were one of the best road draws in baseball to start with.

Many of the games in the earlier years, both home and road would have had larger increases except that many games were sellouts and therefore the increase was capped.

actually struck out more batters than Ryan during those years, 1448 to 1438. Fernando had six consecutive seasons of over 250 innings and it could have been seven without the strike in 1981. Given current trends in pitcher usage, it's likely Valenzuela will be the last pitcher who had six consecutive seasons of 250 innings and a season of 20 complete games.

By 1988, however, all those innings had taken their toll, and Fernando missed part of the season due to a dead arm. He would never be as effective again. Valenzuela pitched two more seasons for the Dodgers with his final highlight being a no-hitter in June 1990.

After all the millions of dollars Fernando had made the Dodgers either directly or indirectly, he was let go in a cost-cutting move. Being cut was bad enough, but

LOS ANGELES DODGERS

Fernando Valenzuela tips his cap to an adoring Dodger Stadium crowd during the electric days of "Fernandomania" in 1981.

the timing was worse. Since it happened late in spring training when most rosters were set, he found it difficult to find a new team. He appeared in two games for the Angels that year. Even though he went on to pitch until 1997, Fernando was angry at the Dodgers for more than a decade, refusing to attend Dodgers games as a spectator, despite living ten minutes from the ballpark, or to participate in Dodger-sponsored events.

But in 2003 the prodigal returned. Valenzuela accepted a color analyst position with the Dodgers Spanish Network, sharing the booth with Jaime Jarrin and Pepe Yniguez. In 2003 Valenzuela was inducted into the Hispanic Heritage Baseball Hall of Fame and in 2005 he was named one of the three starting pitchers on the Major League Baseball's Latino Legends Team. In addition, Fernando became a coach for Mexico in the World Baseball Classic in 2006 and 2009.

Only the words of Vin Scully can put Fernando Valenzuela and Fernandomania in proper perspective. "But in baseball, Fernando…was a religious experience. You'd see parents, obviously poor, with the little youngsters by the hand, using him as inspiration."[7] ∎

Notes

1. Jorge Martin, "25 Years After Fernandomania," *Dodger Magazine*, 18 August 2006.
2. Orel Hershiser gave up 4 earned runs in 82 innings and Don Drysdale gave up 4 earned runs in 81 innings.
3. Mark Heisler, "He Came, He Pitched, He Conquered" *Sporting News 1982 Baseball Yearbook*, 5.
4. Jim Murray, "Fernando Throws Age a Screwball," *The Great Ones*, Los Angeles: Los Angeles Times Books, 1999, 74.
5. Martin, op. cit.
6. Martin, op. cit.
7. Curt Smith, *Pull Up a Chair, the Vin Scully Story*, Washington, DC: Potomac Books, 2009. 185.

Eyeball to Eyeball, Bellybutton to Bellybutton

Inside The Dodger Way of Scouting

Lee Lowenfish

In the highly competitive, insular world of major league baseball, the phrase "The Dodger Way" still retains its hallowed place. The term can be traced to 1942, when Branch Rickey took over as general manager of the Brooklyn Dodgers and created a farm system that surpassed the one he built during his quarter-century with the St. Louis Cardinals. Though Rickey was bought out of Dodgers ownership by Walter O'Malley after the 1950 season, O'Malley understood the importance of scouting and player development. He retained experienced executives Buzzie Bavasi, Al Campanis, and Fresco Thompson, and The Dodger Way remained in force until Walter's son Peter sold the team to Rupert Murdoch before the start of the 1998 season.

What was the secret that produced six pennants and one World Series winner in Brooklyn between 1947 and 1956 and nine more pennants and five World Championship flags in Los Angeles between 1959 and 1988? Al Campanis and Fresco Thompson both wrote about the club's winning philosophy. In The *Dodgers' Way of Playing Baseball*, an oft-republished nearly 300-page instructional book, Campanis explicated the organization's belief in speed and agility and its meticulous attention to detail, everything from the way a player should wear his cap to how he should grip the baseball. Significantly, his discussion of pitching and fielding occupied more than the first half of the book.

In his entertaining, too-long out-of-print 1964 book *Every Diamond Doesn't Sparkle* (David McKay, 1964), Thompson wrote, "Scouting can be distilled into a single sentence: the business of looking for new talent and looking at other people's new and old talent." Sounds so simple, doesn't it? But the process of scouting and delivering sustainable major league talent can be devilishly hard.

Fred Claire, who served in the organization for 30 years and was the last O'Malley general manager, feels that continuity, consistency, and loyalty were the hallmarks of The Dodger Way. Claire says that during his tenure with the Dodgers never did the team go outside the organization to hire a pitching, batting, or third-base coach. Dodgers officials understood that the difficult game of baseball must be taught constantly, mistakes understood and corrected, and an optimistic attitude must always be displayed. In his insightful memoir *My 30 Years in Dodger Blue* (Sports Publishing, 2004), Claire gives credit to a college journalism professor who would not give a student an "A" grade in a feature writing class unless he handed in either three rejection slips or a published article. It was wonderful preparation for being an executive in a sport where missed opportunities are a daily way of life and those who succeed are the ones who know best how to bounce back from adversity.

Another feature of The Dodger Way was personal communication on all levels of the organization, "face to face and bellybutton to bellybutton," in the vivid phrase of super scout Mel Didier (pronounced Did-ee-ay). Author of the absorbing memoir *Podnuh, Let Me Tell You A Story* (written with Texas sportswriter T. R. Sullivan, Gulf South Books, 2007), Didier is a man of many accomplishments. Named after fellow

Left to right: Bobby Miske, Dick Teed, Buzz Bowers, Steve Lembo, Gil Bassetti, and Bill Fesh.

Louisianan, Hall of Famer Mel Ott, he is one of five brothers to have played professional baseball and is the father of former catcher and veteran minor league manager Bob Didier. Mel was also a great two-way football player for LSU, snapping the ball to future Hall of Fame quarterback Y.A. Tittle, and as a linebacker, throttling Charley Trippi in a classic trouncing of the University of Georgia. During his days as a football coach, Mel Didier picked the brain of the legendary coach Bear Bryant and brought Bryant's uber-punctuality and use of tackling dummies into his baseball scouting and development work.

Yet for all his achievements and innovations, Didier's dream was to work side by side with Al Campanis. After the 1975 season his wish came true when he came to the Dodgers from the Montreal Expos, where he had been director of scouting for the expansion National League franchise and took great pride in the development of future Hall of Famers Gary Carter and Andre Dawson, who led the Expos into pennant contention.

Didier considers Al Campanis "the smartest baseball man I've ever been around. Arrogant, at times. A know-it-all at times. But, deep down, he had a great heart." Didier never forgot Campanis's advice: "Mel, if you ever find a guy who is strong in scouting and player development, you do anything you can to keep him and you pay him whatever you can because those guys are hard to find."

Didier did not expect that his first tour of duty with the Dodgers would barely last a season, but another expansion team, the Seattle Mariners and their eager co-owner, entertainer Danny Kaye, beckoned him northward prior to the 1977 season to help the club get started. The scout was reluctant to leave his dream job, but given Walter O'Malley's blessing and a promise that a Dodgers job would always await him, Didier headed to Seattle for what proved to be a disappointing tenure. He discovered that the ownership of the new organization lacked deep pockets and passionate Danny Kaye soon grew disenchanted and withdrew from an active role.

Didier returned to the Dodgers after the 1982 season. Though he missed their 1981 World Series championship year, he played an important role advance scouting the Oakland A's prior to the 1988 World Series. His report stressing that the A's closer Dennis Eckersley always threw a backdoor slider on a 3–2 pitch went into Kirk Gibson's memory bank, and the injured outfielder tapped the knowledge when he hit the dramatic home run in Game One of the Series that set the tone for Los Angeles's five-game upset.

Golfing buddies at the Hudson, New York country house of the Dodgers' New York-area supervisor, the late Steve Lembo, in 1996. *Left to right*: the late Gil Bassetti, Dick Teed, Bobby Miske. Miske was inducted into the Scouts Hall of Fame in Wappingers Falls, New York in July 2010.

Didier also got to observe close-up the respectful if tumultuous relationship between Campanis and manager Tommy Lasorda, a Dodgers lifer who never succeeded in the major leagues as a pitcher and toiled many seasons as a scout and minor-league manager before he succeeded Walter Alston as Dodgers skipper. "[Campanis] used to really get on Tommy about his moves in the game," Didier writes. "'Why did you do this? Why did you do that?'…He made Tommy Lasorda a better manager."

It is one of the tragic ironies of Dodgers and baseball history that Al Campanis was not around to enjoy the 1988 championship. In April 1987, Campanis, who as an infield teammate in Montreal in 1946 taught the basics of second base play to rookie Jackie Robinson, told national TV interviewer Ted Koppel that African Americans lacked the "necessities" to work in the front office. Campanis was unaccustomed to being interviewed on television. His unwillingness to recant his remarks caused such an uproar that owner Peter O'Malley felt obliged to dismiss Campanis from his post as general manager and from the organization as a whole.

Campanis was thus not a part of the all-expenses-paid ten-day trip to Rome and the Italian Alps that Peter O'Malley awarded to all full-time Dodgers employees after the Series triumph. The festive excursion provided a storehouse of vivid memories for all who were in the traveling party. Bobby Miske, who spent 30 years as Dodgers area scout, remembers one overenthusiastic

Bob Miske   **Gary Nickels**   **Clyde Sukeforth**

member of the Dodgers entourage who told everyone encountered that they were meeting the World Champions! When he spoke so loudly in the hallway before an audience with the Pope, a church official interrupted, saying sternly, "Ssssh! This is the Vatican."

The Dodger Way of attentiveness to detail and convivial camaraderie extended to the grassroots of the organization. From 1977 through 1992 Dick Teed served as the Dodgers' East Coast scouting supervisor. In conversation during the 2010 season Teed recalled warmly how the late Steve Lembo, one of his New York metropolitan-area scouts, used to open up his summer home in the Hudson Valley after the end of the minor league season for a joyous weekend with all the scouts and their wives and families. On Friday night everyone gathered to enjoy 20 Maine lobsters sent down by the legendary former Dodgers scout Clyde Sukeforth, the man who introduced Jackie Robinson to Branch Rickey.

On Saturday while the women went sightseeing and shopping, the men talked inside baseball, comparing notes on the long season, and enjoying their annual golf outing. A few scouts like Bobby Miske and the New England-based Buzz Bowers were once-a-year golfers. They left links excellence to the athletic Teed, who though retired as a pro scout stays active as a Little League first-base coach in western Connecticut, teaching the young ones how to hustle and be aggressive on the bases. After their afternoon of frolicking on the golf course, the men would join Steve's wife Josephine Lembo, the daughter of a Brooklyn restaurateur, who always had an Italian spaghetti dinner awaiting them, and all enjoyed another fine evening of food, libations, and friendship.

Love of the game and a willingness to put behind them the disappointments of their playing careers was a common bond for these ivory hunters. Dick Teed and his late brother Bill had both been minor-league

catchers in the talent-rich Brooklyn Dodgers organization. Bill never made the majors and Dick struck out in his only at-bat with the 1953 Brooklyn Dodgers before he was farmed out to a Dodgers minor league affiliate that needed an emergency receiver. "I never could stick in the majors because in those days even a backup had to hit over .250," Teed recalls of an era when there were only 16 major league teams, and the minors were flooded with talented players who never received a chance to establish themselves in the big leagues.

Over two seasons in Brooklyn in 1950 and 1952 Steve Lembo collected only two hits in 11 at-bats. In 1951 he experienced his most notorious part in baseball history when he warmed up Ralph Branca in the bullpen before Branca's fateful meeting with the Giants' Bobby Thomson in the ninth inning of their third and final playoff game. Once he became a scout, Lembo took great solace in signing outfielder Tommy Davis, who won the 1962 National League batting title. (Had Davis not broken his leg sliding he may well have become another Dodgers Hall of Famer.) Lembo also inked another Brooklyn-bred product, southpaw John Franco, who went on to become an All-Star closer for the Mets.

The late Gil Bassetti, another member of the Teed-Lembo scouting brotherhood who was enshrined in 2005 in the Staten Island Yankees (Short Season Class A New York-Penn League) Scouts Wall of Fame, pitched seven seasons in the Giants chain, winning 21 games one year but never rising above Double A. When Bassetti turned to scouting, one of his prize signings was the Dodgers' base-stealing second baseman Eric Young.

Buzz Bowers never got out of Triple A with the Phillies, but he shared a lifelong friendship with his fellow Michigan State Spartan, future Hall of Fame pitcher Robin Roberts. After his years working part-time with the Dodgers, in 1992 Bowers was named by retiring Red Sox scouting legend Bill Enos as his replacement as a New England area scout. Among the major leaguers he has since signed are utility player Lou Merloni and pitcher Carl Pavano, who bounced back from several injury-riddled seasons to become a Minnesota Twins mound mainstay in 2010.

Bobby Miske never played pro baseball although he received an offer from the Kansas City Athletics after graduating from the University of Buffalo. He set out early in life to become both a baseball scout and a basketball referee, succeeding in both to the point where he has been enshrined in nine halls of fame in the combined sports. His latest honor came in the summer of 2010 when a Professional Baseball Scouts Hall of Fame (PBSHOF) plaque was unveiled at Dutchess County Stadium, home of the Class A Hudson Valley Renegades of the New York-Penn League. It is one of the four franchises owned by the Goldklang Group, a sports and entertainment organization that has been a leader in espousing the cause of scout recognition at its other ballparks in St. Paul, Minnesota, Charleston, South Carolina, and Fort Myers, Florida. (In 2008 Buzz Bowers was enshrined in the inaugural year of the Goldklang PBSHOF and in 2008 Dodgers southeastern area scout Lon Joyce was similarly honored.)

Miske was modest in his acceptance speech, saying that he was just another scout who passed on signing Mike Piazza (though the slugging catcher was hardly a prospect, not drafted until the 62nd round mainly as a favor to Tommy Lasorda who knew the Piazza family). Miske said that he hadn't signed any major leaguers but did bring into baseball three players who became scouts. He added that three of his players became extras in the Robert Redford film adaptation of Bernard Malamud's novel *The Natural*.

The scout was too self-effacing in his remarks. After leaving the Dodgers in the wake of a 1993 shakeup in the Northeast division that saw his and Gil Bassetti's departure and the retirement of Dick Teed, he worked as a professional scout for the Yankees where his advance scouting of the Mets in 2000 played an important role in the team's victory in the subway World Series. He moved on to the Mariners for the next eight years and has since returned to the Yankees' pro scouting team.

Although there was an exodus of valued scouts like Mel Didier after the O'Malleys sold the team, Dodgers fans can take solace in knowledge that the organization retains an appreciation for the importance of good scouting and player development. Gary Nickels, the Dodgers' Midwest scouting supervisor since 2003, has been appraising talent for almost 40 years and in 2009 was inducted into the Midwest Scouts Association Hall of Fame. He is also in the Mid Atlantic Scouts Association Hall of Fame. For most of the 1980s the youthful-looking Nickels served as the Cubs Midwest scouting supervisor, where he was instrumental in signing Joe Girardi. "I knew Girardi wanted to finish his engineering degree at Northwestern to keep a promise to his deceased mother," Nickels remembered during an interview before the 2010 Professional Baseball Scouts Foundation dinner in Los Angeles. So the Cubs waited until Girardi's senior year before drafting him in the 5th round and signing the current Yankees manager.

From 1991 through 1998 Nickels was the scouting director for the Baltimore Orioles, where he hired Logan White as an area scout. Today White is Dodgers assistant general manager in charge of scouting and, technically, Nickels's boss, a change in circumstance that both men laugh about. In the search for talent and its fulfillment, the best scouts have always put aside petty matters of rank and prestige in the interests of developing players to their fullest. Though Nickels takes pride in his signing of southpaw Clayton Kershaw as does White for his role in the emergence of first baseman James Loney, they both embrace the larger picture of sustaining team development and constant contention.

Years ago when working for the Cubs, Nickels paused during a lull in a game and mused to Kevin Kerrane, author of still-the-best book on scouting, *Dollar Sign on the Muscle*, "Have you ever thought how much of America the old scouts have seen?"

At a time when the Cold War against the Soviet Union exerted a formidable influence on contemporary American politics, Nickels said, "I wish we had some Russians here tonight so they could see how deep the game goes in our society." And, I might add, how precious and passionate are the scouts who sustain and grow what should always remain our national pastime. ∎

Acknowledgments

Special thanks to baseball scouts Billy Blitzer of the Cubs and John Tumminia of the White Sox for their help in arranging interviews for this article. And to the Goldklang Group and its indefatigable leaders Marv and Jeff Goldklang and Tyler Tumminia for their dedication to recognizing the vital profession of baseball scouting.

Sources

Campanis, Al. *The Dodgers' Way of Playing Baseball with illustrations* by Tex Blaisdell. New York: E.P. Dutton, 1954.

Claire, Fred with Steve Springer. *My 30 Years in Dodger Blue* www.SportsPublishing LLC.com. 2004.

Didier, Mel and T. R. Sullivan. *Podnuh, Let Me Tell You a Story*. Baton Rouge, Louisiana: Gulf South Books, 2007.

Kerrane, Kevin. *Sports Illustrated*. March 19, 1984.

Thompson, Fresco with Cy Rice. *Every Diamond Doesn't Sparkle*. New York: David McKay, 1964.

Dodgers Assistant General Manager Kim Ng Ready to Make the Jump to Top Job

Sherri Eng

Los Angeles Dodgers Assistant General Manager Kim Ng never thought she would become one of the highest-ranking women in the sport. After all, what place did women have in a sport run by the good ol' boys? And yet by the beginning of 2011 she was frequently touted as a sure bet to be the first female general manager in Major League Baseball.

Ng was born in Indianapolis, but grew up in Queens, Long Island, and New Jersey. Her parents—dad, Jin, a financial analyst, and mom, Virginia, a banker—might have preferred the eldest of their five daughters to choose a more traditional profession such as law or business, but young Kim had other ideas. She loved sports—stickball, tennis, skating, and skiing were her activities of choice. Although she lived just a stone's throw from Shea Stadium while growing up, it was the Yankees who captured her heart. "They were pretty good in the '70s and '80s," notes Ng. She went on to play infield for the University of Chicago's softball team.

It is somewhat serendipitous that Ng has emerged as one of the top-ranking women in professional baseball. With her newly minted bachelor's degree in public policy, Ng applied for a variety of jobs at different sports organizations and landed an internship as a research assistant at the Chicago White Sox in 1991. Computers and data analysis were just beginning to gain traction, and Ng was good at it. After three or four months, Ng had impressed the organization so much that management offered her a full-time entry-level job, where she did everything from entering scouting reports to operating the radar gun. She showed a propensity for numbers and soon took over the team's salary arbitration duties. She was later promoted to assistant director of baseball operations.

"I never thought about working in operations for a sports organization. I thought that marketing or sports information would be more likely areas," says Ng in a soft but confident voice. "I just didn't think there were opportunities in operations for someone like me until I went to the White Sox."

Then-White Sox GM Dan Evans was impressed by Ng's analytical ability and attention to detail. Her strong work ethic and dedication to delve into whatever she was working on were traits that convinced Evans that Ng had the makings of a future top baseball executive. "Kim is one of the most inquisitive minds I've ever been around," says Evans, president and chief executive officer of Paragon Sports International, a Pasadena, California-based sports management firm. "She asked really solid questions as to why we were doing certain things. As a result, it made me rethink some of my beliefs and procedures. You could tell that she was going to go far because she had that combination of street smarts, book smarts, and stick-to-it-ive-ness that you can't teach."

Her persistence and drive have kept Ng in a game where the work of scouting, drafting, and developing ballplayers has traditionally been left to men, typically those who played the game at the highest levels. But a sea change in baseball has given rise to GMs without playing experience. Neither Boston Red Sox GM Theo Epstein nor Texas Rangers GM Jon Daniels laced up cleats at the professional level. They are more academic than athletic. Ng believes that the advent of the Internet and the massive amount of readily available statistics and information has leveled the playing field for anyone—man or woman—to get involved with the game. No longer do you have to be an insider to get the inside scoop.

"She's here because of how good she is and how hard she works," says Dodgers GM Ned Colletti.

Her rise to the top could be attributed to the job she took in 1997 as director of waivers and records at the American League office in New York. What might have seemed an odd career move away from baseball operations proved to be just the stepping-stone Ng needed. At the league office, she approved all player transactions and contracts and helped American League general managers interpret and apply major league rules. The job afforded her tremendous opportunity to meet and network with baseball's upper echelon. That's how she met Yankees GM Brian Cashman, who hired her a year later, making her, at the time, the youngest assistant general manager in Major

League Baseball. Under Cashman, she assumed a number of responsibilities, including handling the team's arbitration cases.

Arbitration is an arcane process in which players whose contracts are up and who have at least three, but less than six, years of major league service time can take their team to a hearing to determine their salary. In that hearing, a panel must choose either the player's figure or the team's figure, with no wiggle room in between. Consequently, it behooves both parties to reach a compromise agreement before the case goes to a hearing.

Placing a dollar figure on a human being is not an exact science. While a player's stats can be compared to others playing the same position with the same number of years of service, other factors play into the equation; leadership skills, personality, and attitude should also be considered according to Ng. "I think the intangibles play a big role in whether we want a guy. You never want a bad guy in your clubhouse,"

JUAN OCAMPO/LOS ANGELES DODGERS

The Dodgers players tower over the 5-foot-2-inch Ng as she listens during a Spring Training meeting in Vero Beach, Florida. Ng would like to see more women and minorities enter baseball's ranks.

she says. The Yankees, she notes, wanted very team-oriented players who took care of themselves and handled issues in the clubhouse, thereby making the manager's job easier. "Statistics can tell a story, but they can also lead you down the wrong path," says Ng. "I think that the differences between what you see visually and what you see on paper is very interesting. It makes you look at the game differently."

Ng's uncanny talent for evaluating a player's worth and affixing an appropriate price tag led her to successfully negotiate the contracts of Derek Jeter, Mariano Rivera, and Paul O'Neill, among others, which helped build a team that won three championships. During her four seasons with the Yankees, the team advanced to the World Series four times, winning the World Championship three times.

Ng cites being a part of the 1998 Yankees, who won 114 regular-season games en route to a World Championship, as one of her all-time greatest career moments. "That team embodied a lot of ideals that I believe in—strength in unity, team chemistry, and unselfishness. They were the sum of the parts," says Ng. "That is one of the greatest things you get from sports, is understanding what you can achieve with people who have the same goal in mind. That team did not revolve around any one guy; it was a true team."

In 2002 her former White Sox mentor Dan Evans, then Dodgers GM, lured Ng away from the Yankees to become his deputy as the Dodgers' vice president and assistant general manager. Again, handling arbitration cases has been her forte. In nine winters of handling all arbitration cases for the Dodgers, she has gone to a hearing with just two players: National League Cy Young Award winner Eric Gagne in 2004, and reliever Joe Beimel in 2007. Ng won both cases.

Facing a daunting list of nine potential arbitration cases in 2010—including four former All-Stars, two Gold Glove winners, and two players who finished in the top 10 in the NL Most Valuable Player voting in 2009—Ng reached amicable agreements with all nine players, all before the deadline for teams and players to exchange salary figures. Although three of those players were given two-year deals, Ng signed all nine players for a total of $31.95 million in 2010 salary.

"She's one of the best around," says Colletti. "[Handling the 2010 arbitration cases] was a monstrous task and she came out of it and put the organization in a very good position. It was the best job I've ever seen anyone do."

Prior to the 2011 season, Ng successfully avoided arbitration and signed all three eligible players—Chad Billingsley, Hong-Chih Kuo, and James Loney.

In addition to handling arbitration cases, Ng's duties include negotiating free agent contracts, conducting trade talks, overseeing pro scouting—the department that compiles the information Colletti uses to make decisions on trades or free agent signings—and running Campo Las Palmas, the Dodgers' academy in the Dominican Republic. During the season, a typical day for Ng includes getting an update on the organization's minor league teams, dealing with transactions (placing a player on the disabled list, calling up a replacement, etc.), and making calls to player agents. The rest of the time is spent evaluating players. As she watches from the stands, any number of questions might go through Ng's mind: What does the club need? How can this player improve? How do these players fit into the future?

In 2011, Ng entered her 20th year—12 as an assistant GM—in professional baseball. Her peers say she has paid her dues and has done everything to prove that she is capable of leading a major league team. Still, she keeps getting passed over for the top job—the Dodgers in 2005, the Mariners in 2008 and, most recently, the Padres in 2009.

Still, Ng, 42, does not like to dwell on the fact that she is a rare breed among the rarified baseball elite. She is only one of two women—Jean Afterman who succeeded Ng at the New York Yankees is the other—who currently hold the title of assistant GM, the highest baseball operations position ever held by a woman. What's more, there is no other female within striking distance.

(*Left to right*): Ng, Dodgers General Manager Ned Colletti, and Assistant General Manager, Amateur and International Scouting Logan White await the start of Opening Day in Milwaukee. Ng is one of the few Asian Americans in the game. Bill Singer, a Mets front office employee, made racially insensitive remarks to Ng at the 2003 Winter Meetings and was later fired.

"You have to be persistent to break into this game, and you have to be really good to stay in this game," says Ng. "That takes a daily level of commitment."

Ng's colleagues say that it's just a matter of time before she gets tapped for the top job.

"As I told her [after the Padres interview]: 'This is no longer up to you. You're prepared. You just need the opportunity and someone to believe in you and give you a chance,'" says Colletti. "It's beyond her control at this point. She's done everything she can to put herself in that position. She deserves the opportunity and it will take someone willing to give her the opportunity to make it happen." ■

Sources

The information for this article came primarily from the author's interviews with Ned Colletti, Dan Evans, and Kim Ng.

The Pacific Coast League Ballparks of Los Angeles

Ron Selter

After the Pacific Coast League (PCL) began operations in 1903, it would operate as a virtually independent entity for most of its first 55 years of existence. During that era, the league had at least one and, in most seasons, two franchises in the Los Angeles area that occupied eight different ballparks.

CHUTES PARK (WASHINGTON GARDENS)

Chutes Park was located in a mixed residential area about three miles south of downtown Los Angeles on Washington Boulevard between Grand Avenue and Main Street. Several electric trolley lines served the ballpark, as the site had hosted various amusements, including a beer garden, theater, zoo, and traveling circuses since 1876. The ballpark derived its name from the previous tenant's Chute-the-Chutes thrill ride, though it was also known as Washington Gardens, and the two names were used interchangeably. In December 1900, a simple wooden sports facility was built for baseball and football games. That month a California Winter League game was played, the park's first use for baseball. The Los Angeles franchise of the Califor-

nia League (a predecessor of the PCL) played here during the 1901 and 1902 seasons. Starting in 1903, Chutes Park served as the home field of the PCL's Los Angeles Angels for eight seasons.

The ballpark had several unique characteristics. In the wooden grandstand, only the diagonal section behind home plate and the third base section were roofed, while the first base section was uncovered. A standing-room-only catwalk stood behind the left-field fence and, unlike previous Los Angeles ballparks, Chutes Field had an infield of grass. In 1905 bleachers were added down both foul lines, raising the seating capacity to about 6,000. When the PCL expanded from four to six teams in 1909, one of the new clubs was the Vernon Tigers, which shared Chutes Park during the 1909 and 1910 seasons. Late in 1910, Chutes Park was dismantled and construction was begun for a larger ballpark to be known as Washington Park.

WASHINGTON PARK

Washington Park opened on March 28, 1911 and would become the best-known ballpark in Los Angeles over

A Pacific Coast League game at Washington Park circa 1910.

the next 15 years. Located at Hill Street and Washington Boulevard, Washington Park occupied most of the former site of Chutes Park. The Los Angeles Angels and the Vernon Tigers jointly owned the ballpark, using it as their primary home field.

Washington Park initially seated about 8,000, and consisted of a single-deck roofed grandstand that extended beyond both first and third bases, and wooden bleachers adjacent to the grandstand, down the first and third base lines. The grandstand and home plate were located in the northwest corner of the park, making left field the sun field for afternoon games. After the 1911 season, both foul line bleachers were extended and a section of wooden bleachers added beyond fair right field that connected to the first base bleachers, which increased capacity to about 12,000.

Washington Park's dimensions were, for its time, generous: Left field was 350 feet from home plate and center field was 460, although the right-field distance was 335. To make the pitchers even happier, the left-field and center-field fences were 20 feet high. Sometime between 1911 and 1920, however, the left-field distance from home plate was increased to 375 feet. The first home run over the left-field fence was not hit until October 12, 1920 (by Pete Schneider). No one ever hit a ball over the distant center-field fence. As one would suspect, Washington Park's dimensions made it a poor hitters park. The available data (for the 1918 and 1921–25 seasons) show that Washington Park was last in the PCL in home runs and batting average. The home run park factor was 45, which means that home runs at Washington Park were less than half of the average PCL ballpark.

In late September 1925, Wrigley Field in Los Angeles opened. The Los Angeles Angels' new ballpark was, for its time, a modern marvel, far larger and more fan friendly than Washington Park. The Vernon Tigers did not move to Wrigley Field as their 1925 home season had ended, and by the 1926 season, the Tigers had moved to San Francisco, reborn as the Mission Reds. Shortly after Washington Park's last ballgame was played on September 27, 1925, it was demolished. (The full history of Wrigley Field is covered in this journal by a separate article by Jim Gordon.)

VERNON PARK I

As mentioned above, when the Vernon Tigers joined the PCL in 1909, they built a new ballpark in an industrial suburb four miles southeast of downtown Los Angeles. Located at East 38th Street and Santa Fe Avenue in the city of Vernon, the wooden ballpark had a capacity of only about 4,000, and was not the regular home park of either the Tigers or the Angels. Instead, during the 1909 and 1910 seasons, the two clubs used Vernon Park I for one weekday home game and for the morning game of Sunday/holiday doubleheaders. For the 1911 and 1912 seasons, the weekday games were eliminated. The rationale for this complicated arrangement is not clear, but it may have been due to Vernon's more lenient laws on the consumption of alcohol.

The exact dimensions of Vernon Park I are not known; however, home run data provides insight into the park's approximate dimensions. With home runs averaging 1.03 per game in the 192 games played at the park over five plus seasons, Vernon Park I was the Coors Field of its time. By contrast, home runs at the other seven PCL ballparks averaged much less: 0.34 per game. Based on the home run data, ballpark researcher Larry Zuckerman has estimated the left-field dimension to be 290 feet, perhaps less, center field 440 feet, and right field 330 feet.

A squabble with the City of Vernon moved the Tigers (and the Angels) to a nearby community for the 1913 season, and Vernon Park I sat idle for the next two seasons. On July 9, 1915, the Tigers returned, sharing the ballpark with the Angels for the remainder of the season, after which Vernon Park I was dismantled.

VENICE PARK

After the close of the 1912 season, the Vernon Tigers moved 20 miles west to the seaside community of Venice (California, not Italy). Renamed the Venice Tigers, the club shared its new ballpark with the Angels, playing the morning games of split-site Sunday/holiday doubleheaders just as they had at Vernon Park I during the two previous seasons. Venice Park, located at Washington Boulevard (now Abbot Kinney) and Virginia Avenue (now Venice Boulevard), consisted of a grandstand that seated 3,000 and bleachers that seated 4,000.

The ballpark's configuration would be familiar to those who have attended Little League games. All of the curved outfield fences were the same distance from home plate, 325 feet, according to the *Los Angeles Times*. The outfield fences were three feet high, topped by a six-foot wire screen. This screen permitted fans who drove to the ballpark to view the game from the comfort of their automobiles, which could be parked just outside the left-field and right-field fences. As access was controlled, they must have been charged for the privilege.

Venice Park proved to be far below average as a hitters park. The batting park factors for the 78 PCL games played there between 1913 and 1915 were as follows:

Batting Average	87
Slugging	89
Doubles/AB	107
Triples/AB	81
Home Runs/AB	64

If all of the outfield fences at Venice Park were actually 325 feet from home plate, however, these batting park factors are unbelievable. How could the smallest park in the PCL be far below average in both batting average and home runs? If there was no point in the ballpark farther than 325 feet, how could the triples park factor be as high as 81? Could the actual dimensions have been greater than the 325 feet reported in the *Times*? A study was made of the ballpark and its site. The accompanying diagram, by Larry Zuckerman, using 325 feet as the outfield distance, shows 25 to 30 feet available between the center-field fence and the southern limit of the property, the tracks of the Pacific Electric Railway. Note that center field was the limiting condition for the size of the ballpark. Based on the batting data for the park and by moving home plate five feet closer to the backstop, the estimated outfield

dimensions become 355 feet to all fields. Such dimensions are far more compatible with the batting park factors than the reported 325 feet to all fields.

Poor attendance at Venice Park prompted the Tigers and Angels to return to Vernon in July 1915.

VERNON PARK II

Vernon Park II was ready for the Tigers and the Angels in time for the 1916 season. The new wooden ballpark included a grandstand salvaged from Venice Park and seated about 10,000. Also known as Maier Park, for Tigers owner Eddie Maier, Vernon Park II was used by the Tigers and Angels for five seasons. As at Venice Park, only the morning games of Sunday and holiday doubleheaders were played here. The estimated dimensions were left field 372 feet, center field 395 feet, and right field 315 feet. The right field dimension seems reachable until one considers that the 10-foot wooden fence was topped with a 20-foot wire screen. Whereas Vernon Park I was the Coors Field of its time, Vernon Park II was a pitchers' paradise. In the 110 games played there, only six home runs were ever hit. Over the 1916–19 seasons, Vernon Park II shows an average of 0.05 home runs per game compared to the average of the rest of the PCL ballparks' 0.39 home runs per game.

Midway through the 1920 season, with attendance poor, the Angels and Tigers decided to discontinue using Vernon Park II as a secondary ballpark and thereafter played all of their home games at Washington Park. Through 1925, the Tigers continued to use the Vernon ballpark for spring training. Vernon Park II was torn down sometime in the 1930s, and the site is now occupied by Hannibal Industries, Inc.

GILMORE STADIUM

In 1938, the PCL's San Francisco Mission Reds franchise was purchased by Hollywood interests headed by restaurateur Bob Cobb, and the team, to be called the Hollywood Stars, moved to Los Angeles. The Stars arranged to share the Angels' iconic ballpark, Wrigley Field, for the 1938 season, anticipating that their new ballpark in Hollywood, Gilmore Field, (named for Earl B. Gilmore, the owner of Gilmore Oil, Gilmore Stadium, and the site of

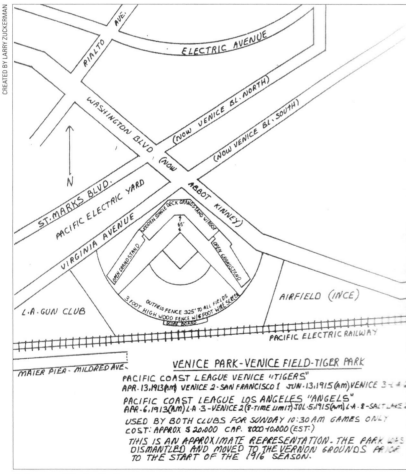

A diagram of Venice Park.

Gilmore Field was the home of the Hollywood Stars from 1939 to 1957. Note how close to the infield the stands were. Home plate was 34 feet from the backstop.

Gilmore Field) would be ready in time for the following season. By April 1939, however, construction was not quite finished. Fortunately, close by was Gilmore Stadium, a football and midget auto racing venue. Gilmore Stadium, an oval steel-and-concrete structure with a capacity of 18,500, was quickly modified for baseball in time for the Stars' first home games. A wire screen was erected behind home plate to serve as the backstop. There were no dugouts. The playing field was laid out with the left-field foul line roughly parallel with the western sideline of the gridiron, producing a left-field dimension of 350 feet. The right-field dimension was a rather short 270 feet, and the right-field power alley (22.5 degrees) 300 feet. To prevent cheap home runs, a pole was placed behind the fence in right center (325 feet from home plate). Any ball hit into the stands to the right of that pole was a ground-rule double. Because of the stadium's oval shape, the left-field distances increased rapidly away from the foul line. All in all, it was an oddly shaped playing field for baseball; left field, with an average distance of 393 feet, was deeper than center field (380 feet) and the right-field average distance was quite short (291 feet).

The Stars hosted the Portland Beavers for a seven-game series, winning four of the seven games, the only baseball played at Gilmore Stadium. The games provided interesting results, the stadium proving quite popular with the hitters. The Stars posted a team batting average of .333, while Portland hit .317. Fifteen home runs were hit over the seven games, a high number for the PCL of 1939. Overall the batting park factors at Gilmore Stadium were impressive:

Batting Average	112
On-Base	112
Slugging	131
Doubles	174
Triples	119
Home Runs	211

GILMORE FIELD

The majority owner of the Stars was Bob Cobb, owner of the Brown Derby restaurant in Hollywood and namesake of the Cobb salad. Several movie stars were shareholders, among them Gene Autry, Gary Cooper, Bing Crosby, and Bob Hope. When Gilmore Field opened on May 2, 1939, some four weeks into the season, many movie stars attended the game to much fanfare. Cobb's wife, actress Gail Patrick, threw out the first pitch.

The ballpark was located on Fairfax Avenue on the west (500 feet west of Gilmore's Farmers Market), between Beverly Boulevard and Third Street. Gilmore Field, seating about 12,000, was an intimate ballpark. Its backstop was only 34 feet behind home plate and the distance from first/third base to the grandstand was 24 feet. No surprise, the foul area was very small. Gilmore Field, one of the first ballparks to be built with lights, consisted of a roofed steel frame and wood single-deck grandstand and open bleachers down both foul lines that reached nearly to the left-field and right-field corners. The playing field was almost exactly symmetrical with left-field/right-field dimensions of 335 feet, left-center/right-center 387, and a center-field dimension of 407. The left-field and right-field fences were wood, 10 feet high, and aligned at 90 degrees to the foul lines. There was a 10-foot high center-field diagonal fence with an 18-foot scoreboard. The average size of left field/right field was 352 and center field was 403. The overall park size of Gilmore Field was 369; by comparison Wrigley Field, the top PCL ballpark for home runs, was 358, and the league average was 362.

Gilmore Field in 1939 was not a good ballpark for hitters. The Stars and their opponents combined for 8.8 runs per game at home vs. 10.8 runs/game on the road. The batting park factors for 1939 were:

Runs/G	84
Batting Average	92
On-Base	89
Slugging	101
Doubles*	101
Triples*	180
Home Runs*	124
BB/Game	71

* Per AB; batting data compiled from box scores in the *Los Angeles Times*

This is a curious result: The park factors for all categories of extra base hits and slugging were above 100, yet runs, batting average, and on-base were markedly below average. All this for a ballpark that had very little foul area, and had the same park size as today's major league ballparks. Two factors contributed to this outcome. First, in 1939 Gilmore Field was the second largest ballpark in the PCL—only Seals Stadium in San Francisco was larger. Second, the billboards mounted on the left-field and right-field fences were very light in color. (They appear to be nearly white in black and white photos.) The billboards extended from the left-field line to nearly dead center, providing a very poor background against right-handed pitchers. This is likely the reason that walks per game were 40 percent higher in road games than in games at Gilmore Field. Gilmore Field was home to the Stars through the 1957 season, when Major League Baseball came to Los Angeles. It was demolished in 1958 and is now the site for part of CBS Television City.

The PCL's tradition of one, and typically two, franchises in the Los Angeles area ended when the Brooklyn Dodgers moved to town after the 1957 season, but not before the league's ballparks had initiated generations of fans to competitive baseball. ■

Sources

Ballparks of Los Angeles, And Some of The History Surrounding Them, by Lauren Ted Zuckerman, 1996, in SABR Minor League History Research Journal Volume I, August 1996.

Los Angeles Times-box scores for games played at Venice Park for 1913–15.

Lawrence S. Ritter, *Lost Ballparks*, Penguin Books, New York, NY, 1992.

Los Angeles' Wrigley Field
"The Finest Edifice in the United States"

James Gordon

Chicago's Wrigley Field, known worldwide, is considered a national treasure. Much less known is its Southern California counterpart. Los Angeles' Wrigley Field was built in the exuberant Roaring Twenties and demolished at the end of the turbulent sixties. Both its birth and demise echo the spirit of the times. The ballpark lived through the Depression, World War II, the postwar baseball boom, the decline of minor league baseball and a brief renaissance as a major-league ballpark. The history of Wrigley is intermingled with that of the City of Los Angeles. It hosted the fiercest rivalry in minor league baseball between the Pacific Coast League (PCL) Angels and Hollywood Stars as well as other baseball, boxing, football, high school and a myriad of community events. And this being Los Angeles, the ballpark appears in many motion pictures.

The story begins in 1921, a few years after William K. Wrigley Jr. became principal owner Chicago Cubs, when he acquired the Los Angeles Angels of the PCL. After a dispute over parking at Washington Park, Wrigley decided to erect his own ballpark. Promising local fans a venue of major-league luxury, Wrigley commissioned architect Zachary Taylor Davis, who had designed Cubs Park (as Chicago's Wrigley Field was then called) and Comiskey Park. Following Wrigley's instructions to pattern the design after Cubs Park, Davis used iron and steel construction and designed a covered, double-decked grandstand from foul pole to foul pole, rarities in the minor leagues at that time. Built at a cost of $1,500,000, six times the cost of Cubs Park, it was dubbed "Wrigley's Million Dollar Palace." Seating about 18,500 in the grandstand and 2,000 in the bleachers, the ballpark was slightly larger than its Chicago counterpart. In later years the left-field wall was planted with ivy to further emulate that ballpark.

THE EARLY YEARS

On September 29, 1925, a crowd of 18,000 attended Wrigley Field's dedication. A month later, *The Sporting News* published an effusive review of the new ballpark. Noting that there was not a sign to mar its beauty, and with an elevator to an observation platform with views from the mountains to the ocean, the newspaper found Wrigley Field to be in a class by itself architecturally, a "real monument to the national game." Major league baseball owners, it argued, would not be able to boast of their parks when they saw this one and would have "to acknowledge that Wrigley has erected the finest baseball edifice in the United States." Observing that the plasticity of today's baseball had caused a cry for larger playing fields, the newspaper reported that Wrigley Field's was among the largest. Home runs have been hit, it acknowledged, but those batters earned them. (It missed, however, the shortness of the power alleys.) Cubs Park may be excellent, *The Sporting News* concluded, "but the Angels have a better one."[1]

The ballpark's first full season was eventful. It began on January 15, 1926, with dedication of the clock tower by Commissioner Kennesaw Mountain Landis. On March 5, the Cubs became the first major-league team to play in Wrigley Field, losing the opener of a three-game series to the Angels. During the regular season, the Hollywood Stars, newly relocated from Salt Lake City, shared the ballpark with the Angels, an arrangement lasting through 1935. The silent comedy movie *Babe Comes Home*, starring Babe Ruth as Los Angeles Angels' outfielder Babe Dugan and Anna Q. Nilsson as his love interest, became the first of many films shot at Wrigley Field. The Angels capped the ballpark's inaugural season by winning the PCL pennant.

In early May 1930, Des Moines of the Western League had introduced lights and night baseball. The Sacramento Senators became the first PCL team to use lights on June 10. The first night game at Wrigley was played on July 22, with the Angels defeating Sacramento, 5–4, in 11 innings before 17,000 excited fans.[2] Southern California had a vibrant winter league featuring major leaguers, PCL players, and usually a team from the Negro Leagues. For the 1930–31 season, the league split into an "official" Southern California Winter League and the Winter League. Playing at Wrigley Field, the Philadelphia Royal Giants participated in the

Expansion of Wrigley Field to more than 40,000 fans by fully enclosing it and adding parking was studied by the Los Angeles to help attract the Brooklyn Dodgers to the city.

Winter League, the first time since Commissioner Allen T. Burns's ban of 1916 went into effect that a Negro League team was able to play ball in a PCL park [3]

In 1932 the New York Giants became the first major-league team to use Wrigley as their spring training headquarters.[4] On September 6, 1933, with the Angels on their way to the pennant, the all-time PCL attendance record of 24,695 was set for a night double header.[5] But by 1934, despite the Angels posting the best record in PCL history, the Depression was hitting Los Angeles hard and attendance was declining. The Angels and Stars drew less than 260,000 in 1934 compared to almost 400,000 the previous year. Hollywood had been losing money for several years, and in 1935 owner Bill Lane prepared to move the franchise to San Diego. The Stars went out in style, ending the season at Wrigley with a doubleheader against the San Francisco Missions. Actor Joe E. Brown amused the fans by umpiring in the second game and then pitching for the Missions with two out in the seventh inning to fan composer Harry Ruby while the rest of the team sat by the mound.[6] The 1938 season saw a reincarnation of the Hollywood Stars when the Missions moved to Los Angeles and played in Wrigley for a year while awaiting the completion of their new ballpark, Gilmore Field, across town. Thus began a local rivalry enhanced by the competition between the west side and the central city/east side of Los Angeles.

From its beginnings, Wrigley Field had served as a community resource for high school athletics, semipro football, charitable events, and boxing. On January 15, 1939, the NFL champion New York Giants beat the All-American Stars in the first Pro Bowl before 20,000.[7] Wrigley was used because the Coliseum Commission would not allow professional sports. The first of two Heavyweight Championship fights was held at Wrigley on April 17, 1939. Joe Louis knocked out Jack Roper before a crowd estimated between 23,000 and 30,000.[8]

After the 1941 season, major league baseball almost came to Wrigley when Don Barnes, St. Louis Browns president, orchestrated a covert deal to move the team to Los Angeles, with the Angels relocating to Long Beach as a Browns farm team. Barnes presented his proposal on December 9 at the Winter Meetings. Although other reasons were cited, the American League unanimously voted against it because of the Pearl Harbor attack two days earlier.[9] The *Los Angeles Times* reported, "That the old gag about bringing major league baseball to Los Angeles was reborn at the American League meeting, but it lived a brief life."[10] The fans continued their support of minor league baseball, and attendance Wrigley Field would prove to be strong as World War II raged on. Because of the fear of a Japanese attack, the Army declared a restriction on night lighting along the Pacific Coast from Canada to Mexico and as far inland as 150 miles in August 1942.[11] The Angels played their last night game on August 7, as fans stood and held lighted matches during the sounding of Taps and the singing of the national anthem.[12]

GLORY DAYS FOR THE PACIFIC COAST LEAGUE

With the war over, in 1946 crowds flocked to the ballpark. The Angels and San Francisco Seals battled for the pennant throughout 1947, finishing in a tie. Home attendance that season had reached 622,485, the all-time record, and nearly 23,000 fans jammed Wrigley for the one-game playoff, with thousands more turned away. With no score in the bottom of the eighth and the bases loaded, Angels outfielder Clarence Maddern hit the first pitch over the left-field wall.[13] Fans have called this the greatest game in Wrigley history.

Near the end of that season, the Angels had televised their first game. However, as the major leagues began televising, interest in the minors declined and many leagues folded. To spur interest and increase broadcasting revenue, the Angels televised more games but attendance further declined. Despite such issues, local fans enjoyed memorable baseball moments, primarily between the Angels and Stars. On August 7, 1952, 23,497 fans attended a Stars-Angels game at Wrigley, the largest paid crowd for a PCL game in Los Angeles.[14] Three day later, Hollywood swept a double header before 17,517 fans, who rioted after umpire Ed Runge called Stars catcher Jim Mangan safe at the plate in the 10th inning of the first game. Cushions were thrown and a fan charged onto the field. After the game, another fan attacked Runge and wrestled him to the ground. The second game was played with 35 extra policemen under the personal direction of Chief William Parker.[15]

The issue of how to bring major league baseball to Los Angeles persisted. No team would come without a major-league stadium, and nobody would create one without a team. Proposals were considered to upgrade Wrigley Field's capacity to 40,000 or 50,000, but, these entailed condemnation of private housing and businesses and could not be accomplished quickly. Although he promoted upgrades, Philip K. Wrigley was not interested in covering the cost. He quietly hired Bill Veeck to sell the ballpark, but Veeck failed to find a buyer at a satisfactory price.[16]

But the local market for major league baseball was demonstrated during a 1955 spring training series between the New York Giants and Cleveland Indians meeting again after the 1954 World Series. In the first game, Willie Mays hit three home runs before 17,893. The next day 24,434 fans packed Wrigley to see Dusty Rhodes slug a pinch-hit homer and Willie Mays make an exceptional catch in deep center field.[17]

THE END OF AN ERA

In August 1955, after Walter O'Malley announced that the Dodgers would not play at Ebbets Field after 1957, Los Angeles city officials began working to attract the Dodgers. On February 21, 1957, the Los Angeles baseball world exploded when the Dodgers announced that they had bought Wrigley Field and the Angels for $3,000,000 plus their Fort Worth franchise.[18] The Angels' final season at Wrigley Field seemed anti-climatic as the anticipation of major-league baseball permeated the city. The Angels fared poorly; the fans' primary interest was Steve Bilko's pursuit of Tony Lazzeri's home run record. The last PCL games were played in Wrigley, with San Diego sweeping a double header before 6,712. During the first game, the club received anonymous calls that there was a bomb in the dugout. The players were moved to the bullpens until the police checked the dugouts. However, the game was not delayed nor was the crowd informed.[19]

The Dodgers' announcement that they would move to Los Angeles for the 1958 season came on October 8, 1957, one day after the Los Angeles City Council approved the transfer of Chavez Ravine to the Dodgers in exchange for Wrigley, with the idea of expanding the old park while the new one was built.[20] Seating could be increased to 28,000 or 29,000 by enclosing the outfield with double-decked stands, the bleachers would be moved back towards Avalon Boulevard, and a 12-foot screen added in left. Then, the "soap opera" of where

Wrigley Field's 150-foot office tower housed 13-foot clocks on its four sides that could be seen from all parts of the city, making the ballpark the iconic symbol of baseball in Los Angeles for more than 35 years. The dedication plaque reads: "This tower was erected by W. K. Wrigley, Jr., in honor of the baseball players who gave or risked their lives in defence of their country in the Great World War."

the Dodgers would play began, oscillating among Wrigley, the Coliseum, and the Rose Bowl. Expansion of Wrigley was reduced to 27,000, 26,000, and then to 24,000. Wrigley Field was found lacking; it had too few seats, too small a playing area, terrible parking, poor public transportation and it was situated in a declining neighborhood. Baseball Commissioner Ford Frick called it a "Cow Pasture." He didn't want to see Babe Ruth's record of 60 home runs broken there.[21] On January 17 the Dodgers and the Coliseum Commission agreed on a two-year contract.[22] There would be no major league baseball at Wrigley Field—at least not yet.

Now owned by the city, and with the PCL Angels relocated to Spokane, Wrigley Field was used for various events. On August 18, 1958, Wrigley held its second Heavyweight Championship fight with Floyd Patterson retaining the title over Roy Harris before a crowd of 17,000.[23] In 1959, the television show *Home Run Derby* began filming and aired for 26 weeks.[24] The show was a nine-inning contest between two of the top sluggers of the era, providing the inspiration for the Home Run Derby now part of the All-Star Game festivities.

Then, in December 1960, the American League awarded an expansion franchise to Gene Autry christened the Los Angeles Angels. They were to play one year at Wrigley and four years at Dodger Stadium. The Los Angeles press criticized O'Malley for not sharing the Coliseum and for forcing an unfair lease upon the popular Autry. Some of their comments related to Wrigley. Sid Ziff predicted rough sledding with parking conditions that were prehistoric, rundown neighborhood, with $75,000 has-beens. Mel Durslag called

Wrigley "an obsolete concrete shack."[25] Al Wolf said "Mob scenes at Wrigley Field, with the Coliseum empty, will arouse resentment among fans who believe O'Malley maneuvered the Angels into that small, park-ingless park."[26] He added, "It is unfortunate that the club must open for business on short notice in an abandoned minor league park." Nevertheless, the City undertook renovations at a cost of $275,000 to Wrigley: fresh paint inside and out, replacement of the sod and the seats, improved restrooms, refurbishment of the tower offices, and installation of radio and TV booths in an enlarged press box.

Wrigley Field hosted its first regular season major league game on April 27, 1961, after opening ceremonies featuring Commissioner Ford Frick and Ty Cobb.[27] Sportswriters predicted the expansion team would be lucky to win 50 games, but the Angels won 70. General manager Fred Haney had played at Wrigley from 1929 through 1934 and managed the Hollywood Stars from 1949 to 1952. He was familiar with the park and structured the Angels accordingly. Thus the Angels were an excellent home team in their first season, winning 46 games for a .561 percentage.

The characteristics that made Wrigley a home-run paradise are important. The power alleys were a short 345 feet; the foul poles were a respectable 338.5 feet and 340 feet, and center field was a robust 412 feet. However, the fences were angled toward the infield more than 9 degrees. Thus the distance to the wall decreased as one moved away from the foul lines. The minimum distance to the wall was about 335 feet in left and right, making the power alleys, left and right, and left-center and right-center easy distances. Wrigley Field obliterated the minor league record for home runs with 248, a record that lasted until 1996 when 271 homers were hit at mile-high Coors Field. How good a hitters park was Wrigley? The home run park factor was 180. Almost twice as many homers were hit at Wrigley than at the average American League ballpark.

On October 1 the Angels' Steve Bilko hit the last home run at Wrigley Field, a pinch-hit smash over the left-field wall with two out in the ninth inning.[28]

After the Angels departed for their four-year stint in the Coliseum, Wrigley Field staggered on for 7½ years as a venue for local events. Its final highlight came on May 26, 1963, when a crowd of more than 35,000 attended the largest civil rights rally ever held in Los Angeles, where Martin Luther King Jr. said, "We want to be free whether we're in Birmingham or Los Angeles."[29] August 1965 was a traumatic time in Los Angeles as civil unrest broke out and spread over the South Central area, culminating in what would be known as the "Watts Riots." Many federal, state, city, and private commissions analyzed the causes of the unrest. One contributing factor was a lack of long-promised community services including parks, health and senior citizen facilities, and pressure built to have Wrigley Field better serve the community. In 1966, Wrigley was converted for soccer as arguments continued over final plans and funding. Finally, in March 1969, Wrigley Field was demolished to make way for the Gilbert W. Lindsay Community Center, which includes health facilities and a park with baseball fields still in use today. Wrigley Field had admirably served as a baseball and community sports center but its time had passed. Fond memories will always linger. ∎

Movies Filmed at Wrigley Field, Los Angeles

1927	Babe Comes Home	1949	It Happens Every Spring
1927	The Bush Leaguer	1951	Angels in the Outfield
1929	Fast Company	1951	Meet Danny Wilson
1932	Fireman Save My Child	1951	Rhubarb
1933	Elmer the Great	1953	The Kid from Left Field
1934	Death on the Diamond	1957	Fear Strikes Out
1935	Alibi Ike	1958	Damn Yankees

Compiled by the SABR Ballparks Committee

Notes

1. *The Sporting News*, 29 October 1925, 3.
2. *Los Angeles Times*, 23 July 1930, 1.
3. William F. McNeil, *The California Winter League – America's First Integrated Professional League*, McFarland & Company, 2008.
4. *Los Angeles Times*, 18 February 1932, A11.
5. *Los Angeles Times*, 7 September 1933, A9.
6. *Los Angeles Times*, 23 September 1935, A10.
7. *Los Angeles Times*, 16 January 1939, 21.
8. *Los Angeles Times*, 18 April 1939, 1.
9. *Chicago Daily Tribune*, 10 December 1941, 33.
10. *Los Angeles Times*, 10 December 1941, 10.
11. *Los Angeles Times*, 5 August 1942, 1.
12. *Los Angeles Times*, 8 August 1942, 11.
13. *Los Angeles Times*, 30 September 1947, 8.
14. *Los Angeles Times*, 8 August 1952, C1.
15. *Los Angeles Times*, 11 August 1952, C1.
16. Ned Cronin, *Los Angeles Times*, 8 February 1955, C3.
17. *Los Angeles Times*, 21 March 1955, C1.
18. Frank Finch, *Los Angeles Times*, 22 February 1957, 1.
19. Frank Finch, *Los Angeles Times*, 16 September 1957, C1.
20. Frank Finch, *Los Angeles Times*, 9 October 1957, 1.
21. *Los Angeles Times*, 12 January 1958, C1.
22. Frank Finch, *Los Angeles Times*, 18 January 1958, 1.
23. Paul Zimmerman, *Los Angeles Times*, 20 August 1958, C1.
24. Joe King, *The Sporting News*, 2 March 1960, 8.
25. *The Sporting News*, 14 December 1960, 7.
26. Al Wolf, *Los Angeles Times*, 19 December 1960, C1.
27. Braven Dyer, *Los Angeles Times*, 28 April 1961, C1.
28. Braven Dyer, *Los Angeles Times*, 2 October 1961, C7.
29. Los Angeles Public Library Photo Database, #00032099, 1963.

When the Angels and Stars Ruled Los Angeles

Richard E. Beverage

Long before the Dodgers moved to Los Angeles and the Angels sprang into being three years later, professional baseball and its rivalries had been a central part of the Southern California sports scene.

Los Angeles had its first team of professionals in 1890, then joined the fledgling California League in 1892. When this league folded after the 1893 season, Los Angeles was out of Organized Baseball until 1901 when it joined a new version of the California State League. That league evolved into the Pacific Coast League in 1903. The Loo Loos, as the club was first known, won that first pennant in a runaway. In a 211-game schedule they won 133 games and finished 27½ games ahead of second place Sacramento. Los Angeles won pennants in 1905, 1907, and 1908. Clearly, the club was the dominant force in the PCL.

But in a pattern that would repeat itself over the decades, the Angels/Loo Loos were not able to keep the city to themselves. In 1909 a new franchise began play in Vernon, a small industrial enclave located about nine miles from downtown Los Angeles. The Tigers played just a few games within the city limits of Vernon, mostly on Wednesday and the first game of the Sunday doubleheaders. The rest of their home games were played at Washington Park, the home of the Angels. After July 1, 1920 Vernon played all of its home games in Los Angeles.

Vernon remained in the Pacific Coast League through the 1925 season. The club did not draw well in either Vernon or Los Angeles. In 1913 the club moved to Venice, on the Western side of the city, but after two fruitless years there returned to its original site in Vernon. The Tigers were unable to build much of a fan base until 1918, when they finished in first place during a season truncated by World War I. Vernon repeated as champions in 1919 and 1920, but Tigers fortunes declined rapidly after a second place finish in 1922.

Meanwhile, the Angels had been purchased by William Wrigley Jr. in August 1921. Wrigley also was the majority stockholder of the Chicago Cubs, and although the two clubs were separate entities, common ownership gave the Angels a definite competitive advantage in Los Angeles. Relations with the Vernon owner, Edward Maier, began to worsen.

When Wrigley purchased land for a new ballpark in south central Los Angeles, he made it clear that the Vernon club could not play its games there. The Tigers would have to find a new home in 1926.

In November 1925 Maier sold the Vernon club to San Francisco interests who immediately announced that the franchise would be moved there. That presented an opportunity to Bill Lane, owner of the Salt Lake City Bees. The Bees had been a member of the PCL since 1915. It had not been a success either on the field or at the box office. Salt Lake had never finished higher than second place and usually hovered around the .500 mark. Attendance had never exceeded 160,000 annually and was generally near the bottom of the league. Even the second place team of 1925, which featured the play of Tony Lazzeri and his 60 home runs, could draw no more than 1,300 per game.

The other PCL owners had complained about the high cost of travel to Salt Lake and the small crowds. Lane moved to take advantage of the open territory in Los Angeles. He and Wrigley had become friends, and the Angels owner offered to share his new ballpark with Lane's club beginning in 1926. The club played in Los Angeles but took the label of the Hollywood Stars. Informally, it was generally called the Sheiks, after the Hollywood High School athletic teams.

The Sheiks/Stars were expected to be a pennant contender during their first year in Wrigley Field, but they finished in sixth place. The Angels won their first pennant under the Wrigley regime, finishing 10½ games ahead of Oakland. Surprisingly, Angels attendance declined to 273,202 in 1926 while the Hollywood club drew 212,830.

A few years previously the Chicago Cubs had introduced Ladies Day at Cubs Park. Female fans could enter the park at no charge on certain days of the week, and the policy seemed to stimulate attendance. The Angels adopted a similar policy in 1925. But then Mr. Wrigley went one better in 1928—every day was Ladies Day, not only for the Angels games but for

The trigger for the biggest brawl in Pacific Coast League history. Hollywood Stars outfielder Ted Beard slides spikes-high into Angels third baseman Murray Franklin, August 2, 1953.

Seconds later, Beard comes up swinging.

The brawl spreads as Angels catcher Al Evans winds up for a swing at umpire Joe Iacovetti.

Fortunately for Evans, the punch misses.

Evans moves to crowd Iacovetti.

Hollywood games as well! The other club owners protested the loss of all that revenue from games played in Los Angeles, and no voice was louder than Bill Lane's. He revolted against the policy and canceled Ladies Day on June 3. But the Angels continued to open the gates to the women at any time. Finally, Wrigley agreed to pay the other clubs their share of the lost revenue for some games and confine Ladies Day to weekdays only in 1929. But the damage to the friendship with Bill Lane had been done. No longer were the two men on friendly terms, and relations would deteriorate further over the next seven years.

Hollywood fortunes improved in 1928, and for the next four years the club enjoyed its greatest years in Los Angeles. The Sheiks won their first pennant in 1929 when they defeated the Mission club in a season-ending playoff and won again in 1930 when they routed the Angels in the playoffs. There were great players on those two Hollywood champions, most of whom are forgotten today. The best known was pitcher Frank Shellenback, who won 295 games during a Pacific Coast League career that spanned over 19 years. Other important Sheiks were Mickey Heath, Dave Barbee, Otis Brannan, Dudley Lee, John Bassler, and Cleo Carlyle. Except for Bassler, none of these men had significant major league careers, but they contributed greatly to the two pennant winners.

But Hollywood's fortunes declined after that, and Bill Lane's team won no more pennants in Wrigley Field. Both the Angels and the Stars were hit hard by the Depression, but Los Angeles fared better, partly because of their relationship with the Cubs, who supplied the Angels with good talent. They won the pennant in 1933 and then overwhelmed the PCL in 1934 with what may have been the greatest minor league team in history. It won both halves of a split season and a total of 137 games. No other Coast League club came close to that mark. Featured players that year were Frank Demaree, the league MVP, pitcher Fay Thomas, who posted a 28–4 record, Jim

Oglesby, Jimmy Reese, and Jigger Statz. The success of the Angels that year had a negative impact on attendance throughout the league, and no one was hurt as much as Hollywood. The core of fans that the Stars had developed over the years vanished. By 1935 Hollywood was in last place, and attendance was less than half of what it had been four years earlier. Bill Lane was getting desperate, and when the Angels informed him that his rent would increase to $10,000 in 1936, he decided to move his ballclub. The city of San Diego agreed to build him a new ballpark, and in February 1936 the Hollywood Stars became the San Diego Padres.

But after a two-year hiatus, the Stars would be back. At the end of the 1937 season the Mission club of San Francisco received permission from the league to move to Southern California and would play once again in Wrigley Field in 1938, with the stipulation that it would be for only one year. The second version of the Hollywood Stars would have to find their own ballpark for the 1939 season.

The Stars were sold to a group of Los Angeles investors, fronted by Bob Cobb, owner of the Brown Derby Restaurant chain. Shortly after the sale, Cobb announced the club would have its own ballpark. Gilmore Field, which actually *was* in the Hollywood area, was opened in May 1939, and the Stars finally had their own identity. Their move into new quarters created the heated rivalry between the Stars and Angels, who would play each other four series a year in what was frequently called the Heavenly Series.

During the early years of the rivalry, the Angels were especially dominant. They won pennants in 1938, 1943, and 1944 and finished one game out of first place in 1942. During those years the Angels took the season series by wide margins over the Stars in all but one year. Their close relationship with the Chicago Cubs provided them with an abundance of good players, a luxury that Hollywood did not have. The Stars were consistently a second division team in that period. They had no working agreement with a major league club until 1946, when they entered into a limited agreement with Pittsburgh. They finished above .500 for the first time under the Cobb regime and finished ahead of the Angels for the first time.

Los Angeles won the PCL pennant in 1947, but that was the last success the Angels would have for nine years. They slipped to third place in 1948 and then crashed to the cellar in 1949. Conversely, the Stars were beginning the greatest period in their history. They entered into a working agreement with the Dodgers and with the fine players supplied by Brook-

lyn won their first pennant in 1949 under the leadership of Fred Haney. Chuck Stevens, Jim Baxes, Irv Noren, and Frank Kelleher formed the core of that team, which many Stars fans thought was the best team in their history. Hollywood would win pennants in 1952 and 1953 and have the best record in the PCL during the 1950s. They took control of the Heavenly Series, winning 7 of the last 9 years.

Like Hollywood cowboys who thought the town wasn't big enough for both of them, the rivalry between these two clubs wasn't confined to the fans. The players didn't like each other. There were frequent incidents on the playing field which culminated on August 2, 1953. Fireworks broke out during the first game of a Sunday doubleheader before an overflow crowd. Frank Kelleher was hit by a pitch from Angels hurler Joe Hatten in the sixth inning and charged the mound, wrestling Hatten to the ground. Both benches cleared, punches were thrown, and Kelleher was ejected. Ted Beard was sent in to run for him, and when the next hitter singled to right field, Beard raced all the way to third where he slid into Angels third baseman Murray Franklin with spikes flying. Franklin came up swinging and both benches emptied once again. This was a real fight that inspired Police Chief William Parker, who was watching the game at home on television, to send a brigade of his officers to the park to break up the melee. Several players suffered cuts, bruises, and black eyes. When the fighting subsided, Beard, Franklin, Gene Handley, and Fred Richards were gone, and the reserve players were sent to the clubhouse for the remainder of the day. The donnybrook was featured in the national press, including the popular magazine *Life*.

Once it became known in late 1957 that the Dodgers were coming to Los Angeles, the Angels and Stars were doomed. The franchises were moved to Spokane and Salt Lake City, respectively, and the great rivalry was over, to be replaced by the Dodgers-Giants rivalry that the Eastern clubs brought with them. But fans of the old Pacific Coast League retain their fond memories of what was really a Heavenly Series. ■

Sources

Los Angeles Times, 1926–57.
Los Angeles Examiner, 1926–57.
Pacific Coast League Record Book, 1956–57.
Reach Official Baseball Guide, 1903–40.
Spaulding Official Baseball Guide, 1925–40.
Spaulding-Reach Official Baseball Guide, 1941.
Sporting Life, 1903–15.
The Sporting News, 1903–57.
The Sporting News Baseball Guide and Record Book, 1942–43.
The Sporting News Official Baseball Guide, 1944–58.

Rounding Third and Heading for Home

Fred Haney, L.A.'s Mister Baseball

James Gordon

Fred Girard Haney touched all the bases in a 65-year baseball career that led him from athletic stardom in high school to the general manager's office of the Los Angeles Angels. Along the way, he was a player, coach, scout, World Series winning manager, broadcaster, and general manager. On the field, Fred was a fierce competitor, disputing calls and plays with opponents, umpires, and fans. Off the field, he was a devoted family man, with many lifelong friends, and a heart for charitable works, particularly those involving youth, veterans, and baseball.

Haney was born April 25, 1898[1] in Bernalillo, New Mexico Territory, the fourth and youngest son of William J. and Frances (Fannie) Haney. After the family relocated to Los Angeles, Fred attended Polytechnic High School, where he was a four-year letterman in three sports. Named twice to the All-California Interscholastic football team,[2] holder of several swimming titles, a member of the water polo team, and the city's junior handball champion,[3] Haney was one of the first great high school athletes of Los Angeles.

MINOR LEAGUE BALL PLAYER

After a partial year with the Class B Portland Buckaroos, Haney tried out with the Pacific Coast League (PCL) Los Angeles Angels for the 1919 season and made the team. Haney is listed as being 5-foot-6 and 170 pounds; unsurprisingly, he acquired the nickname "Pudge." Despite his weight, he was fast and used his speed to advantage throughout his baseball career.

He made the Angels squad again in 1920 as a backup. That June he married his high school sweetheart, Florence, and the two began a life and baseball partnership that would last 57 years. Shortly after their wedding, Fred was sent to Omaha of the Class A Western League where he blossomed.[4] Haney was an aggressive negotiator and for the 1921 season achieved a clause that granted him one-fourth of the purchase price if he were sold to the majors. Haney's play at Omaha attracted the Detroit Tigers who purchased his contract for $5,000 and four players: Babe Herman, future Hall of Famer Heinie Manush, George Grantham, and Bill Baumgartner. Haney got his $1,250 but when he asked for more because of the players, he was asked which quarter of the players he wanted. For years, Haney liked to tell his fellow Angeleno Babe Herman that he owned twenty-five percent of him, and the Babe usually responded with, "Get out your knife and start cutting."[5]

MAJOR LEAGUER

In 1922, Ty Cobb, beginning his second year of managing the Tigers, developed an affinity for the brash, hustling youngster and gave Haney an opportunity to play a key reserve role. Fred took full advantage of the opportunity, batting a remarkable .352 and playing several positions. He got national attention in mid-season in *The Sporting News*. "Manager Ty Cobb has gotten some wonderful work out of recruits…. A notable instance is Fred Haney who was called up from Omaha…. One of the strong points in Haney's favor is that he has the old never quit spirit highly developed, and that is just what Cobb demands."[6]

Shortly after this article appeared, the fiery rookie got his first suspension and fine.[7,8] Cobb influenced much of Haney's approach to the game of baseball. The two shared a sense of competitiveness, aggressiveness, and desire to win, and would remain lifelong friends. Fred stayed with Detroit through the 1925 season. In a September 23 game at Fenway Park, Howard Ehmke beaned Haney; he was knocked unconscious and carried from the field. After the season, Haney was traded to the Boston Red Sox. The Haneys' only child, their daughter Patricia (Patsy), was born in Michigan during the season.

Haney won the starting third base job for the Red Sox but hit only .221, although he did lead the team in stolen bases. Some have attributed his hitting drop-off to being bat shy after the beaning. In July 1927 Fred was sold to the Chicago Cubs and subsequently sold to Indianapolis (Class AA-American Association), where he started at third base and hit well.[9]

Fred returned to Indianapolis for the 1928 season and had the best year of his career. He hit well with power and led the league in stolen bases. This was Haney's breakout year as a base stealer, and it would become his hallmark on the field. When the St. Louis Cardinals purchased his contract,[10] he made an unusual demand. If he did not make the team, he wanted the right to purchase his release or to be released to a PCL team. By now he had an insurance business with 29 branches in California, and if he were to be in the minors, he wanted to be near his work.[11]

PCL STAR

On May 7, 1929, he was sold to the Los Angeles Angels of the PCL. He was an immediate sensation, hitting well, stealing bases, and energizing the Angels. On September 16 Fred used some of his old football skills by throwing what was termed an illegal block into Hollywood shortstop Dud Lee to break up a double play. The umpire failed to call interference and the Angels rallied for three runs to help their victory. Fred led the league with 56 stolen bases even though he played only two-thirds of the season.

The 1930 season was another excellent one for Fred Haney. Early in the year he had a streak of 36 errorless games at third base.[12] He was the first man to lead the PCL in steals for two consecutive seasons.[13]

Haney's expectation of another banner year in 1931 ended in March when he had one kidney removed.[14,15] It was thought that Fred would miss the season, however he was "officially"[16] welcomed back to the team on June 24, when the game was stopped as he came to bat and he was presented a huge basket of flowers by his admirers at Paramount Studios, where he worked as an electrician during the offseason.[17] At the end of August, Fred was in the middle of a riot in Seattle, which ended in a forfeit; police and firemen had to use fire hoses to disperse the crowd of 8,000.

In 1932 Haney was given his first unconditional release in 14 seasons of baseball.[18] The following year Haney signed to play third base for the Hollywood Stars, the Angels' arch rivals. Fred played well in 1933 and again the next year. In June 1934, Fred severely spiked Angel catcher Walt Goebel who was hospitalized for several days because the wound was too badly bruised to stitch.[19] Given the bad blood between the teams, the Angels thought that it was intentional. Florence once related a story about sitting in the stands

Manager Fred Haney, wearing the Hollywood Stars' new shorts and lightweight rayon jerseys that debuted April 1, 1950, visits with Brooklyn Dodgers executive Branch Rickey at Gilmore Field.

during Fred's playing days when the fan next to her remarked, "Wouldn't you hate to be married to a hot-tempered pepper pot like that?" She added, "Nobody would ever believe that as excitable as Fred was as a player and as colorful as he is as a manager, he has always been a mild easy-going person at home."

MINOR LEAGUE MANAGER

In November Fred moved to another level in his career as player-manager of the Toledo Mud Hens. He was recommended by Frank Navin, owner of the Detroit Tigers.[21] Fred's fiery nature did not remain in Los Angeles. In June he protested a doubleheader loss at Columbus because the umpire delayed the first game while a telegram was sent to league president Thomas Hickey changing the Columbus roster during the game because of an injury.[22] The next day Fred was still seething and vigorously protested a call. He was ejected and, when he refused to leave the field, was escorted out by the police and suspended. He also made the league all-star team and led the league in stolen bases.[25]

In January 1936 Fred had a serious operation at Good Samaritan Hospital in Los Angeles,[26] that ended his every-day playing career but did nothing to stem his fighting spirit. During a June 20 game, Fred took exception to manager Burleigh Grimes riding the Toledo pitcher. They came to blows near third base and had to be separated by the police.[27] The 5-foot-10 Grimes made short work of Fred, knocking him down and then trying to carve up Fred's face with his spikes. Fred managed for two more years in Toledo, garnering praise from *The Sporting News* for his fiery leadership that kept the team in the 1937 race by winning games the experts said that they had no right to win.[29]

MAJOR LEAGUE MANAGER

Fred's success in Toledo caught the attention of the St. Louis Browns who were looking for a new manager—someone who would not command a large salary. Fred accepted their offer. Although some people offered their condolences, Fred viewed the Browns job as an excellent opportunity and expected to deliver a .500 team with improved pitching. It did not happen; the Browns finished last in 1939 and sixth in 1940. After the Browns started the 1941 season poorly, Haney was fired.[30] The Browns were not done with Fred; to save money they assigned him to manage Toledo, now a Browns farm team, where he stayed through the 1942 season.

THE BROADCAST BOOTH

At the end of the 1942 season, Fred called it quits in Toledo, citing the lack of authority to make player deals.[31] But he really wished to return to Los Angeles, where his daughter Patricia was in high school. Haney became the radio announcer for both the Angels and Stars home games. He had kept his Hollywood connections from his days at Paramount and was instrumental in having Bing Crosby wear a St. Louis Browns uniform in the movie *Going My Way* that was released when the Browns were winning their only pennant.[32]

Controversy arose late in the 1947 season. Philip K. Wrigley, owner of the Angels, wanted to broadcast road games and sought a broadcaster more partial to the Angels. He also wanted Haney fired from the Stars job, because he feared the new broadcaster would not be able to compete with Haney's style, knowledge, and on-air persona. Haney was defended vigorously in the local papers through a letter writing campaign to the Angels. Fred was praised as the best broadcaster the Coast has ever had and for almost single-handedly keeping baseball on the radio alive during the war.[33,34,35] The campaign worked; the following season Fred broadcast the Stars home and away games on KLAC.[36] That year also brought the Haneys their first grandchild.

MANAGERIAL SUCCESS WITH HOLLYWOOD

On November 4, 1948 the Stars asked Fred Haney to become their manager.[37] Haney requested and eventually got a three-year contract with full authority over player deals.[38] Before he signed, Fred contacted Branch

Rickey and got a promise that the Dodgers would add Hollywood to their farm system.[39] He was also allowed to continue as program director at KLAC and keep his radio show.

Haney was an excellent broadcaster. His work on the air and his support of youth, charities, public service, and baseball brought him a host of friends and admirers in and out of the game. He ended each broadcast with, "This is Fred Haney, rounding third and heading for home."[40] Little did Fred know that in his career, already spanning 30 years, he was only approaching second base.

Haney assessed the Stars as lacking talent and, by the start of 1949 spring training, 16 of the 25 players on the 1948 roster were gone. His motto was, "Win today, for tomorrow it may rain."[41] Haney warned the players to hustle on every play or be ready to be released.[42] The team was dubbed the Comets, Hurricanes, and Shooting Stars because of their running and aggressive play. They won the pennant by 5½ games. The press started calling him Frederick the Great. He was named *The Sporting News* Minor League Manager of the Year.[43]

On the first Saturday afternoon of the 1950 season, the Stars dropped a bombshell on the baseball world by appearing on the field in shorts. Fred asserted that the rayon T-shirts and shorts that resembled track suits, worn for day games and warm night games, would give his players more speed and change the decision on some close plays. The papers called the uniform "scanties," and opposing players teased the Stars mercilessly throughout the season.

During the 1951 season Haney initiated a successful plan with Ty Cobb to promote the election of critically ill Harry Heilmann to the Hall of Fame.[44] Shortly before the end of the year, Fred was hospitalized with viral pneumonia.[45] Florence had the unenviable chore of keeping Fred quiet as she supervised his convalescence in Palm Springs. As he recovered, she drove him to spring training games and cooked while trying to make sure he got sufficient rest.

BACK TO THE MAJORS, WITH PITTSBURGH

After the Stars won the 1952 pennant, Branch Rickey, now with the Pittsburgh Pirates, offered the managerial job to Haney. Fred said that he took the job out of obligation to Rickey for the help he had provided to the Stars.[46] Haney now had the dubious honor of managing Pittsburgh, the worst team in baseball.

Fred spent three tough years managing the Pirates "Kiddie Corps." Rickey had signed a large number of players and instructed Fred to play the kids even if they were not the best so as to build for the future. They finished a dismal last each year. On September 25, 1955, Fred received a registered letter from Branch Rickey dismissing him as manager. Fred's contract would have automatically renewed if he had not been notified by midnight on that day.[47] Fred was bitter over being coldly dismissed by letter when Rickey had promised him a face-to-face meeting.

THE PINNACLE IN MILWAUKEE

Wanting to remain in the majors, Haney accepted a one-year coaching offer from the Milwaukee Braves for the 1956 season.[48] The reaction in Milwaukee was that this was one of the best moves the Braves had made since moving from Boston, as Haney would bring hustle, competitiveness, and baseball strategy.[49] In June, with Milwaukee languishing in fifth place, Haney was appointed interim manager.[50] The Braves then went on a tear, winning 11 consecutive games, and stayed in contention throughout the year. On September 11 with the Braves one game ahead, Fred was rehired for the 1957 season for the magnificent job that he had done.[51] However, on the final Saturday of the season, the Braves lost a 12-inning heartbreaker to St. Louis 2–1 to fall one game behind, and the next day the Dodgers won to clinch the pennant.

During the offseason, the now retired Jackie Robinson said, "The Milwaukee Braves lost the pennant because two or three key players were night-clubbing until 6:15 A.M. while the Braves were in Pittsburgh."[52] In his farewell speech to the club after the last game, Haney said, "You had a good time boys. Have a good time this winter. Because when we meet again next spring, you're going to have the toughest so and so you've ever run into."[53] True to his promise, Fred worked the Braves exceptionally hard during spring training and prophetically told the team, "You may hate me in the spring but you'll love me in the fall when you pick up your World Series checks."[54]

On June 15, Fred got the team leader he wanted, Red Schoendienst, from the Giants.[55] When the Braves clinched the 1957 pennant, Fred said, "This is the thrill of a lifetime. I knew the boys would come through, and what a great way to do it."[56] In his fortieth year in baseball, Fred Haney made it to the World Series. For the seventh game, Fred had a tough decision to make. He chose Lew Burdette to start over Warren Spahn. Lew led the Braves to a 5–0 win to give Haney and the Braves the World Championship. Fred was now a hero in Milwaukee. He was named National League Manager of the Year.[58] He was rehired for 1958 with a $40,000 salary, his highest salary in professional baseball.[57]

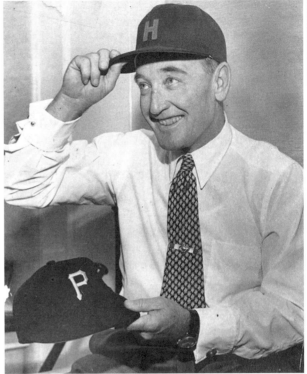

Fred Haney swaps his first place Hollywood Stars cap for a last place Pittsburgh Pirates cap as he takes over the helm of the worst team in baseball.

One event in his busy offseason typified Fred Haney. Fred's brother Ralph saw a polio-crippled teen-aged boy, Bill Culver, simulating playing the different positions on the diamond and catching pitches on an empty school playground. It was a major struggle for him with a withered arm and a weak leg. Ralph wrote to Fred asking him to send a ball and Braves hat that he could give to the boy, because he admired his courage. Fred did more. He arranged an assembly on the playground of the school in front of the students and, with his arm around Bill, presented him with an autographed Braves baseball, a Milwaukee T-shirt and cap, and a World Series program while he spoke about baseball and life.[59]

Haney led the Braves to another pennant in 1958, losing the World Series to the Yankees, and lost the 1959 pennant in a playoff to the Dodgers. During the 1959 World Series, Fred resigned as manager of the Braves. In midseason, he had said that this might be his last year. There was speculation in the press whether he quit or was pushed out; however, what is most likely is that he made demands on Braves owner Lou Perini for more authority that were not granted, and he quit.

NATIONAL TV BROADCASTER

Haney was ready to return home and be with his family. He quickly signed with Los Angeles television

119

station KCOP to host *Major League Baseball Presents* on Saturday evenings. Fred then landed a plum three-year contract to televise NBC's *Game of the Week*. A review of Fred's work that season said that he described the action as though it were radio but that he had a flair for bringing in colorful anecdotes that added a definite flavor to the telecasts.[60]

ANGELS' GENERAL MANAGER

When Gene Autry won the Los Angeles franchise of the American League at the Winter Meetings in December 1960, he quickly hired Haney as the general manager.[61] Fred would set the standard for future expansion teams. He hired Bill Rigney as field manager and moved to the player draft. Fred had friends all over baseball and called on them for advice on players, particularly those in the minors. Buzzie Bavasi shared the Dodgers evaluations and Casey Stengel provided information from the Yankee scouting reports. Rigney wanted to draft young players for the future but Haney overruled him with a mix of young players and veterans with reputations to compete with the Dodgers for local attention. Haney also wanted to get power hitters for Wrigley Field. The Angels drafted 30 players, 28 from the majors and two from the minors. Eight were over 30, 18 were in their twenties, and four were teenagers. The gems were two teenagers, Jim Fregosi and Dean Chance.

Haney's next task was to hire a staff and he brought together an outstanding front office including Marvin Milkes, Cedric Tallis, and Roland Hemond. At the end of January, Haney and Hemond negotiated a working agreement with their first minor league club, the Dallas-Fort Worth Rangers of the Class AAA American Association.[62] Haney organized the refurbishment of Wrigley Field, developed a spring training facility in Palm Springs, and carried out over 20 trades to improve the nascent Angels. Although pundits predicted that they would be lucky to win 50 games in their inaugural season, they won 70. Since that time, 13 more expansion teams have entered the major leagues and none has equaled that win total yet in their opening season. Moreover, his structuring of the team for Wrigley led to a 46–36 home record. No expansion team since has achieved a winning season at home in their inaugural year, either.

For the 1962 season the Angels moved to the Dodgers' new park in Chavez Ravine, which was

Fred and Florence Haney, a 57-year baseball partnership.

pitcher-friendly as opposed to the bandbox at Wrigley. Fred restructured the team for this park, making multiple trades and bringing up young players. By July 4 the Angels were in first place, ultimately finishing third with an 86–76 record. For his work, both *The Sporting News* and UPI named Haney as Major League Executive of the Year.[63]

Fred Haney continued as general manager of the Angels for six more years, orchestrating the club's move to Anaheim and the development of its image in Orange County. After the 1968 season, Gene Autry suggested that it was time for the 70-year-old Haney to retire and offered him a consulting position at the same salary. Fred knew that this position had no authority or even formal input but acquiesced out of friendship for Autry.

Fred continued to follow the Angels, attending many games and advising Gene Autry. As his vision began to fail, Florence drove him to the games. On November 9, 1977, Fred suffered a fatal heart attack at his Beverly Hills home.[64] Two years later, in 1979, the Angels won the American League West and entered the playoffs. Gene Autry honored Fred by asking Florence to assist him in throwing out the first ball for Game 3 and having her throw out the first ball for Game 4.[65] In 1980, the team established the Fred Haney Memorial Award to recognize the outstanding rookie in spring training.[66]

Florence Haney lived to be nearly a hundred before passing away in 1998. She and Fred are buried at Holy Cross Cemetery in Culver City, California. Their gravestones represent what was important to them in their lives: "BELOVED HUSBAND FATHER • GRANDFATHER"; "BELOVED WIFE MOTHER • GRANDMOTHER." ■

Notes

1. There is conflicting information on Fred's year of birth as 1896, 1897 or 1898. I have chosen 1898 because that is what is on his tombstone.
2. *Los Angeles Times*, 26 August 1934, F2.
3. *The Charleston Gazette*, 10 November 1938.
4. *Los Angeles Times*, 5 June 1920, 18.
5. *Los Angeles Times*, 6 November 1947, 14.
6. *The Sporting News*, 6 July 1922, 1.
7. *Los Angeles Times*, 24 July 1922, III2.
8. *Los Angeles Times*, 4 May 1930, F3.
9. BaseballReference.com, Minor League DataBase.
10. *Los Angeles Times*, 18 December 1928, B2.
11. Moberly, MO *Monitor Index and Democrat*, 15 February 1929, 2.
12. *Los Angeles Times*, 6 June 1930, A13.
13. *Los Angeles Times*, 14 December 1930, F5.
14. *Los Angeles Times*, 25 March 1931, A13.
15. *Los Angeles Times*, 8 December 1938, A13.
16. *Los Angeles Times*, 16 June 1931, A11.
17. *Los Angeles Times*, 25 June 1931, A11.
18. *Los Angeles Times*, 1 September 1932, A9.
19. *Los Angeles Times*, 5 June 1934, A9.
20. *Los Angeles Times*, 9 April 1951, C2.
21. *Los Angeles Times*, 22 November 1934, A11.
22. Massilon, OH *Evening Independent*, 17 June 1935, 3.
23. Emporia, KS *Daily Gazette*, 18 June 1935, 8.
24. *Los Angeles Times*, 12 August 1935, A11.
25. Waterloo, IA *Daily Courier*, 23 December 1935, 9.
26. *Oakland Tribune*, 23 January 1936, 23.
27. Lima, OH *News*, 21 June 1936, 2.
28. Ada, OK *Evening News*, 17 November 1936, 10.
29. *The Sporting News*, 30 September 1937, 3.
30. *Los Angeles Times*, 5 June 1941, 21.
31. *Los Angeles Times*, 24 September 1942, A10.
32. *Los Angeles Times*, 6 October 1944, 10.
33. *Los Angeles Times*, 5 September 1947, A8, A9.
34. *Los Angeles Times*, 11 September 1947, 11.
35. *Los Angeles Times*, 14 September 1947, A6.
36. *Los Angeles Times*, 15 September 1947, 11.
37. *Los Angeles Times*, 5 November 1948, C1.
38. *Los Angeles Times*, 11 November 1948, C1.
39. *Los Angeles Times*, 7 September 1952, B7.
40. Richard Beverage, *The Hollywood Stars*, Arcadia Publishing, 2005.
41. *Los Angeles Times*, 16 January 1949, 28.
42. *Los Angeles Times*, 29 March 1949, C2.
43. *Los Angeles Times*, 25 January 1950, C2.
44. *Los Angeles Times*, 10 July 1951, C3.
45. *Los Angeles Times*, 12 January 1952, B4.
46. *New York Times*, 12 December 1952, 45.
47. *New York Times*, 26 September 1955, 27.
48. *Los Angeles Times*, 26 October 1955, C1.
49. *The Sporting News*, 2 November 1955, 9.
50. *New York Times*, 17 June 1956, B1.
51. *New York Times*, 12 September 1957, 44.
52. *New York Times*, 13 January 1957, S1.
53. *Los Angeles Times*, 14 January 1957, C6.
54. *Los Angeles Times*, 29 October 1957, C4.
55. *New York Times*, 17 June 1957, 40.
56. *Los Angeles Times*, 24 September 1957, C1.
57. *New York Times*, 20 October 1957, S5.
58. *New York Times*, 24 October 1957, 45.
59. *Los Angeles Times*, 21 November 1957, C4.
60. *Los Angeles Times*, 4 June 1960, B5.
61. *Los Angeles Times*, 9 December 1960, C1.
62. *Los Angeles Times*, 31 January 1961, C3.
63. *Los Angeles Times*, 24 October 1962, B5.
64. *Los Angeles Times*, 9 November 1977, A1.
65. John Hall, *Los Angeles Times*, 8 October 1977, D3.
66. 1999 Anaheim Angels Media Guide.

A Game I'll Never Forget
Los Angeles Defeats San Francisco in 1947 Playoff Game

Al Parnis

On Monday night, September 29, 1947, 22,996 fans, with hundreds in the aisles and thousands more turned away, saw a game with all the elements of a great classic: fine pitching, sparkling defensive plays, dramatic offense, and an exciting finish.

The cities of San Francisco and Los Angeles have always been rivals. In 1947 the rivalry coalesced around their Pacific Coast League entries—the San Francisco Seals and the Los Angeles Angels.

The Angels and the Seals were the class of the league. The Seals had fine starting pitching. Cliff Melton, Al Lien, Bob Chesnes (an All-Star selection), and Jack Brewer completed 60 percent of their games and the starting staff of six won 90 of the team's 105 wins. The double play combination of Roy Nicely, an All-Star selection, and Hugh Luby was the best in the league. Outfielder Don White led the team with 213 hits and hit .292. Neil Sheridan, an All-Star selection, hit 16 home runs in spacious Seals' Stadium, had 9 triples, 95 runs batted in, and hit .286. He was a real asset defensively as well, as he threw out 24 runners.[1] Dino Restelli at .292 and Joe Brovia at .309 proved to be valuable as well. What they didn't have was a lot of good reserves. They lost Battle Sanders, Charles Henson, Bernie Uhalt, and Neil Sheridan for significant time and had no similar talent to replace them.[2]

Los Angeles, on the other hand, was a power team. They led the league in home runs with 151 (33 more than second place Oakland) in hitter-friendly Wrigley Field. John Ostrowski and Cecil Garriott, both All-Star selections, had over 20 home runs. Larry Barton and Eddie Sauer showed a lot of power as well. The double play combination of Bill Schuster and Lou Stringer rivaled the duo of Nicely and Luby. Pitching was led by Cliff Chambers, an All-Star selection, with 24 wins, Red Adams, and Red Lynn.[3] Along with these three, the Angels had the Fireman of the Year Jess Dobernic. He appeared in 55 games with 13 saves and 8 wins. The last two weeks of the season he relieved 6 times, pitched 15 innings, and gave up 6 hits.[4]

At the end of July, it had seemed Los Angeles was going to win the pennant in a walk. But the power

stopped. From August 12 to September 16 they won 18 and lost 19 while San Francisco won 25 and lost 12.[5] Both teams rallied over the final two weeks, but wound up in a tie.

Since the teams had split their season series, there would have to be a playoff, and the Angels won the coin toss for home-field advantage. The game was to be played the next night, September 29, at Wrigley Field in Los Angeles.[6]

What a vivid memory for an eleven-year-old boy, enjoying his first full baseball season! And what great seats! On the day of the game, somehow my lovable dad had been able to get five choice seats ten rows behind home plate for the first playoff game in Pacific Coast League history.[7]

From there I watched as Jack Brewer of San Francisco and Cliff Chambers of Los Angeles pitched inning

Cliff Chambers, winning pitcher of the 1947 PCL playoff game between the Los Angeles Angels and San Francisco Seals, autographs the cast of injured boxer Eddie Malone.

1947 Angels team photo, Clarence Maddern top row, second from left.

after inning of scoreless baseball. Ground out, strike out, ground out, fly out—rarely a meaningless single. Seals threats were quickly erased by two double plays. The Angels did have one serious threat in the bottom of the fourth inning. Leadoff man Cecil Garriott worked Jack Brewer for a walk. Bill Schuster was safe on an error. Big Ed Sauer made an out. Clarence Maddern, the cleanup man, also walked. Now Jack Brewer was in a real mess. Seals second baseman Hugh Luby came to the rescue, however. He stabbed John Ostrowski's hard grounder, stepped on second quickly, and threw a strike to Bill Matheson at first for the double play.[8]

Then came the unforgettable Angels eighth inning. After the first batter, pitcher Cliff Chambers, made an out, feisty leadoff man Cecil Garriott began the destruction of the mighty Seals, the 1946 champions, when he worked a nervous Jack Brewer for a walk. The next batter, Broadway Bill Schuster, always trouble, called for a hit and run. The ball just eluded second baseman Luby as he was running to cover second base. The speedy Garriott raced to third. First and third, only one out. Brewer was now more visibly shaken as slugging outfielder Eddie Sauer stepped to the plate. One mistake and the Seals would be behind 3–0. Trying to keep the ball inside to avoid a home run, a too-careful Brewer hit Sauer. The bases were loaded; Hollywood could not have written it any better. The tension and excitement were high for me and thousands of other fans as victory was in sight for our beloved Angels. Clarence Maddern, the dangerous cleanup man, was up, and there was no place to put

him. Brewer had to throw strikes. He wound up and threw his best pitch, a good hard fastball, for a strike. But the man in blue did not get a chance to call it as Maddern slammed a long, high blast over the left field wall onto 41st Place. The stands erupted, and I felt that there just may be something to this game of baseball.

That night, it was not an instant that brought everyone to their feet. It was a masterfully pitched game that heightened the suspense with each hitter. Which pitcher would be the first to falter?

That night, Clarence Maddern triumphed; Jack Brewer was left powerless. Now the Angels were in the driver's seat. Only three more outs were needed for L.A. to become the Pacific Coast League Champions. Everybody knew that the Angels would never surrender this lead. The bases-loaded home run was too devastating. That one blow was too much for any team to overcome. Brewer did recover some as he struck out third baseman John Ostrowski, but first baseman Larry Barton added another nail to the Seals' coffin with a solo shot into the right field bleachers. Finally, second baseman Lou Stringer closed out the inning.

As expected, the Seals did next to nothing in the top of the ninth inning. Left fielder and cleanup man Dino Restelli walked, but was quickly erased as third baseman Ray Orteig hit into the third Seals double play of the night. There was no way Cliff Chambers was going to give up anything at this point, and first baseman Bill Matheson obliged by making the final out of the game.

Why did the Angels win?

1947 San Francisco Seals: Jack Brewer, top row, sixth from right.

Chambers's pitching was outstanding. He gave up only five hits and two walks. San Francisco's leadoff men never got on. The middle of the Seals' order—Neil Sheridan, Dino Restelli, and Ray Orteig—got one hit amongst them. The Seals' hits came from the bottom of the order. The Angels made three double plays, the pitcher's best friends. The Angels' eighth inning? A first batter walk, a timely single just eluding the second baseman, a power hitter up who was a real threat, and the fourth hitter, Clarence Maddern, who had been the hottest Angels hitter in the latter part of the season. All these elements in the Angels' favor led to a dramatic and unforgettable finish.

Today, many, many years later the same excitement that I experienced in 1947 is just as strong and vivid as it was on that September night. Baseball has a certain drama and tension that no other game can claim. While the action is not as frenetic as in other team sports, this tension builds inning after inning in a well pitched game. ∎

Notes

1. *Pacific Coast Baseball News*, October, 1947, Los Angeles, 3.
2. Willie Runquist, *Pacific Coast League Almanac, 1947*, Self-published, Union Bay, B.C., 96.
3. Ibid, 87.
4. Ibid, 87.
5. Ibid, 65, 66, 67, 71, 73, 74, 76, 78.
6. Runquist, 2.
7. *PCL Baseball News*, 1.
8. *PCL Baseball News*, 1.

The Bucs in San Berdoo

Fred R. Peltz

Although the arrival of Major League Baseball in Southern California is usually dated to 1958, when the Brooklyn Dodgers moved to Los Angeles, big league clubs had roots in the area going back several decades. The Chicago Cubs began training in L.A. in the spring of 1903, and the White Sox played an exhibition game in Riverside in 1914. From 1924 to 1934, the Pittsburgh Pirates trained in the central California town of Paso Robles. The club then got a pitch from a San Bernardino civic group led by Harrison Sporting Goods, the regional supplier of Spalding Sporting Goods, the chief provider of equipment to the big leagues.

As longtime resident Bill Harrison told the *San Bernardino Sun* in 1999, his parents, William and Laura Harrison, owned Harrison Sporting Goods and put the request to the Spalding Company, which relayed it to the Pirates. The invitation had merit for several reasons. San Bernardino, a citrus-growing center of a region known as the Inland Empire, enjoyed a benign climate. Located 50 miles east of L.A. and the Pacific Ocean, the city had grown in prominence as the gateway to Southern California, given its intersecting highways—including the marvelous Route 66—and railroads. The city's transportation hub made it convenient to play the other big-league clubs who trained at that time in Southern California: the Chicago White Sox in Pasadena, and the Chicago Cubs on Catalina Island. The St. Louis Browns trained in San Bernardino in 1948, then several years in Burbank (1949–52), and returned to San Bernardino in 1953. The Philadelphia Athletics trained in Anaheim in 1940–42 and the Cleveland Indians in Tucson, Arizona, 1947–1992, adding to the competition, as did the New York Giants, who trained in Phoenix 1947–50 and 1952. The Triple-A teams of the Pacific Coast League provided further opportunities for games. The Pirates agreed to make San Bernardino's Perris Hill Park their spring training home in 1935, playing there off and on until the end of the 1952 exhibition season.

San Berdoo, as it is popularly known, was an attractive spring training site for other reasons. The city had a population of about 40,000 in 1935 and sits at the base of the towering San Bernardino Mountains, where for a few years the Pirates stayed at the Arrowhead Springs Hotel, five miles from the city below. With its 36 springs, the hotel was a well-known spa frequented by Hollywood celebrities. The hotel was devastated by a forest fire in 1938 but was soon rebuilt. When it re-opened in December 1939 entertainers Judy Garland, Al Jolson, and Rudy Vallee were there to celebrate the occasion. Each spring the Pirates rubbed shoulders with radio and film celebrities.

A few years later the club moved its headquarters downtown to the California Hotel, another favorite stop for Hollywood stars and other notables, as it was located across the street from the West Coast Theater, which hosted several movie premieres. Charlie Chaplin, Bette Davis, and John Wayne were among those who signed the hotel's guestbook. Some Pirates dabbled in the Hollywood scene, such as Pirates manager Frankie Frisch, who used an off-day in 1941 to make the short drive to Palm Springs to appear on Jack Benny's radio show.

In those years, clubs tended to shift spring training sites often, and Pittsburgh was no exception. After initially training in San Bernardino in 1935, the Pirates spent the next spring in San Antonio, Texas, before returning to San Bernardino through 1942. Pittsburgh then trained in Muncie, Indiana, during the rest of World War II (1943-45), spent 1946 back in San Bernardino, then trained in Miami, Florida in 1947, and in Hollywood in 1948. The Pirates' springtime returns to town were always cause for civic celebration. The arrival time of the team's train at the Santa Fe railroad depot downtown was announced in the *San Bernardino Sun*, players were greeted with music by the San Bernardino High School band, and the city's mayor and the queen of San Bernardino County's National Orange Show joined the reception committee.

For most Inland Empire residents, Perris Hill Park provided their only means of seeing a major-league ballplayer up close. The expansion of big-league teams west of the Mississippi River was still decades away, as were televised games, and local baseball fans' visual impressions of their favorite players were limited to snippets on movie newsreels, magazine photos, newspaper reproductions, and images on Wheaties boxes. The Pirates may have often experienced lean seasons after training in San Bernardino—Pittsburgh's best finish in those years was second in 1938 and 1944—but local fans were treated to an array of stellar ballplayers and managers when the Pirates were in town. At Perris Hill, fans not only could watch big-league players in person, they could see several who were among the best in the game's history. The 1935 Bucs, for instance, were led by Honus Wagner (by then a coach and mentor), manager Pie Traynor, Arky Vaughan, and the Waner brothers, Paul and Lloyd, known as "Big and Little Poison." The Pirates also had Truett "Rip" Sewell, the right-hander known for his looping "eephus" pitch. Harry "Cookie" Lavagetto played for Pittsburgh 1934–36 before moving to the Brooklyn Dodgers. And Albert "Al" Gionfriddo—forever remembered for robbing the Yankees' Joe DiMaggio of a double in the 1947 World Series when Gionfriddo was playing his last major-league game as a member of the Dodgers—spent most of his four seasons with the Pirates. During the late 1940s and early 1950s, fans always thrilled to see the Bucs' left fielder Ralph Kiner, who won or shared the National League home-run title in all seven of his seasons with the club. Kiner frequently commuted to Perris Hill from Alhambra, where he had grown up.

Through the years, local fans also got to see other stars come to Perris Hill to play against Pittsburgh, such as Gabby Hartnett and Billy Herman of the Chicago Cubs, Luke Appling and Jimmy Dykes of the Chicago White Sox, and Philadelphia Athletics owner-manager Connie Mack. Even the lowly Browns offered future star power with Los Angeles-born infielder Johnny Berardino, who later would become a TV soap-opera star on *General Hospital*.

Through it all the Pittsburgh players remained "fun-loving guys and [were] having a good time" during the spring, attorney Ron Skipper told the *Sun*, adding that "they signed balls and they didn't swat you away." Skipper, whose family lived a few blocks from the California Hotel, had an especially keen interest in the team because his uncle was Bob Elliott, the seven-time All-Star outfielder and third baseman. His career included playing for the Pirates from 1939 to 1946 and winning an NL Most Valuable Player award after he moved to the Boston Braves.

San Bernardino was still growing but retained its small-town flavor, and ballplayers could easily be spot-

Honus Wagner (left) gives Johnny Rizzo, promising Pittsburgh outfielder purchased from Columbus, a few pointers during an exhibition game.

ted when they weren't on the diamond. Jack Brown, who later became chairman of the Stater Brothers supermarket chain, recalled how he and his friends watched games at Perris Hill and then scouted other locations to see their heroes. "When we got done with the game, we'd come back to downtown San Bernardino on our bikes and park them at the California Hotel and wait for the team to come down and go to dinner," Brown told the *Riverside* (CA) *Press-Enterprise* in 2005.

Built in 1927, Perris Hill was a diamond in the truest sense, with no rounding off of the center-field fence. It was 354 feet down the lines and 451 feet to dead center field. The ballpark later had a $10,000 overhaul that turned it into a facility that could host pro baseball. Perris Hill was one of the few parks that had lights for night play, courtesy of the New Deal's Works Progress Administration (WPA). Only a belt-high wooden fence down the third base line separated the players' bench from the fans. A kid could easily walk up to Honus Wagner, tap him on the shoulder, and walk away with an autograph by the man many consider the best shortstop ever. Tickets ranged from 50 cents to $1.50, and one could even see big-league ball for as little as 25 cents when the Pirates played an intra-squad game at Perris Hill.

For some local residents, Perris Hill offered employment. George Beck, who read meters for the local gas company, supplemented his income by serving as the public address announcer at Perris Hill and other venues. For $15 a day, Beck would announce the line-ups from each manager and read advertisements to the crowd "so that the Pirates could pay for the lights."

There was one other star-crossed Pirate of note who briefly played at Perris Hill in 1950: 19-year-old Paul Pettit. After a remarkable high school career in Harbor City, California, where Pettit threw six no-hitters and struck out 27 batters in one 12-inning game—the most since Walter Johnson in 1905—movie producer Frederick Stephani signed the young pitcher to a 10-year personal services contract for $85,000. Stephani wanted to film the life story of an athlete but couldn't afford an established star, so he bet on Pettit's future. Three months later, Stephani—in effect acting as Pettit's agent while retaining the movie rights to his life—sold Pettit's contract to the Pirates for $100,000. The St. Louis Cardinals and other teams cried foul, but Commissioner Happy Chandler's subsequent investigation found no wrongdoing.

Pettit had become the first $100,000 "bonus baby," and he spent two weeks at Pirates rookie camp at Perris Hill in 1950. Then he was assigned to the Double-A New Orleans Pelicans where he worked hard to merit his bonus. But, "for all the money the Pirates spent, there was no pitching coach in New Orleans to monitor him," John Klima wrote in his book *Deal of the Century*. "Pettit was not trained. He was simply handed the ball. It was baseball in the dark ages." In the third week of the season, Pettit hurt his elbow and, while favoring the injury, his shoulder. He finished the season 2–7 and had only two short stays with the Pirates, in 1951 and 1953. He reinvented himself as a power-hitting position player in the Pacific Coast League and in Mexico, but was never given another shot in the major leagues.

The end of World War II brought new ownership for the Pirates, who were purchased in 1946 by a syndicate that included actor-singer Bing Crosby. Also coming on board that year was Ralph Kiner, who recalled how Crosby, his kids in tow, often showed up at Perris Hill for Pirates' practice and to take part in pepper games. He said Crosby treated the players well. When the Pirates went to Los Angeles for a game, he would take the team to Chasen's for dinner. But Crosby's charity and Kiner's slugging success on the field didn't mean much at contract time. In late 1950, the Pirates hired Branch Rickey, famous for his years running the Brooklyn Dodgers, as their general manager. Kiner, coming off one of his best seasons, expected a raise, but Rickey responded, "We finished last with you, we can finish last without you." Largely due to

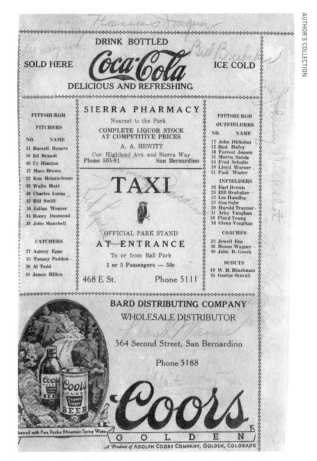

Images from the author's scrapbook evoke memories of long afternoons spent at Perris Hill Park.

continued salary disputes, Kiner eventually was sent to the Cubs in June 1953 as part of a 10-player trade.

In an odd twist, given Southern California's vaunted climate, it was weather that caused the Pirates to abandon San Bernardino for good after the spring of 1952. Branch Rickey praised the field, the hotel accommodations, and the city's cooperation, but he had soured on the weather after the rains that year were among the worst in Southern California history, with numerous practices and games cancelled. Instead Rickey accepted an offer to move spring training to Havana, Cuba. The following year San Bernardino enjoyed one more big league spring with the Browns, whose 1953 roster included legendary pitcher Satchel Paige, but that marked the end.

Perris Hill Park has remained connected to sports. In 1983 the field was renamed John A. Fiscalini Field, after the San Bernardino high school standout and UC Berkeley All-American outfielder, who later played in the Pirates minor league system from 1948 to 1950. In 1987, the ballpark became home to a single-A team, the San Bernardino Spirit of the California League. The city spent more than $1 million on improvements to

SAN BERNARDINO DAILY SUN

Perris Hill Ballpark, circa 1930–1940.

the park during that period, increasing the seating capacity to 3,500 by 1996. The Spirit's roster in 1988 included Ken Griffey Jr., then an 18-year-old Seattle Mariners prospect. In 58 games with the club, he batted .338. *Baseball America* named him its single-A player of the year.

Actor Mark Harmon, the team's largest shareholder at the time, also visited Fiscalini Field in 1988, bringing Hollywood with him. The final scenes of Harmon's movie *Stealing Home* were filmed at the field, with Harmon wearing a Spirit uniform. After the 1992 season, the Spirit's ownership changed, and the team moved to a new stadium, the Epicenter, in nearby Rancho Cucamonga.

The city of San Bernardino, in order to meet changing minor league standards and thus keep professional baseball, built a $16.5-million facility, now called Arrowhead Credit Union Park, which opened in 1996. It is currently the home of the Inland Empire 66ers, the Angels' single-A affiliate in the California League. City Parks superintendent Ed Yelton maintained in 1997 that the old ballpark was "far from dead." The manicured diamond that once hosted the likes of Honus Wagner, Paul Waner, and Ralph Kiner now is used for youth, high school, and college baseball games, soccer tournaments, and even church revivals. Said Yelton: "I envision Fiscalini Field being here another 50 years." ∎

Acknowledgments

The author wishes to acknowledge Sue Payne, docent Arda Haenszel California Room, Norman F. Feldheym Central Library, San Bernardino, California; Sue Peltz; James F. Peltz; Joan Gonzalez; William Swank; and Al Parnis for their assistance.

Sources

Books

John Thorn, Pete Palmer, Michael Gershman, and David Pietrusza, *Total Baseball*, Fifth Edition, Viking Penguin, 1997.

Periodicals

Spring Memories," Mark Muckenfuss, the *Riverside* (CA) *Press-Enterprise*, March 29, 2005.

"SB's no stranger to Baseball," Gregg Patton, *San Bernardino County Sun*, 21 March 1999.

"Picture Stars Participate in Full Program," *San Bernardino Daily Sun*, 17 December 1939.

"S.B.'s team, announcer recalls," Nick Leyva, *San Bernardino Sun*, 28 July 1984.

"Fiscalini's upkeep grounds for concern," Danny Summers, *San Bernardino Sun*, 18 March 1997.

Internet

Klimaink.com, John Klima Baseball Writing, *Deal of the Century*.
Ed Burns
Baseball Reference.com Encyclopedia of Players
Wikipedia, the free encyclopedia
http://hwof.com/star/television/johnberardino/2354
Steve Treder, *The Hardball Times*, "The Branch Rickey Pirates," 10 March 2009.
http://seattletimes.nwsource.com/html/mariners/2012145723, 5 July 2010.
Geoff Young, *The Hardball Times*, "Produce great men, the rest follow," 9 June 2010.

Winter Baseball in California
Separate Opportunities, Equal Talent

Geri Strecker

For most black players during the early 1900s, baseball was a year-round occupation. Much has been written about African American involvement in the Cuban Winter League and with barnstorming teams that played against white major leaguers. However, less is known about other offseason baseball opportunities for black players, including the fact that many Negro League stars spent winters playing ball on the West Coast. Long before Satchel Paige's All Stars faced Dizzy Dean's barnstorming major leaguers during the 1930s, Oscar Charleston's "Bear Cats" mauled Irish Meusel's All Stars in Southern California during the winter of 1921–1922. Such pre- and post-season competitions between black and white teams occurred throughout the era of segregated baseball.

Among the Negro Leaguers who played winter ball on the West Coast, Raleigh "Biz" Mackey reigns supreme, playing 18 winters in the Golden State and maintaining an impressive .366 batting average with 28 home runs. Other multi-season stars include Mule Suttles (8), Norman "Turkey" Stearnes (9), and James "Cool Papa" Bell (12). Among the pitchers were Satchel Paige (56–7), Chet Brewer (43–13), and James "Cannon Ball" Willis (41–10). Wilber "Bullet" Rogan spent six winters in California and dominated both as a pitcher (42–14) and batter (.362 with 15 home runs).[1]

In his book *The California Winter League: America's First Integrated Professional Baseball League* (McFarland, 2002), William F. McNeil discusses opportunities that African American ballplayers had to compete against their minor and major league counterparts. However, the story is not quite so clear, and mislabeling all winter baseball played in California as "California Winter League" ignores the uneven color lines that existed in that time and place.

The season most illustrative of this point occurred during the winter of 1921–1922, when future Hall of Famers Ty Cobb, Harry Heilmann, Rogers Hornsby, George Sisler, Oscar Charleston, Raleigh "Biz" Mackey, and Jose Mendez traveled west after the regular Major League or Negro League season to play winter ball—but not against each other. That season, the official California Winter League was reserved only for major and minor league players, which meant that all participants were white. To promote attendance, the four CWL teams signed major league players as managers: San Francisco Seals, Ty Cobb (Detroit Tigers); San Francisco Missions, Harry Heilmann (Detroit Tigers); Los Angeles Angels, Rogers Hornsby (St. Louis Cardinals); Vernon Tigers, George Sisler (St. Louis Browns).

Cobb's temper during this period was particularly volatile. In the bottom of the fourth inning of a November 19 game against Vernon, he threw a fit over a missed call (Lu Blue threw out George Sisler at second, but the umpire missed it) and refused to leave the field when ejected from the game. The chief umpire ultimately declared a forfeit, and league president Frank Chance fined Cobb $150. On November 20, the *Los Angeles Times* headline read, "Tyrus Cobb is Somewhat Sad," and the article predicted the Tiger "may leave California flat on its back by never returning after the close of the present winter season. Life's road sure is becoming rocky for the greatest ball player of all time." He had batted only 1 for 3 the previous day and slumped out of the batting lead; meanwhile, his San Francisco Seals were mired in last place. Discontented with his CWL experience, and clearly not interested in staying to play against the Colored All Stars, Cobb left California on December 7, vowing never to play or manage winter ball there again.[2] Cobb's attitude toward the black players was not unique among the major and minor leaguers.

Although Southern California provided winter opportunities for black ballplayers, during the regular season African American teams had to scramble for games, playing whatever semipro and military clubs would accept their challenge. They could not be part of a regular league because the all-white Southern California Managers' Baseball Association held tight control over the semipro circuits. A few of the best black teams still managed to thrive, however, and the strongest during the summer of 1921 was the Alexander Giants.[3]

The club had opened a new ballpark at 32nd and

BATTING AVERAGES AND FIELDING PERCENTAGES OF JAMES P. WHITE'S COLORED ALL-STARS 1921-22 FOR 33 GAMES, COMPILED BY OFFICIAL SCORER WM. M. WATSON

	G	AB	R	H	2B	3B	Hr	Sac	SB	O	A	E	Av.	Per.
Charleston	21	79	22	32	7	6		2	7	44	4	2	405	.960
Blackman	21	74	16	30	4	2	3	5	1	25	36	7	405	.897
Mackey	31	123	19	47	8	5	3	4	5	126	87	6	382	.964
Carr	33	134	24	45	8	5	3	3	6	74	18	5	336	.948
Hawkins	30	116	22	39	10	3		5	5	133	17	3	336	.980
Pullen	12	46	4	15	1	1	1	2		87	8	2	326	.979
McNair	32	124	24	36	6	6	2	2		45	15		290	1.000
Foote	2	7		2	2					2	1		286	1.000
Fagen	32	121	17	33	3	1	2	1	3	59	69	7	280	.948
Moore	22	80	11	22	4	3		2		47	39	12	275	.878
Jeffries	22	63	11	16		2		4	2	12	16	3	254	.903
Mendez	24	82	12	20	3	3	2	3	3	50	56	6	244	.946
Ward	10	37	7	8	1		1	1	1	14	1	2	216	.882
Taylor	13	32	3	5		2		1		4	23	2	156	.931
Baugh	1										1			
Team's totals	33	1118	192	350	57	39	17	35	33	720	341	57		
Team's Average	:	:	:	:	:	:	:	:	:	:	:	:	280	.881

California Eagle, March 4, 1922, page 6.

Long Beach Avenue in the Nevin area of Los Angeles on May 2, 1920 (interestingly, the same day the Indianapolis ABCs and Chicago Giants played the first Negro National League game in Indianapolis). During their brief 16-month history, the Alexander Giants played 142 games. In 1920, their record was 55–15–2 (.786), and in 1921 they had dominated their opponents 60–10 (.857). But in late September 1921, the Alexander Giants' grandstand burned to the ground.[4] The loss of this ballpark shifted much of the black community's interest to another African American team, the Los Angeles White Sox.

In early October 1921, the White Sox incorporated as The White Base Ball and Amusement Association with the following officers: Frank Howard, president; J.E. Walton, secretary; J.H. Graham, treasurer; James P. White, general manager; and Alonza (Lon) Alfred Goodwin, field manager. This new business structure generated financing for establishing a new headquarters, improving the team's ballpark, and recruiting an impressive roster for the winter season.[5]

The team's "new and well furnished" headquarters was at 1419 E. 12th Street (two miles southwest of their ballpark). This gave the management and players a convenient place to "congregate and discuss the game without infringing upon some one's pool room and barber shop rights." They saw this move toward professionalization of the business as "a step in the right direction." This business structure allowed them to sustain the team in an otherwise increasingly seg-

regationist climate. (During the winter of 1921–1922, the Ku Klux Klan moved into California and held their first recruitment rally in Los Angeles on Wednesday, January 11, with hundreds in attendance).[6]

The White Sox played at Anderson Park, which by 1921 was better known as White Sox Park, in the Boyle Heights area of East Los Angeles.[7] The field was deemed suitable to white professional and semi-professional clubs, and its proximity to teams from the California Winter League offered the White Sox a unique opportunity to compete against assorted teams of major and minor league players. Because of the expense of fielding an all-star team and attracting strong opponents, the White Sox increased ticket prices over summer rates, to 50 cents general admission, 75 cents grandstand, and 1 dollar box seats.[8]

In mid-October 1921, the *California Eagle*, a weekly African American newspaper in Los Angeles, announced, "During the next five months the new [White Sox] concern will devote its energy toward promoting a top notch brand of big league baseball ably managed by Alonza Alfred Goodwin [who] will have absolute charge of the maneuvers of the ball club which winters here this season." Goodwin had been manager of the Los Angeles White Sox for ten years, and he was already "busy drafting one of the greatest aggregations of baseball performers…either black or white, gathering stars from the various clubs of the [Negro] National League." His initial recruitment goal for the team he would call the Colored All

Stars is mind-blowing: Oscar Charleston, Wilber Rogan, John Donaldson, George Carr, Hurley McNair, Walter Dobie Moore, Bob Fagan, Frank Warfield, Bill Riggins, and Bill Drake.[9] While this is not the team Goodwin ended up with, his ultimate line-up was almost as impressive:

Oscar Charleston, cf
George Carr, rf
Bob Fagan, 2b
Lemuel Hawkins, 1b
Walter Doby Moore, ss, p
Jose Mendez, ss
Tom Ward, lf, rf
Henry Blackman, 3b
Neil Pullen, c
Raleigh "Biz" Mackey, c
John Taylor, p
Jim Jeffries, p, rf
Hurley McNair, p, lf

Many of these players were legends in professional black baseball. During the 1921 Negro National League season, Oscar Charleston had played for Charlie Mills's St. Louis Giants. It had been this great player's best season, with an astonishing .426 batting average. In the fifty games for which we have box scores, he stole 28 bases and made 79 hits, including 14 doubles, 10 triples, and 14 home runs. What makes this record even more impressive is that these box scores are mostly from games against top opponents, like Rube Foster's Chicago American Giants, C. I. Taylor's Indianapolis ABCs, and the Kansas City Monarchs. While Charleston usually spent winters in Cuba (and won batting titles there in 1920, 1922, and 1924), he opted to stay in the United States during the winter of 1921–1922 and went to Los Angeles to play for Lon Goodwin's Colored All Stars.

Because Negro National League teams back east each had different postseason barnstorming obligations, the White Sox team was not complete until late November, but they began playing games in early October. This created an opportunity for local talent to play alongside the stars. During the regular season, catcher Neal Pullen had been captain of the El Segundo team. He was skilled behind the plate but became the back-up catcher when Biz Mackey arrived from Indianapolis, where he had spent the season with C.I. Taylor's ABCs. Another player—Henry "Heinie" Blackman—had played first base for the Alexander Giants. A threat at the plate, he had hit an inside-the-park home run during an August game.[10]

The official California Winter League season—with four all-white teams—spanned from October 8 to December 11. As it was winding down, baseball promoter and Los Angeles White Sox owner Joe Pirrone signed a group of major and minor leaguers to form a white all-star team that would face his White Sox (also known as the Colored All Stars, the Colored Giants, and the Bear Cats) during the remainder of the winter. Pirrone secured Irish Meusel to manage the team and recruited several notable players:

Bill McKechnie (Pittsburgh Pirates/Minneapolis Millers AA)
George Cutshaw (Pittsburgh Pirates)
Tony Brottem (Pittsburgh Pirates)
Lew Fonseca (Cincinnati Reds)
Tony Boeckel (Boston Braves)
Earl Sheely (Chicago White Sox)
Lee Thompson (Chicago White Sox)
John "Red" Oldham (Detroit Tigers)
Lu Blue (Detroit Tigers)
Don Rader (Philadelphia Phillies),
Bob Fisher (Minneapolis Millers AA)
Rowdy Elliott (Sacramento PCL)
Slim Love (Vernon PCL)

Some of these men had also been playing on CWL teams and gradually joined Pirrone's or other all-star teams as the CWL schedule wound down. This blurs the boundaries between league competition and other non-sanctioned games, but the mix of major and minor league talent still offers a rare opportunity to see how African American players performed against their white contemporaries.

While the CWL was still in full swing, the Los Angeles White Sox defeated "Pirrone's minor leaguers"

CHARLSTON JOINS L. A. WHITE SOX.

With the signing of Charlston, home-run swatter, the L. A. White Sox club is now complete. Charlston hails from the St. Louis Giants and is said to have established a record last summer for home runs in the Negro National Baseball League. Mendez, famous Cuban Giant star, joined the club last week.

Los Angeles Times, November 26, 1921, section 2, page 11.

(mostly players from the Pacific Coast League), 6–4, on October 9, in their first fully competitive game of the 1921–1922 winter season. The regular season opener came three weeks later on October 29, with another victory (4–0) against Joe Pirrone's All Stars, which by then had more major leaguers in the line-up. To gather public interest and show off their new uniforms, the White Sox held a big parade beginning at noon and leading to the ballpark for the afternoon game.[11]

During the first half of their winter season, the Colored All Stars played well but struggled with Sunday games, losing five weeks in a row. In an October 30 game against Pirrone's All Stars, the White Sox faced Red Oldham, who had an 11–14 record for the Detroit Tigers in 1921. The black team batted well and scored 8 runs, but Baugh, a less known local black pitcher, gave up 6 runs in 1⅓ innings, so Goodwin sent Biz Mackey to the mound. Amazingly, the White Sox came back to an 8–8 tie in the eighth, but then the white All Stars pulled ahead again, winning the game, 10–8.[12]

The following Sunday, November 6, the White Sox faced Pirrone's All Stars again. In a questionable decision, Goodwin chose to pitch John "Steel Arm" Taylor (brother of C.I., Ben, and Candy Jim). On any other day, this would have been a sure bet, but the Chicago American Giants ace had gotten off the train from Illinois a mere four hours before the game and had not trained for several weeks. The *California Eagle* reported, "The results are sad, sad to relate without the free use of a bandana…. The first five men to face Mr. Taylor piled enough lumber on him to build a hotel." After 4 runs in only 7 minutes, with no outs, Goodwin pulled him and put in McNair. The reliever fared better but was still no match for major leaguer Bill Pertica, who had a 14–10 record with the St. Louis Cardinals in 1921. The White Sox lost, 12–9.[13]

On November 12, Taylor took the mound again against Fisher's All Stars (another team of major and minor leaguers). This time he was rested and ready and shut out his opponents, 4–0. The *California Eagle* reported, "John did about everything to Bob Fisher's big bush leaguers that the rules on baseball etiquette call for: he walked none, allowed 2 little singles, poled a triple and single himself and left four standing at the platter wondering where the elusive pill went through their stick."[14] The *Eagle*'s "Sports and Amusements" columnist William Mells Watson scored most of the games and contributed colorful commentary in his weekly summaries.

On November 15, 16, and 17, the White Sox easily swept a mid-week series from the Dyas All Stars, yet another white team. Then the following week, the already strong White Sox began transforming into a powerhouse when Cuban Jose Mendez of the Kansas City Monarchs arrived and replaced Doby Moore at shortstop.[15] The unpredictability of game outcomes shows just how evenly matched teams were. On November 19 in a game against the Pacific Nationals, McNair gave up five runs in two innings, so the manager sent in "the dependable utility wonder, Raleigh Mackey, [who] stepped on the slab and won his struggle 11 to 7." Pitching is always fickle, and the following day, seasoned veteran John Taylor lost the first game of a doubleheader, 6–3. Jim Jeffries, from the Indianapolis ABCs, won his game, 8–5.[16]

In late November, more top minor and major leaguers were showing up on opponents' rosters. On November 24, John Taylor gave up only four hits against Edington's major league stars, winning 2–1. His opponents on the mound were Slim Love of the CWL-leading Vernon Tigers and George "Sarge" Connally, who had debuted with the Chicago White Sox during the regular season.[17]

In announcing the Colored All Stars' next series against Calpaco, the *Los Angeles Times* noted, "Oscar Charleston, the colored Babe Ruth, arrived from St. Louis yesterday and immediately joined White's aggregation." The following day, the *Times* elaborated, "With the signing of Charleston, home-run swatter, the L. A. White Sox club is now complete. Charleston hails from the St. Louis Giants and is said to have established a record last summer for home runs in the Negro National League." Everyone expected the slugger to "attract a crowd."

The Calpaco team was a mix of major and minor leaguers, featuring Blue and Oldham (Detroit), Pinch Thomas (Cleveland), James Washburn (Wichita WL), and Ray Bates (Seattle PCL).[18] The Colored All Stars won the Saturday game 4-2 but continued their string of Sunday losses in the first game of a doubleheader, followed by a tie in the second, when the umpire called it due to darkness in the sixth. The *California Eagle* commented, "Notwithstanding that Oscar Charleston (the famous Colored Babe Ruth of the St. Louis Giants) was camping in the outfield, still Jim White's 'Bear Cats' failed to grab off either of the Sabbath twin performances with the big league Calpaco nine." Charleston was 1 for 4 in the first Sunday game and 1 for 3 in the second (a triple and a single).[19]

While Southern California's mild climate is ideal for year-round baseball, the weather still caused problems. Rain and sometimes high winds could wreak havoc with the schedule. On December 3, a game versus Calpaco was cancelled when a "rip-roaring Santa

Ana storm" blew down "the entire north and south side fence [and left it] lying mangled on the ground." On December 17 and 18, it rained so hard that the *California Eagle* declared that "fish were swimming around the bases, bringing sorrow to the management and disappointment to the several thousand fans." Rainouts were so common that the California Winter League had actually spent $3,000 on a rainout insurance policy; teams collected $34,000. The Colored All Stars did not have that luxury and suffered at the will of the weather, sometimes losing an entire series, such as around Christmas, when rain claimed three games against the Vernon Tigers. Record crowds had been expected at White Sox Park.[20]

Fortunately, in good weather the games without rain drew many fans. In early December, with Charleston, Mendez, and the rest of his starters now in full form, Goodwin enjoyed increasing coverage in both black and white newspapers. The latter even began praising black players. On the morning of a December 4 game against Calpaco, the *Los Angeles Times* praised Charleston as the "home run swatter of the St. Louis Giants." Then, after the Colored All Stars had lost five straight Sunday games, John Taylor defeated Red Oldham, 7–2. The *Times* wrote, Calpaco

Irish and Bob Meusel in 1923.

was "unable to stem the tide of hits." Mendez and Fagan had both hit home runs, while Charleston went 1 for 3, was hit by a pitch, and scored twice. During the first inning, Calpaco's shortstop became angry after a called third strike and pushed the umpire. Surprisingly, such tensions were actually rare in contests between the Colored All Stars and white professional teams.[21]

Goodwin had assembled a crack team and on any given day any player could offer a tremendous performance. Often that was Mackey, the team's catcher, who at the time was still young and fast enough to be a threat on the basepaths. A December 11 pitchers' duel against Art Krueger's All-Stars was tied "in the eighth and...drifted into the eleventh still knotted when old man Mackey hammered out a sweet two sacker and skeeted across the gravy dish when pinch hitter Henry Blackman broke up the argument with a timely single."[22]

Kruger's team included Fred Haney (former Angel, PCL), Carter Elliott (Chicago Cubs), and Slim Love (Vernon, PCL, and soon-to-be CWL champions). But these men were no match for the White Sox offense. On December 13, the *Los Angeles Times* gave the following statistics: "Lem Hawkins and 'Slim' Blackman of the L.A. White Sox club are both hitting an even .400 for the fifteen games of winter ball... Other leading batters are Mackey .351; Charleston .300; Foote .286; Fagan .285." A few days later, the mainstream paper conceded, "White's team is composed of high class professional players."[23]

In mid-December, White Sox manager Lon Goodwin retired and left Jim White to manage the team with Oscar Charleston as captain. The *California Eagle* called Goodwin "the greatest baseball manager in the West." But, they added, "Charleston is thoroughly capable, having acted in this capacity in the Negro National League many years." This was also the week when the California Winter League was wrapping up, and the *Eagle* commented that the league's official closing would be "a relief to the gate receipts at the White Sox Park." After the Vernon Tigers won the California Winter League pennant, comedian Carl Sawyer took over the team and began playing games against the Colored All Stars. Vernon had their entire championship team intact, except for George Sisler and Jimmy Austin. Their manager was Irish Meusel, outfielder of the 1921 World Series champion New York Giants. On December 17 the Tigers won, 5–3, with John Taylor defeating Sam Lewis.[24]

On January 7 and 8, 1922, the Colored All Stars made easy work of Calpaco in a three-game series

(9–3, 4–3, 14–0). The *California Eagle* wrote, "Jim White's chief of staff, Oscar Charleston, the Colored king of swat and his pack of twin-six assistants, with malice aforethought, last weekend and Sabbath coaxed the high-toned and prettily uniformed squad of Calpaco diamond stars into their bull-pen and then turned on 'em and smacked them for three rows of Chinese pot houses in as many games." The first game on Sunday took eleven innings. Then, "Manager Charleston smacked a triple; Mackey...whaled a sacrifice to center and Oscar railroaded home at least three inches to the good." Charleston went 3-for-5 in that game. Mackey pitched, and "ten [white opponents] left with the wood on their shoulders and sorrow in their hearts."[25]

The Calpaco team included "Red" Oldham (Detroit), Chet Thomas (Hartford EL), Ray Bates (Seattle PCL; Indians 1913, Philadelphia Athletics 1917), Pete Schneider (Cincinnati 1914–1918; Yankees 1919; Vernon 1921 PCL), Harold "Rowdy" Elliott (Sacramento PCL; Boston Braves 1910, Cubs 1916–1918, Dodgers 1920), and Johnny "Trolley Line" Butler (Wichita WL).

After sweeping Calpaco, the Colored All Stars again turned their attention to the Vernon team. Tigers coach Irish Meusel and his brother Bob, of the AL champion New York Yankees, both wanted to play for the team, as did Johnny Rawlings (Giants) and Bill Piercy (Yankees). However, fearing that top major leaguers from the World Series might fall in contests against top Negro Leaguers, Commissioner Landis had barred them from barnstorming. The players petitioned Landis to reverse his ruling, which he finally did on January 9. Bob and Irish Meusel, and John Rawlings all joined the Vernon Tigers for a five-game series with White's Colored All Stars, beginning January 14. Coach Meusel also signed pitcher Bill Pertica of the St. Louis Cardinals to pitch the Sunday game on the 15th. The Vernon team's expected lineup included seven current and former major leaguers: Johnny Bassler and Lu Blue (Detroit), Irish Meusel and Johnny Rawlings (NY Giants), Bob Meusel (Yankees), Bill Pertica (St. Louis Cardinals), Tony Boeckel (Boston Braves), and Carl Sawyer (of Vernon, but formerly with Washington Nationals).[26]

The Colored All Stars won the opening game against Vernon, 3–2. Charleston's men had been behind 2–0 until the ninth but then rallied with three hits and three runs. The crowd was the biggest of the season thus far, and fans lined the outfield, topped only by the following day's "Sabbath mob [which] was the greatest ever crammed in the enclosure." Perhaps fans were there to see the White Sox captain even

more than the major leaguers. The *Eagle* wrote, "If brainy Oscar Charleston wasn't pulling one of his famous drag-shot bunts safely, he was lambasting a double or hot and sizzling grass cutter to the outfield." The Vernon team won the Sunday game, but only by a single run, 7–6. John Taylor had given up two home runs, but Charleston went 3-for-4 with a double and a stolen base. By Tuesday, Commissioner Landis was reconsidering the wisdom of allowing MLB players to participate on an "all-professional team" in such match-ups.[27] The Colored All Stars also won their next two games against Vernon. The *Los Angeles Examiner* called the contests "important tilts" and emphasized how much the major leaguers had been training for the games. After their 4–3 victory on January 21, the *Examiner* headline read, "Sox Trounce All-Stars." And the following day, Charleston, Mackey, and Carr all hit triples off Bill Pertica in the 5–4 win. *Examiner* sportswriter Frank A. Kerwin also noted that Yankees slugger Bob Meusel was "riled up" over these "defeats of the Majors."[28]

On January 28 and 29, the Vernon-White Sox rivalry continued, with a set of "winner take all" contests, meaning that the victor of each game would claim 100 percent of the gate. Bill Pertica won the Saturday contest for Vernon, 15–10, but it was a total slugfest, with 2 home runs, 7 triples (2 by Charleston), and 9 doubles. The Sunday game was another rainout. The following weekend, the "winner take all" series continued, with the Colored Stars taking the Saturday game 5–4, and Vernon claiming the Sabbath contest, 5–2. This left the season at 4–3, in favor of the Colored Stars—with five of these games won by only a single run. Before the Saturday game, the *Examiner* had announced that these would likely be the last games, but with the White Sox ahead, they planned one more weekend.[29]

The game on February 11 was called off due to wet grounds, and the Colored Stars took the Sunday contest, 13–8, bringing the winter series to 5–3. The *Los Angeles Examiner* admitted, "White's colored All Stars walked away with the game" and even praised the team leader: "Oscar Charleston, slugging outfielder, hit three doubles." The teams met only twice more.[30] Vernon took the penultimate game, but after the February 25 capstone, The *California Eagle* declared: "[John] Taylor White Washes Meusel's Majors 6 to 0 in Last Clash." The story mocked the losers:

> Evidently Irish and Bobby Meusel didn't care about facing Oscar and his gang in the last fracas of their schedule which ended so disastrously

last Saturday as neither of them showed up for hostilities so the results were aerographed to them in order to cheer them up as they start on their way to training camp—Meuselites "Zero," Colored Hope Destroyers 6.[31]

Besides proving himself an able leader, Charleston generated impressive offensive performance, batting .405 overall during the winter season. In 21 known games, he had 79 at-bats, with 32 hits, 6 triples, and 7 doubles, plus 7 stolen bases and 22 runs scored. On March 4, *California Eagle* sports writer William Mells Watson celebrated Charleston:

OSCAR CHARLESTON KING OF SWATTERS THROUGHOUT SEASON HITS .405, FIELDS .960 When general manager Jim White drafted "bambino" Oscar Charleston to the Angel City last fall, he imported without a doubt the second greatest living baseball performer in the entire universe, the great Babe Ruth being his only peer.[32]

After claiming a definitive victory over the major leaguers, 7–4, the Colored All Stars fell to financial pressures. Leaving Los Angeles, they barnstormed against local and semipro teams throughout southern and central California, where they continued dominating all opponents.

Studying the 1921–1922 California Winter League and the state's less organized barnstorming season demonstrates several important points. Most importantly, it proves that these Negro League players could stand up against major leaguers. This justified Commissioner Landis's concerns about major league championship players facing Negro Leagues All Stars during the offseason. While Ty Cobb chose to leave California before he might have faced Oscar Charleston and the White Sox, we still learn something about these players. In the CWL, the San Francisco Seals' weak season showed that Cobb was not an effective manager and that his playing skills were becoming less reliable. Meanwhile, when Charleston took over managing the Colored All Stars, he demonstrated great potential, which would later show in his successful career as a manager with several Negro

League teams, most notably the 1932–1938 Pittsburgh Crawfords. ∎

Notes

1. Center for Negro Leagues Baseball Research www.cnlbr.org/DefiningNegroLeagueBaseball/WinterLeagueTeams/tabid/59/Default.aspx.
2. *Los Angeles Times*, November 21, 1921, B2; *Los Angeles Examiner*, 8 December 1921, sec. 2, 4; *Los Angeles Times*, 12 December 1921, 17.
3. *California Eagle*, 12 August 1921, 6.
4. *California Eagle*, 1 October 1921, 6.
5. *California Eagle*, 15 October 1921, 6.
6. *California Eagle*, 26 November 1921, 6; *Los Angeles Examiner*, 13 January 1922, 1.
7. Sanborn Fire Insurance Maps for Los Angeles, California, 1906-January 1951, volume 14, 1921, plates 1417, 1418, and 1419.
8. *California Eagle*, 29 October 1921, 6.
9. *California Eagle*, 15 October 1921, 6; *California Eagle*, 1 October 1921, 6.
10. *California Eagle*, 19 August 1921, 6.
11. *California Eagle*, 29 October 1921, 6.
12. *California Eagle*, 5 November 1921, 6.
13. *California Eagle*, 12 November 1921, 6.
14. *California Eagle*, 19 November 1921, 6.
15. *Los Angeles Times*, 17 November 1921, sports 3; *California Eagle*, 19 November 1921, 6; *Los Angeles Examiner*, 17 November 1921, sec. 2, 4.
16. *Los Angeles Times*, 20 November 1921, A9; *California Eagle*, 26 November 1921, 6; *Los Angeles Times*, 21 November 1921, B1.
17. *Los Angeles Times*, 25 November 1921, C3.
18. *Los Angeles Times*, 25 November 1921, C3; *Los Angeles Times*, 26 November 1921, B11; *Los Angeles Times*, 26 November 1921, B11.
19. *Los Angeles Times*, 27 November 1921, A10; *Los Angels Times*, 30 November 1921, C3; *California Eagle*, 3 December 1921, 6.
20. *California Eagle*, 10 December 1921, 6; *California Eagle*, 24 December 1921, 6; *Los Angeles Times*, 13 December 1921, C3.
21. *Los Angeles Times*, 4 December 1921, A10; *Los Angeles Times*, 5 December 1921, B9.
22. *California Eagle*, 17 December 1921, 6.
23. *Los Angeles Times*, 13 December 1921, C2; *Los Angeles Times*, 17 December 1921, B14.
24. *California Eagle*, 17 December 1921, 6; *California Eagle*, 17 December 1921, 6; *California Eagle*, 24 December 1921, 6.
25. *California Eagle*, 14 January 1922, 6; *California Eagle*, 14 January 1922, 6.
26. *Los Angeles Examiner*, 31 December 1921, sec. 1, 13; *Los Angeles Examiner*, 10 January 1921, sec. 1, 12; *Los Angeles Examiner*, 12 January 1922, sec. 1, 15.
27. *Los Angeles Examiner*, 20 January 1922, sec. 1, 14; *California Eagle*, 21 January 1922, 6; *Los Angeles Examiner*, 16 January 1922, sec. 1, 14; *Los Angeles Examiner*, 17 January 1922, sec. 1, 10.
28. *Los Angeles Examiner*, 21 January 1922, sec. 1, 12; *Los Angeles Examiner*, 22 January 1922, sec. 1, 16; *Los Angeles Examiner*, 23 January 1922, sec. 1, 12; *Los Angeles Examiner*, 28 January 1922, sec. 1, 12.
29. *Los Angeles Examiner*, 29 January 1922, sec. 1, 18; *Los Angeles Examiner*, 5 February 1922, sec. 1, 13; *Los Angeles Examiner*, 6 February 1922, sec. 1, 14.
30. *Los Angeles Examiner*, 12 February 1922, sec. 1, 14;13 February 1922, sec. 2, 4.
31. *California Eagle*, 4 March 1922, 6.
32. *California Eagle*, 4 March 1922, 6.

Jeane Hoffman

California Girl Makes Good in Press Box

Jean Hastings Ardell

The battle women have faced to gain access to Organized Baseball's locker rooms is, by now, well documented. Throughout the 1970s, many ballplayers were shocked, *shocked*, when increasing numbers of female sportswriters breached the privacy of that sanctum, with some declaring it merely an excuse to ogle athletes in a state of undress. Less known—and less understandable—are the obstacles such women faced to gain access to the press box, where presumably their male colleagues were fully and decently clothed.

Indicative of the era was the experience of the *Cleveland News*' award-winning investigative reporter Doris O'Donnell, whom an editor sent to cover the Cleveland Indians' eastern road trip in May 1957. O'Donnell's presence as a female sportswriter became the story, with much analysis of her figure, and she was excluded from the Yankee Stadium press box. (O'Donnell, incidentally, was a role model for a local

teenager named Dorothy Jane Zander, known later to SABRen as Dorothy Seymour.)

Twenty years before O'Donnell, however, 17-year-old Jeane Hoffman worked out of the press box at Wrigley Field, home of the Los Angeles Angels of the Pacific Coast League.[1] Despite her youth, Hoffman already had sportswriting experience. At Los Angeles High School she had studied journalism and cartooning, served as girls sports editor for the school's semi-annual publication, and at age 15 was publishing sports cartoons in the *Hollywood Citizen-News*. Covering baseball, football, and hockey for that publication, she became the youngest regular writer in the history of the Pacific Coast League.

But Hoffman had her eye on major-league markets. In 1940, having learned of an opportunity at the *Philadelphia Evening Bulletin*, Hoffman and her mother, Ada, drove across the country at the rate of 600 miles a day. She got the job. As a writer-cartoonist, she was a regular in the Shibe Park press box, reporting games and drawing three-column sports cartoons. In 1942, Hoffman became the "first girl scribe" to cover spring training in Florida. She took advantage of her roving assignment to interview Bob Feller and Sam Chapman, then stationed at the Roanoke (Virginia) Naval Training Station, before continuing to Florida to cover the Cardinals, Tigers, Yankees, Reds, Phillies, Giants, and Red Sox.[2] By then, she had a job in the heart of the major-league baseball universe, New York City, with a by-line under her column "From the Feminine Viewpoint," in the *New York Journal-American*.

"I don't know how she managed to get that job," said her friend Rosalind Massow, who worked at the newspaper as a copygirl. "The *Journal-American* was not notable for its women reporters. She must have been very convincing. I do know that the guys at the sports desk liked her—they were not competitive with her."[3] In an article that year entitled "No 'End' to Jokes, Girl Finds, in Yankee Stadium Press Box," Hoffman took on the issue of access, writing with humor but nevertheless making her point:[4]

Jeane Hoffman, shown here with her daughter Valerie McIntosh and Walter O'Malley, enjoyed a relaxed friendship with the Los Angeles Dodgers owner.

Jeane Hoffman brought her reporter's notebook and cartoonist's sketch pad to Yankee Stadium in 1940. Shown here interviewing Yankee teammates Joe Gordon (left), Lefty Gomez, and Joe DiMaggio (far right).

We note that *The Sporting News* has been running a handy guide service on "How to Crash the Press Box," alias "No Women or Dogs Allowed."… We would like to add our two-bits' worth (Confederate coin). But prepare yourself; this one's gonna be different! To begin with, we haven't a complaint in the world against the Gentlemen of the Press. …The boys have been darn nice to us. When we toured Florida last spring, we didn't have more than 250 jokes played on us, and no more than 50 jesters tried to steer us into the players' un-dressing room.

In an article syndicated in the Associated Press, she had accurately predicted a Cardinals-Yankees World Series; she closed out the season writing features on the World Series.

"Famous Woman Sports Writer Begins Series in Times Today"
– *Los Angeles Times*, September 16, 1951

In January 1944, Hoffman became engaged to Thomas Allen McIntosh, a first officer in the British Merchant Marine, and they married in Portsmouth, Virginia, on February 15 of that year. Hoffman and her husband remained on the East Coast for several years before returning to Los Angeles in 1951, whereupon the *Los Angeles Times* hired her to write a weekly feature on

sports. That November she gave birth to Joan Margaret, the first of three daughters. In September 1957, as Brooklyn Dodger fans faced the unthinkable, Hoffman published an 11-point analysis of the benefits attached to L.A. becoming a major-league city. The *Times* found it necessary to insert the following explanation at the beginning of the essay:[5]

(Jeane Hofmann, authoress of the following story, is qualified to discuss the importance of major league baseball to Los Angeles. She spent 12 years in Philadelphia and New York at major newspapers there, covering all sports, before she came to *The Times*. She knows the baseball picture there and here thoroughly.)

Hoffman laughed or shrugged off the patronizing comments and attitudes that attended her presence as a sportswriter. "Mom had a way about her…. She always seemed to have a very good knack for getting her story," recalls her middle daughter, Valerie McIntosh, who thinks Jeane found support and encouragement from her own mother.[6] Valerie's younger sister, Diane McIntosh, agrees. "Grandma had gotten a divorce and owned a number of rental properties. Our grandmother was very independent, so I can only imagine… that she fully supported her daughter. They were both women ahead of their time."[7]

Hoffman continued to cover the Dodgers' move

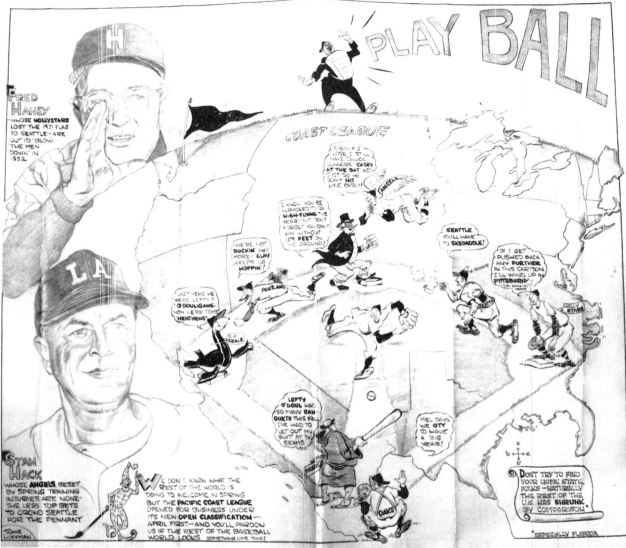

Jeane Hoffman's skill as a cartoonist helped open doors for her work as a sportswriter.

west, and their plans for a new stadium in Chavez Ravine. She profiled Vin Scully and the Dodgers' front office executives, including Buzzie Bavasi. In May 1965 Dodgers' owner Walter O'Malley circulated a memo to the front office: "Jeane Hoffman (McIntosh) has been retained by me 'on special assignment.' She will be furnished an office and will have Department Head courtesies. Calling cards will read 'Assistant to the President.'"[8] Her job entailed filling Dodger Stadium when the team was out of town and during the offseason, and she took on the assignment with enthusiasm, booking events from R.V. shows and bull fights to the National Football Foundation and Hall of Fame Scholar-Athlete Awards banquet in the Stadium Club and the filming of an Elvis Presley movie, *Spinout*.

In an undated letter sent to O'Malley during spring training 1966, Hoffman began, "Dear Walter, Well,

how are all the heroes down in Vero?" and went on to alert him about the prospect of the Beatles performing at Dodger Stadium that August.[9]

Her daughters often accompanied their mother to the ballpark. Valerie McIntosh, whose godmother was Eleanor Gehrig, recalls, "being bounced on the knees of Drysdale and Koufax…. We saw lots of games—we always sat up on the club level by the offices. Mom covered everything in L.A., from the Rams, to John Wooden's UCLA basketball team, to Santa Anita Race Track, and lots of tennis. At the Christmas party she always held, all the sports people in town came."[10]

By the mid-1960s the women's liberation movement was gaining momentum; American women were beginning to act upon their professional dreams. Within a few years, increasing numbers of women began covering baseball, and the press box signs forbidding women access came down. But in 1966 Jeane

Hoffman had already had it all—marriage, family, and a successful career in a man's field—for two decades. Her success can be attributed to talent, a healthy sense of humor, the support of a strong mother, and, perhaps, starting out in sportswriting so young that she simply did not accept the status quo. In late spring of 1966 an award was established in her name: The Theta Sigma Phi-Jeane Hoffman Unique Coverage Award. Several months later, however, on September 29, 1966, she was at home recovering from a virus when she was stricken with a pulmonary embolism. She died at age 47, leaving her husband and three daughters aged 15, 13, and 11. As that year's World Series got under way, her former colleague at the *Times*, Sid Ziff, recalled her career:[11]

> Jeane could have made the newspaper in any department but she had her mind made up to write sports and nothing would discourage her. *We used to remind her it was too tough for a girl to make it in sports. There was a rule against allowing them in the press boxes. They couldn't get into the dressing rooms. She was invading a man's world. With her talent why not go to the city side?* Nope, Jeane loved sports and the people in it. It was her world. She conquered it. She put on the gloves with prize fighters and caught the pitches of Bob Feller.

As this article neared completion, Hoffman's two surviving daughters revisited her legacy. Diane McIntosh's nine-year-old son was preparing a school report on his grandmother's career, and Valerie McIntosh, who studied journalism at San Diego State University and later worked in radio, reported finding among her mother's files a manuscript entitled "No Place for a Lady"—an ironic title given Hoffman's ability to maintain her feminine identity while thriving in the press boxes, newsrooms, and business offices of the sports media. ∎

Notes

1. The spelling of Hoffman's name appears in some by-lines and publications as "Hofmann."
2. "Draws As She Writes," 3 December 1942. (National Baseball Hall of Fame and Museum.)
3. Rosalind Massow, telephone interview, 25 February 2011.
4. Jeane Hofmann, "No 'End' to Jokes, Girl Finds, in Yankee Stadium Press Box," *New York Journal-American*, no date. (National Baseball Hall of Fame Library.)
5. Jeane Hoffman, "Big Boon".
6. Valerie McIntosh, telephone interview, 13 February 2011.
7. Diane McIntosh, e-mail to the author, 13 February 2011.
8. 3 May 1965, Memo, Walter F. O'Malley to All Department Heads. (Courtesy Peter O'Malley.)
9. Jeane Hoffman, letter to Walter O'Malley, undated, 1966.
10. McIntosh, telephone interview.
11. Sid Ziff, "Series Fever," *Los Angeles Times*, 4 October 1966.

Contributors

DAVID KIRK ANDERSON SR. joined SABR in 1980 and was an original member of the Allan Roth Chapter. His article "All Time College All-Star Teams" appeared in SABR's 1983 *Baseball Research Journal*. **DAVID KIRK ANDERSON JR.** has been an active SABR and chapter member since age eleven. Now a collegian, he researched much of the data for this article.

JEAN HASTINGS ARDELL lives in Corona Del Mar, California, where she works as a writer, editor, and teacher, with baseball a continuing subject of interest. She is author of *Breaking into Baseball: Women and the National Pastime* (Southern Illinois University Press, 2005), and received the *Baseball Weekly*/SABR award in 1999.

FRANCISCO E. BALDERRAMA is Professor of Chicano Studies and History at California State University Los Angeles and also serves on the planning committee and the advisory board of the Latino Baseball Project: the Mexican American Experience. Balderrama has taught "Mexican American Baseball: An Oral History Approach" at Cal State LA with particular attention to directing students in conducting interviews of players and fans. The golden age of amateur and semi-professional baseball for Mexicans in East Los Angeles, which instilled ethnic pride and identity during the early 20th century, is a major research area of Balderrama. This interest led Balderrama to co-author with Richard Santillan *Mexican American Baseball in Los Angeles* (Arcadia Press, 2011).

DICK BEVERAGE is a former President of SABR and a longtime fan of the Pacific Coast League. He is the founder of the Pacific Coast League Historical Society, an organization devoted to preservation of the memories and history of the Pacific Coast League during the years before major league baseball came to the West Coast.

ROB EDELMAN is the author of *Great Baseball Films* and *Baseball on the Web*. His film/television-related books include *Meet the Mertzes*, a double-biography of *I Love Lucy*'s Vivian Vance and fabled baseball fan William Frawley, and *Matthau: A Life*—both co-authored with his wife, Audrey Kupferberg. He is a film commentator on WAMC (Northeast) Public Radio and a contributing editor of *Leonard Maltin's Movie Guide*. His byline has appeared in *Base Ball: A Journal of the Early Game*, *Baseball and American Culture: Across the Diamond*, *Total Baseball*, *The Total Baseball Catalog*, *Baseball in the Classroom: Teaching America's National Pastime*, and *The Political Companion to American Film*. He authored an essay on early baseball films for the DVD *Reel Baseball: Baseball Films from the Silent Era*, 1899-1926, and has been a juror at the National Baseball Hall of Fame and Museum's annual film festival. He is a lecturer at the University at Albany, where he teaches courses in film history.

SHERRI ENG is a lifelong San Franciscan and diehard Giants fan. She has written for *Giants* magazine since 1996—her first article being a profile on Barry Bonds. She was the Giants' editorial coordinator 1999–2000 and had the once-in-a-lifetime experience of helping the team move from Candlestick Park to AT&T Park (formerly Pacific Bell Park)—a momentous event that she never thought would happen considering the team's impending move to Florida in 1992. She considers the Giants' winning of the 2010 World Series a dream come true. Over the years, she has grown to like that other baseball team across the Bay and now follows and writes about the Oakland A's.

JAMES GORDON retired from TRW/Northrop Grumman after forty years as an aerospace and nuclear engineer to concentrate on baseball and being a grandfather. His joy is attending baseball games around the country and documenting aspects of Los Angeles baseball history. Having been born in Brooklyn, he is genetically and emotionally a Dodger fanatic, although he reached Los Angeles fifteen years before the team arrived.

ROLAND HEMOND has served as Special Assistant to the President and CEO of the Arizona Diamondbacks since August 2007. During his sixty-year career in the front offices of Organized Baseball, he is a three-time recipient of the Major League Executive of the Year Award (recognized by UPI and *The Sporting News* in 1972, *The Sporting News* again in 1989, and by the Associated Press in 1983). Four awards have been named in his honor: by the Chicago White Sox, for those dedicated to bettering the lives of others through personal sacrifice; by *Baseball America*, for major contributions to baseball scouting and player development personnel; by SABR, for executives who display great respect for baseball scouts; and by the Arizona Fall League, for meritorious service to the League. In 2011 the National Baseball Hall of Fame awarded him the Buck O'Neil Lifetime Achievement Award.

PAUL HIRSCH is the owner of Paul Hirsch Professional Communications, a marketing and public relations firm in Danville, California, where he lives with his wife Debbie and two children. Paul has been a SABR member since 1983, is a past president of the Lefty O'Doul chapter, and has served on the SABR Board of Directors since 2007. His work has been published in BioProject books on the 1969 Mets and 1947 Dodgers.

MAXWELL KATES is an accountant based in the Toronto area. He has lectured at the Limmud Conference at York University and at the 2006 SABR Convention. His writing has appeared in *Elysian Fields Quarterly* and *The National Pastime*, along with books, which include *Sock It To 'Em Tigers* and *The Miracle Has Landed*. He attended his first Angels game in 2002, where he became the proud owner of a rally monkey named Alphonse. Although Alphonse vanished a few years later, he has been rumored to have been sighted in the outer reaches of Gatineau, Quebec.

JEFF KATZ loves baseball so much that he and his family moved to Cooperstown in 2003, just to be close to the Hall of Fame. Since then, Jeff's work has been published in the anthology *Play It Again* (McFarland, 2006) and his own *The Kansas City A's & The Wrong Half of The Yankees* (Maple Street Press, 2007), the latter receiving national attention. More recently, Jeff has turned to his other love, rock & roll, with his inventive blog *Maybe Baby* (or, *You Know That It Would Be Untrue*).

GREG KING has been a SABR member since 1993 and co-founded the Sacramento Chapter in 1994. A public historian by professional training, he taught ten years at CSU-Sacramento. He joined the Parsons Transportation Group in San Francisco in 2009 after retiring from the California Department of Transportation, where he served as an environmental manager.

FRANCIS KINLAW has contributed to 11 SABR convention publications and written extensively about baseball, football, and college basketball. For better or worse, he is old enough to have listened to Nat Allbright's re-creations of Brooklyn Dodgers games on radio and grown familiar with Ebbets Field through the magic of black-and-white television. A member of SABR since 1983, he resides in Greensboro, North Carolina.

MARK LANGILL is the Publications Editor and Team Historian of the Los Angeles Dodgers. A member of the front office since 1994, he previously covered the ballclub as the beat reporter for the *Pasadena Star-News* 1989–93.

BOB LEACH played first base for the 1972 Sierra High School baseball team, a CIF semi-finalist. At the University of Southern California, he was a member of the 1974 NCAA Champion Baseball team as well as the 1975 and 1976 teams. In 1980 he was head coach of USC's junior varsity as well as assistant baseball coach at Duarte High School, where he has taught for 34 years. He frequently attends USC baseball games and plays in the annual alumni game, collecting a single and double in the 2010 contest. Each summer he visits the wonderful "retro" ballparks around the country. He is the author of the recently published biography of Rod Dedeaux: *Never Make the Same Mistake Once*.

LEE LOWENFISH, a member of SABR since 1976, won the 2008 Seymour medal for his biography *Branch Rickey: Baseball's Ferocious Gentleman* (University of Nebraska Press, hardback 2007; paperback 2009). He was deeply honored in January 2010 when the New York Professional Baseball Scouts Hot Stove League gave him the James Quigley Memorial Award for "baseball service."

DON MALCOLM received a copy of *The Baseball Encyclopedia* (first edition) for his birthday as an aging child—and the rest of the world has regretted it ever since. He edited the iconoclastic, controversial *Big Bad Baseball Annual* from 1995-2001. He is currently completing two books about film noir, *The Dark Embrace* and *Noir in the Sixties*, while continuing to edit the *Noir City Sentinel*, the acclaimed house organ of the Film Noir Foundation.

ANDY MCCUE had the skills of Ken Oberkfell scaled down to park softball leagues. He is now mostly retired while serving as president of SABR.

TOM NAHIGIAN grew up in the Boston area and remains a fan of the Red Sox, Celtics, and Bruins. A SABR member since 1983, Tom enjoys the baseball writings of Bill James and Roger Angell. He and his wife make their home in Pasadena. He enjoys playing Strat-O-Matic Baseball and reads as many baseball books as he can. Tom wrote the article on Fred Lynn for the SABR Biographical website.

KERRY YO NAKAGAWA is founder of the non-profit Nisei Baseball Research Project (www.niseibaseball.com). He is founding curator of the "Diamonds in the Rough" exhibit that has been displayed at the National Baseball Hall of Fame in Cooperstown, Japanese Baseball Hall of Fame in Tokyo, and museums around the country. He was the associate producer and actor in the feature film *American Pastime*.

RICK OBRAND taught in Los Angeles city schools for 39 years. He was selected as a "Hero in Education" and Teacher of the Year in 2008. He also was included numerous times in "Who's Who Among America's Teachers." Married and the father of two sons, he currently is the historian for the Los Angeles City Schools Sports Hall of Fame. He is the author of many articles and booklets on high school sports stars.

AL PARNIS is a retired high school English teacher and adjunct college professor. He has taught courses in baseball history and baseball literature. As a lifelong Angeleno his baseball loyalty is to the City of Angels, now the Dodgers, in years past the Los Angeles Angels of the Pacific Coast League, whose memory is kept alive by his long membership in the Pacific Coast League Historical Society.

FRED R. PELTZ enjoyed his first taste of major league baseball in the late 1930s, watching Pie Traynor's Pittsburgh Pirates spring training in San Bernardino, California. In 1947 while playing Junior League ball, he earned a trip to the World Series in New York and witnessed Jackie Robinson in his debut year. Peltz had a limited career pitching in the Sunset and Pioneer Minor Leagues from 1948–51. In 1954 he played with Dave Bristol on Army's XVI1 Corps Championship team in Japan. Before retiring from newspaper advertising in Riverside, California, Peltz learned of SABR from co-worker, Andy McCue. He credits McCue with introducing him to the wealth of available resources and camaraderie of SABR. Peltz has been married to Sue for 57 years and currently lives in San Clemente, California. They have five children and six grandsons.

HOLLY PRADO has published ten books that encompass the genres of poetry, fiction, and autobiography. Her poetry and prose have appeared numerous publications, among them *The Paris Review*, *The Kenyon Review*, and *The American Poetry Review*. She's been active as a writer and teacher since the early 1970s in the Southern California literary community, a community she values greatly for its exuberance and variety of voices. Honors include First Prize, 1999 Fin de Millennium LA Poetry Award and the Certificate of Recognition from the City of Los Angeles in 2006 for her achievements in writing and teaching, along with her influential participation in the literary community. Since 1978, she and her husband Harry Northup have cheered loyally for the Dodgers from the top deck at Dodger Stadium.

STEPHEN RONEY is a lifelong Angels fan, starting when they actually played in Los Angeles. He has been a SABR member since 1984 and the president of the Allan Roth Chapter since 1999. He currently lives in southern Orange County, California and works as a computer programmer in Irvine.

RICHARD SANTILLAN is a Professor Emeritus of Ethnic and Women's Studies at California State Polytechnic University, Pomona, where he has taught for 31 years. He also serves on the planning committee and advisory board of the Latino Baseball Project: The Mexican American Experience. Dr. Santillan has written extensively on Mexican American baseball history in the Midwest United States. He is a longtime Los Angeles Dodgers fan with special interest on Mexican American players who have played for the Dodgers since the team's arrival in 1958. Dr. Santillan is co-author with Dr. Francisco E. Balderrama of *Mexican American Baseball in Los Angeles* (Arcadia Press, 2011).

RON SELTER is a retired economist, formerly with the Air Force Space Program. A SABR member since 1989 and a member of the Ballparks, Minor League, Statistical, and Deadball Committees, his area of expertise is twentieth-century major-league ballparks. A frequent presenter at SABR regional meetings and national conventions — Selter has a particular interest with ballparks and their effect upon batting, he served as text editor for *Green Cathedrals* (2006 edition, SABR) and as a contributor to *Forbes Field* (McFarland, 2007). He is the author of *Ballparks of the Deadball Era* (McFarland, 2008).

GERI STRECKER teaches English and Sport Studies at Ball State University. She is writing a biography of Hall of Famer Oscar Charleston and a history of baseball and diplomacy in the Philippines prior to World War I. She is also editing a collection of columns by Dave Wyatt, the first great black sportswriter. Her article "The Rise and Fall of Greenlee Field: Biography of a Ballpark" (*Black Ball*, Fall 2009) received the McFarland-SABR Research Award.

ERIC THOMPSON is a retired high school mathematics teacher living in Solon, Ohio. Thompson received a Bachelors Degree from Kent State University in 1963 and a Masters Degree from Illinois Institute of Technology in 1968. Thompson's focus is on major league baseball's expansion from 1960 to 1962.

BOB TIMMERMANN is a librarian who lives in South Pasadena, California. He has given research presentations at earlier SABR conventions on the life of Harry Kingman as well as Japanese baseball.

TOM WILLMAN was born in Los Angeles. His first magical view of a great ballpark was of LA's Wrigley Field, watching the Pacific Coast League Angels. A longtime Southern California journalist, he spent some years collecting reminiscences of the game as it was played in the 1910s and '20s. He last wrote about Jimmie Reese in *Northern California Baseball History*, published for the 28th National SABR Convention in 1998.

VICTOR WILSON, a SABR member since 1984, has been a baseball and Braves fan ever since his fourth grade teacher, Miss Braun (a nun from Milwaukee) "beat it into him" in 1955. His major interests have been adjustment of player statistics (cross era and ballpark adjusted) with major associates being Pete Palmer, Michael Schell, and Ron Selter. His all time favorite players over the years have been Eddie Mathews, Sandy Koufax, Hank Aaron, Fernando Valenzuela, Greg Maddux, and now Tim Lincecum.

DON ZMINDA has worked for STATS LLC since 1992, first as the company's Director of Publications and more recently as Director of Research. A member of SABR since 1979, he is the author or editor of more than a dozen books about baseball, including the SABR publication *Go-Go to Glory: the 1959 Chicago White Sox*. A native of Chicago, he has lived in Los Angeles since 2000.

Notes